More Praise for *It Can Be Fixed*

"Here is a timely book for all of us. Whatever our partisanship or ideology, we have a common interest in a well managed government. Roger Johnson has gone to Washington (and survived) and now gives us his wisdom and common-sense recommendations that will hopefully ignite a national dialog on what should be a national policy issue—the need for professional management of government. His sense of humor and anecdotes add to the compelling nature of his call."

—Jack W. Peltason,
coauthor of *Government by the People* (20th edition, 2003)
and President Emeritus, University of California

"In a town dominated by lawyers and accountants, it is good to hear what a professional manager has to say about fixing problems in our government's operations."

—James R. Mellor, Retired Chairman and CEO,
General Dynamics Corporation

"The book gives the reader a living insight into the inner circles of the Washington world. Roger reveals a realism of politics from a nonpolitician who is repaying his country for the heights his personal achievements have taken his family in this democracy. He concludes with a genuine workable means of removing the risk of qualifying and selecting tomorrow's leaders. An easy read for such a serious topic."

—Harold C. McCray, Founder and Chairman of
McCray, Hewett & Associates
An Executive Search Firm

IT CAN BE FIXED!

YOUR UNMANAGED GOVERNMENT

By

Roger W. Johnson

CLAREMONT GRADUATE UNIVERSITY PRESS

CLAREMONT, CALIFORNIA

ISBN 0-9758782-0-4

Library of Congress Control Number: 2004109489

TABLE OF CONTENTS

Dedicated to my wonderful wife Janice,
who has been my inspiration and my partner
in all things for 48 years.

FOREWORD

I began to write this book in 1998—in the middle of President Clinton's second term. It was set aside twice as I took on two separate "turn around" jobs, first as CEO of an international not-for-profit organization, and subsequently as the CEO of a small public company. In early 2003 I decided to dedicate whatever time was needed to finish it, because as the months and years passed it became increasingly clear that the problems resulting from the lack of professional management skills and experience in Washington were accelerating at an alarming rate, bringing the country closer to financial and operational crisis. It was also clear that this huge gap in our federal management capability was bipartisan. The election of a Republican president in 2000 not only failed to stop the trend, but only served to further amplify the problems.

Therefore, although the examples I use are from the mid-90s, I believe they are more appropriate today than they were then. The negative impact of the lack of professional management experience and skills in Washington ranges from the structural flaws brought into public focus by the 9/11 Commission hearings to the poor implementation of otherwise good policies and programs. In the process, billions of dollars are wasted—but the problems caused go far beyond dollars and what most people associate with poor management of our government. An additional sense of urgency began to drive me to complete the work when I concluded that neither political party was getting close to addressing this huge issue of professional management. In fact both parties were running away from it. Actions that hide the problems and/or push them off to the future are becoming more and more blatant. In depicting the age-old saying of "hear no evil, see no evil, speak no evil," the donkey and the elephant could easily be used instead of the monkeys.

I realize that the subject of professional management can be very dry, but I hope the anecdotes and real-life examples I use will make the book an easy and enjoyable read. Most important, I hope it will be seen as a call to arms for the millions of concerned Americans who have all but given up on being able to have any impact on the federal government.

I

STRANGER THAN YOU
CAN IMAGINE

IN JANUARY OF 1993 I BECAME WHAT THE EXECUTIVE search industry calls a "target candidate" for a the position of CEO of an operation about which I knew very, very little—except that it was very, very big.

At the time, I was chairman and chief executive officer of Western Digital Corporation, a Fortune 500 company that designed, manufactured, and sold computer hard disk drives. Headquartered in Orange County, California, we had operations all over the world. I could reflect with pride upon my ten years at Western Digital. In 1982, the company was just coming out of bankruptcy, had revenues of $40 million coming mostly from a wide range of semiconductors, and employed about 600 people. By 1991, an exceptionally competent and close-knit team had turned Western Digital into a $1 billion company with more than 7,000 employees operating in twenty-six countries, a leader in the highly competitive disk drive industry. Today it is still a leader in the industry with annual sales of approximately $3 billion.

I had spent more than twenty years in the high-tech field. Most of that time had been in management positions of disk drive companies, Memorex and Western Digital in particular. I had also spent fourteen years with General Electric—mostly in defense-related businesses with products that ranged from the Polaris submarine missile guidance systems to the flight control devices for the F-111.

Now I was being "courted," as the executive search people put it, to run an operation in which I would be responsible for more than 20,000 employees. It pumped $60 billion a year into the economy. It had offices and facilities all over the country, a fleet of automobiles (but no corporate jets) larger than the corporate fleets of any Fortune 500 company. The majority of employees were in locations far distant from the head office—Boston, New York, Philadelphia, Atlanta, Chicago, Fort Worth, Kansas City, Denver, San Francisco, and Seattle.

The person attempting to recruit me was persuasive and charming. Unlike someone from executive search firms (also known as "head-hunters") like Spencer Stuart or Heidrick & Struggles, he did not give me the usual briefing on things like the organization's culture and core values, profiles of its key executives, or the other usual things—information often presented in elaborate workups inserted in fancy binders. Moreover, he gave me no detailed list of the "specs" for the position, the requirements that the candidate must meet as defined by the search committee of the board of any corporation looking for someone to fill a senior executive position. It was a most unusual recruitment by a very different sort of recruiter.

And—even though at the end of what turned out to be a very brief recruiting process I knew little more about the job than I did when I first got the phone call asking me to take it—I said yes.

Depending on how one looks at it, 1993 would prove to be either an *annus mirabilis* or, in the phrase of Queen Elizabeth, an *annus horrilibis*. Actually, it was an interesting blend of both.

I found myself passing through the looking glass, from the familiar territory of business—the private sector—into a world of which I knew little—the public sector. The "recruiter" was the President of the United States, William Jefferson Clinton, and the job was Administrator of the General Services Administration.

Headquarters would be Washington, D.C., a place I had been to many times, but always as an "outsider." I discovered, very quickly, that once I became an insider I would, like Alice in Wonderland, have to run twice as hard to stay in the same place.

I was soon to find out what the specs of the job were—and nothing, but nothing, in my previous experience had prepared me for what it would be like to become the Administrator of the GSA. On the face of it, I didn't fit one crucial spec that Washington's peculiar political and bureaucratic culture expected of someone being appointed to this position. I was an Orange County Republican who would become the highest-ranking Republican political appointee at that point in a Democratic administration.

The GE years had made me familiar with government procurement practices. In my disk-drive years I had become *quite* familiar not only with my own industry, but also with our customers—that is, the computer makers such as IBM, Compaq, Dell, Hewlett-Packard, and others.

At Western Digital, based on my GE experience, I was very cautious regarding government business. In my judgment, the costs and risks of doing business with the government were high. We primarily sold to government through manufacturers' "rep" companies. Other value-added resellers bought our drives, modified them, or tested them to government specs. I found that most of our customers had similar issues. But since the government represented much larger business for them, percentage-wise, they didn't want to completely abandon that market. Therefore, most either established a completely separate Federal Division—IBM, GE, and UNIVAC, for example, did this—or they sold to value-added resellers who had been set up specifically to do business with the government.

It was a way of creating a *cordon sanitaire* against the infections and plagues that could result from having too much of your business tied to the whims and regulations of the federal government. Defense contractors, of course, have no such qualms. Far from it— they are a part of what President Dwight Eisenhower called "the military-industrial complex," run by a concert of Congress, the Pentagon, and the contractors.

You have to get inside of the culture peculiar to Washington, D.C., however, and run the risk of being "infected" or at least strenuously educated, in order to understand how the system works, to navigate the millions of pages of rules and regulations, understand the even more vital *unwritten* rules of working, and often gaming, the system before you can begin to comprehend how things really are done in the place where they spend most of the money.

When President Clinton called me that January and asked me to take on the job of running the GSA, he also asked me "to help Al Gore 'reinvent the government,' as we are calling our efforts."

"Of course! I will help in any way possible, but what is the GSA?"

"The General Services Administration," he said, and then I understood. I knew that the GSA was a huge monolith in American government, but just how immense it was I would not learn until later.

"This is a perfect slot for you because it runs the day-to-day operations of the government," the President added. "It deals with things you've been doing all your life. Your talents in planning, business, common-sense decisions, and getting things done are made to order for the GSA. Someone will call you with all the details—I still have to figure out myself as to who will be doing what. Thanks for agreeing to come. One more thing: Please hurry up and get here!"

★   ★   ★

It was not long after my arrival in Washington before I discovered that what was required of me in my assignment at the GSA was nothing like what I had expected. The President was wrong. Completely and absolutely wrong. Nothing I had done, none of my successes (and lessons learned from occasional failures) in some thirty years of management, not only in large corporations but also with nonprofit organizations, seemed to be useful in the capital city!

Yes, the GSA ran the day-to-day operations of government— from purchasing paper and pencils to building courthouses. Inexplicably, at least to me, they did it without almost any of the professional management tools that most of us take for granted. They did it, or at least tried to do it, with laws, rules, and regulations. Although I found that federal workers were just as smart, just as dedicated, just as hardworking and honest as any employees I ever had in the "outside" world, they were locked in a system that almost guaranteed money would be wasted and good policies and programs would be poorly implemented—with the added result that the citizens of the country would all but give up on a government that couldn't be trusted to manage *anything* effectively.

In a phrase, good people were being devoured by a bad system. At the roots of the systemic problems were things I could address by using fundamental tools of management, while others then and now require a "reinvention of government" that goes far beyond the achievements of the Clinton Administration, changes made in the face of formidable opposition, changes that were substantial and important, but just the first steps in a long, long journey.

Just as I had a lot of company in my enthusiasm in my first days in Washington, I was not alone in my subsequent frustration and even despair.

In time, many of the great expectations ground to a halt as a result of a combination of missteps by the administration, an unbelievable atmosphere of partisanship, and the lack of a "big picture" within the institutions of government, the last preventing them from dealing with more than one or two issues at a time. The term "multitasking," so familiar in successful corporations, was not in the Washington dictionary.

As the days and weeks went by and I became more and more immersed in the details of the management issues facing the reinvention process as it related to the huge GSA organization, I began to see that the opposition to what I felt were obviously needed changes was coming from both sides of the aisle. I am not aware of many government insiders with experience as senior executives of large companies as well as nonprofits who were cast in a position of running an enterprise as huge as the GSA, who have ever told the full story of their experience. While this book recounts some of what happened during the Clinton years, its larger goal is to outline, briefly and clearly, massive problems that can be solved only by the American people. It is both a cautionary tale and a road map of sorts, a road map for change. That change emphatically will not come from within the culture of Washington, D.C. As you will see, many of the core values and implicit rules in Washington are all about *resisting* change. So it is up to the public, to the voters, to insist on the right kind of changes.

In the middle of those hot summer days some 225 years ago when a relatively small group of individuals were creating our Constitution, Benjamin Franklin walked out of the hall after the end of one session and was asked by a bystander, "What kind of government are you giving us?"

"A republic," Franklin responded, "if you can keep it!"

The least we can do is learn to manage it more effectively.

2

SCREWING UP A ONE-CAR PARADE

"THE GOVERNOR OF ARKANSAS IS ON THE PHONE," SAID my assistant Maralyn Olsson.

It was November 1991. In Newport Beach, California, I was in my office, taking care of business, as the saying goes, as chairman and chief executive officer of Western Digital. A call from Bill Clinton was the last thing I expected. I didn't have any significant connections with the Democratic Party—and I had never met the Governor. (If Maralyn hadn't told me he was the Governor of Arkansas, I would have had no idea who Bill Clinton was. Such was probably the case with most Americans at the time—but that would soon change!)

As the son of a labor union president in Hartford, Connecticut, I grew up in a very liberal atmosphere. However, after graduation from college (I was only the second on both sides of our family to attend college), I became exposed to different political views—and to income taxes—so I became a Republican.

Although I had voted Republican since I first saw a ballot box in 1956, I had never been active in partisan politics. However, over the preceding few years I had become involved with national economic and trade issues through my work with the American Business Conference, a nonpartisan group of 100 CEOs of fast-growing companies founded by Arthur Levitt, who, at the time, was CEO of the American Stock Exchange and would later be Chairman of the Securities and Exchange Commission (SEC) under President Clinton.

"Hello, Roger. I'm Bill Clinton and I'm running for the Democratic nomination for President," the rather friendly voice on the phone continued, "and I read a *Los Angeles Times* story last week that said you were upset with your party and President Bush. Well, I have some concerns in the same area, as you might expect. Hopefully we could talk about some of the issues, and perhaps both make a positive contribution."

I was a bit taken aback with "Bill," as he called himself, implicitly inviting me to do the same, but I responded something to the effect that, yes, I was upset with the Republican leadership in general and with President Bush in particular. However, I wasn't sure I was *that* upset!

"Can we talk for a few minutes?" Clinton asked again.

"Sure," I replied, "I'd love to hear your thoughts on the economy and how we can get out of the mess we're in now. And, if you have devised a platform for your campaign and want to share other ideas, I would enjoy learning your thoughts about improving our education system."

We talked for about a half-hour. Minute by minute I become increasingly impressed with the depth of Clinton's understanding of the issues and the seeming lack of ideology in his suggestions. This was particularly important to me at that time because it seemed that all I was getting from my own party leadership was slogans and ideological sermons, while being politely brushed off.

As we talked, I reflected that a Bush Cabinet member, Commerce Secretary Robert Mosbacker, had just visited with me a week before in my office, but had basically denied that the country was in an economic slump. Obviously, Mosbacker was not studying the same markets or reading the same national indicators that I was! Now, Clinton was ten times more interested in my views than my Bush-appointed visitor had been! Something was wrong with my interface with higher-ups in the Republican Party, and I did not think it had to do with me. If anything, I have always been *realistic,* even at the expense of political correctness.

A month or so earlier I had chaired an American Business Conference meeting in Washington with another Bush appointee, Treasury Secretary Nick Brady, who told a group of CEOs from very successful companies that the reason banks were not lending them money to expand was probably because they were not creditworthy! You can imagine the impact this had on the audience. The Republicans probably lost every future vote in the room. How much better it would have been had Brady addressed the very real problems of the economy and had sought suggestions from the *Who's Who in American Business* lineup of executives listening to him.

In my view, both Mosbacher and Brady were completely out of touch with reality and, I suspected, so was their boss.

By contrast, in our conversation Clinton shared his enthusiasm, backed by a deep knowledge of the situations—about reducing the federal debt so that long-term interest rates could come down, about providing incentives for companies to begin retraining workers for the "new information society," about bringing down the cost of health care, and about a long list of other substantive ideas that he would put in place if he were President.[1]

I did not agree with all of his ideas, but it was surely refreshing to talk to a politician who was obviously bright, articulate, and wanted to spend a great deal of effort to fix things. Clinton seemed to be a doer, not just a talker.

I was very impressed and I asked him if he would mind talking to a friend of my wife and me, Kathryn Thompson. Kathryn was also a Republican, and like my wife Janice and me, she was getting quite upset with what we perceived to be President Bush's aloofness from the real economic issues in the country. But it wasn't only the economy that had her upset. As a major Republican contributor, she had been invited to attend a small gathering of a select group of other major Republican contributors. Kathryn was not

---

[1] See Appendix 2: Roger W. Johnson, "Jumping Parties over the Economy," Los Angeles Times, September 2, 1992.

only a significant contributor but was also a very successful real estate entrepreneur in her own right. So one can imagine her reaction when Clayton Yeader, Chairman of the Republican National Committee at the time, approached her at the reception with all of his southern charm and asked, "Now, just who do you belong to, little lady?" Bye-bye, Clayton!

Bill Clinton and Kathryn talked a couple of days later. She, too, was very impressed with the Governor of Arkansas. We talked, and as a result we invited the Governor to come to Orange County to meet with what we thought would be a small group of other concerned Republican friends. The time was set for early in the next month.[2]

★ ★ ★

Bill and Hillary Clinton arrived in Orange County on the morning of December 6, 1991. My good friend Bob Blair, a top-notch public relations executive, met the Clintons at the local airport and brought them and a couple of others, including Mickey Kantor (who later became the United States Trade Representative and Secretary of Commerce), to the Pacific Club in Newport Beach.

A couple of days before the arrival of our guests, Bob Blair had told me that our little event, planned to be casual, was "taking off." Each day more people learned about it, and we kept getting requests to attend. Further, the press sniffed a good story, and media people also sought to be among those in our "private" meeting.

But nothing Bob had said could have prepared us for what we found waiting for us that morning at the Pacific Club. We had expected only ten or twenty people, but there was a *line of people*— more than 100—waiting to join the breakfast! We let in as many as the room could hold, but had to turn away many others. We were at once surprised and delighted, and I am sure that Governor and Mrs. Clinton felt as warmly welcomed here as they had been anywhere else in the early days of their campaign.

It was quite a scene! Every television network, all of the cable companies, and at least a couple dozen newspaper and magazine

---

[2] See Appendix 1: Invitation letter to the Clinton breakfast.

reporters were on hand—so many that they had to be set up in a separate room for what turned out to be a major news conference following the breakfast. Who could have imagined that a casual telephone call to me from Bill Clinton would have caused a veritable media earthquake!

I said I was a realist. And at this breakfast, candidate Bill Clinton revealed himself as a realist as well. Soon, there was the strange sight of old-line Republicans from Orange County—the very seat of party conservatism—applauding a *Democrat!* I watched for the first time as Bill Clinton captivated a gathering of the "opposition," who, remarkably, kept interrupting him with applause as he made one common-sense suggestion after another.

Afterward, we went into the press conference where I publicly endorsed him. At the time, Clinton was one of seven seeking the Democratic nomination, a race that normally would not have been of concern to me. After all, incumbent George Herbert Walker Bush was getting an over 70% favorable rating in the polls, and for me and other Republicans, he was a shoo-in. How could he ever be stopped? And, who was this upstart from Arkansas, anyway?

Later that night we got a call from Clinton thanking us and speculating that this event probably would "break him out of the pack." Coverage of the news conference had run as the number one or number two story on the six o'clock broadcasts of all of the networks and cable news channels.

Before we knew it, Janice and I were deeply involved in the Clinton campaign! It is remarkable that in life one chance thing can lead to another, sometimes dramatically changing the course of events. And so it was for both of us. In time, Mr. and Mrs. Roger Johnson would be in Washington, D.C., and would not only be working for but would also be the friends of President and Mrs. Bill Clinton.[3]

But even with these highly placed connections the government train—at least the part we were on—too often veered off the track. What makes things go off the rails is the logic of unintended legislative and regulatory consequences. Government is not a business;

[3] See Appendix 3: David J. Lynch, "Republicans Celebrate in Arkansas," *Orange County Register*, November 4, 1992.

it can't be driven by considerations central to business—ROI, profits, the bottom line, earnings per share, and market cap. But versions of the basic tools of management, things learned in business schools and through hard experience in companies of every size and sort, are not only applicable to achieving goals in government's delivery of goods and services—they are indispensable. Unfortunately such tools are all too frequently dispensed with even when they are, theoretically, in place—or they simply don't exist.

3

THE "B" TEAM

THE FACT THAT GOVERNMENTS HAVE A VERY poor record of effective management will come as no surprise to most people. Governmental management, or the lack of it, has been the subject of everything from some very funny but sad jokes to dozens of serious books and countless articles. Similarly, poor management has been the subject of a wide range of presidential and congressional committees and commissions over a number of years. The GAO (General Accounting Office), as well as the Inspectors General of various agencies, put out a steady stream of scathing reports for years exposing all shapes and sizes of government waste, fraud, and abuse. We even saw the successful Clinton-Gore '92 presidential campaign make "Reinventing Government" a significant part of its platform. However, even with all of this attention, it seems clear, at least to most of the American people, that nothing much ever changes. As President Clinton said to me one day in 1994 while discussing the Reinventing Government initiatives, "The American people think we would screw up a one-car parade—and they're probably right!"

Most of the studies of management in government have dealt primarily with flaws such as ineffective organizational structures, lack of clearly defined responsibilities and the resulting lack of clear accountability, the absence of or incorrect use of measurements, and the absence of or improper use of incentives. Some of the studies delve into the social and cultural issues associated with people's attitudes about government, such as perceived performance versus expectations of performance, or the impact of the huge growth of government not only in terms of dollars and employment levels but also in the broadened programmatic reach of government.

I do not want to imply that the findings in these important works are not valid and relevant; the issues they raise certainly must be addressed. However, these studies make two fatally flawed assumptions: first, that there are people in government who understand the problems and know how to fix them; and second, that there is a political will to take on the task. It has been my experience and now my conviction that neither is true—at least to the extent necessary to make any meaningful or sustainable changes. It wasn't until I came to these conclusions that I could come to grips with the questions that haunted me during my first frustrating months in Washington at the GSA. Why haven't these issues already been addressed if everyone seems to agree that they are a major part of the problem? With all of these good works, why has there been no real improvement in the management of government? Why has nothing changed? Is it because the people involved lack the necessary intelligence? Is it because they are dishonest and somehow purposefully misuse the system for their own gain? Are they lazy and constantly seek to do as little as possible?

Conventional wisdom says that all of the above are true. However, it has been my experience, and, more important, the findings of scholars with better credentials than mine, that in the main, those involved in governmental management do not lack intelligence and are hardworking, honest, and dedicated people. During my own term as the Administrator of the GSA, I found that the typical federal worker had a work ethic equal to or better than any group of employees I had had ever worked with in the private sector.

Then what was wrong? Why haven't things changed?

Well, my personal and painful experience revealed the reasons why. It's the management—stupid!

* * *

Having never served in government before, I was naive and ill prepared for what I found. After the first year of frustration, I began to make some progress in achieving meaningful change within the agency. However, that was not accomplished without a very high level of opposition, including unwarranted attacks, personal investigations, and threats. These assaults further frustrated and angered me. I had come to Washington with the sole purpose of responding to President Clinton's request to join his administration "to help Al reinvent government."[4]

I certainly had nothing personal to gain by taking the assignment. I was just trying to do my part in government service. I was used to people challenging my ideas and at times disagreeing with my approach to a problem—but why all the personal attacks, and why so vitriolic? As time passed, however, a surprising pattern of issues began to emerge. I slowly came to the realization that the opposition was not because people disagreed with what I was trying to do, but because they had no *idea* of what I was trying to do. The government was not being *mis*managed; it wasn't being managed at all! The research findings on ineffective organization structure cited above, the lack of clearly defined responsibilities, the absence of measurements, and other institutional shortcomings are all clearly major failings of government operations. However, the implicit assumption that those responsible know how to fix the problems is surprisingly wrong. That helps explain why nothing has changed.

It finally dawned on me why the actions and programs that I proposed were unfamiliar to most and indeed threatening to many. It was the embedded culture that I was challenging, and it was the embedded culture that was striking back. The meanness and vitriol were just extensions of the Washington climate that had turned personal character assassination into an art form. "Roger, don't take it personally." At the time I couldn't relate to that admonition even though it was coming from the President, the Vice President, and several others. These attacks were personal, hateful, and hurtful.

---

[4] See Appendix 4: Letter from Roger Johnson to Vice President Albert Gore (Re: National Policy Review early observations).

It took quite awhile, but I finally recognized that the attacks really weren't personal, but rather the weapon of choice to repel a newcomer's challenges to the status quo. The fact was that people just didn't understand my motives, let alone my tactics. Further, they didn't know how to do what I was proposing. They had no prior experience with even the most simple management techniques, procedures, and processes that seemed so obvious to most of us in business. Therefore, I was an external threat that had to be defeated.

This observation was reinforced when I decided to do a mini-survey of the backgrounds of the senior agency management—political and career. "Tell me what you've been doing for the past twelve years," I asked the new political appointees in the GSA. (Republicans had held the White House and therefore all of the executive branch appointees for the preceding three terms.)

"Well, I've been working on K Street for a lobbyist for the last few years, and before that I was at the Brookings Institute," said one.

"I was on Senator X's staff for five years and then did graduate work at Georgetown," replied another.

"I have been in a law office working on consumer issues."

"I've been working in Congressman X's home office."

The jobs were different, but the pattern was clear, and except for the Deputy Administrator, who had been recruited from a large Chicago real estate developer, the others had little or no experience that would have given them any professional management skills. Not satisfied, I dug a little deeper.

"What about your earlier career?" I asked.

"I studied political science at Georgetown University and then worked as a campaign assistant for our local Congressman."

"After college—with a degree in urban planning—I joined the Department of Transportation as a planning analyst."

The other responses varied somewhat but again the pattern was clear: Their academic work had been in areas like political science, law, and social sciences, and their work experience garnered in jobs in the political process or government/quasi-government units (lobbying, think tanks, public policy law, etc.). There were a few exceptions. For example, the GSA's Chief Financial Officer, Dennis Fischer, was well trained in sound financial processes; he turned out to be indispensable to the change process. And Julia Stash, the Deputy Administrator, came to Washington from a private sector real estate company and led major reforms in the federal buildings operations—but she would leave in frustration after two years.

Although I didn't undertake a formal survey, my continuing assessment of the other Cabinet officers, agency heads, Congressmen, Senators, and various staff showed the same pattern of training and experience. There were a few who had some management skills, or at least understanding, and tried to continue to "do the right thing." However, they were and still are almost always overwhelmed by a system that has little foundation in the basics of professional management.

Why should this be a surprise? The laws, rules, and regulations have been developed over the years by thousands of elected, appointed, and career people who have no understanding of management issues and no incentives—good or bad—to try to gain that knowledge. In fact, the vast majority of those in the governing process are lawyers. Why are we then surprised by the complexity of the layer upon layer of regulations that seem to be compounding each year? The entire enterprise of management in the private sector—tested and proven by the necessity to turn a profit in a public company or consistently break even in a not-for-profit, while, at the same time, pleasing customers—had not been tapped by the biggest enterprise of them all: the federal government.

The impact of this lack of professional management capabilities in government reaches far beyond Washington. In his book, *Managing in the Next Society*, Peter Drucker comments that

> the cost of these [government] rules and regulations threatens to strangle small business. According to the government's Small Business Administration, the annual cost of [government] regulations, government required paper work, and tax compliance for U.S. businesses with fewer than five hundred employees was $5,000 per employee in 1995 (the last year for which data were available)—a 25 percent surcharge on top of the cost of wages, health care, insurance, and pension, which was around $22,500 in 1995 for the average small

business employee. Since then the cost of government related paperwork is estimated to have gone up another 10 percent.[5]

Drucker also makes the following observation:

> Even more onerous than these costs are the enormous demands
> that regulations place on management time and attention. In the
> twenty years between 1980 and 2000, the number of laws and reg-
> ulations regarding employment policies and practices grew by 60
> percent. . . . All of these require reports, and all threaten fines and
> punishment for noncompliance, even if unintentional. According
> again to the Small Business Administration, the owner of a small
> or even midsized business "spends up to a full quarter of his or her
> time on employment related paperwork.[6]

Drucker continues by pointing out that one of the results of this
avalanche of rules and regulations on the private sector is the outsourcing of activities ranging from human resource functions to
the assembly of products in the *maquiladoras* (the manufacturing
plants on the Mexican side of the U.S. border). He says, "I would
argue that the avoidance of onerous paperwork is a stronger
incentive for manufacturing companies to go 'off shore' than the
often questionable labor savings."[7]

Although the private sector employers have more alternatives
than do government employers as they try to respond to inane regulations, sometimes the private sector also reacts in ways that are
counter to otherwise well-intended regulations. Professional management inside the government would have a spillover effect in the
private sector, as rational regulations replaced inane directives.

Just how important this deficiency is can be seen best by looking at some specific situations. For example, the President and the
Vice President had made specific commitments to reduce the size
of government. When I arrived officially at the GSA in June 1993

[5] Peter F. Drucker, *Managing in the Next Society* (New York: Truman Talley Books/St.
Martin's Press, 2002), pp. 114–115.

[6] Peter F. Drucker, *Managing in the Next Society* (New York: Truman Talley Books/St.
Martin's Press, 2002), p. 116.

[7] Drucker, *Managing in the Next Society*, p. 117.

(I first had to go through the confirmation process), many actions were already under way in other agencies. My experience told me that the first, easiest, and least painful way to reduce headcount was simply by not replacing people who leave the organization voluntarily (i.e., the attrition rate).

Within a few days of my swearing in I asked about the GSA attrition rate. I was told that it was "very low." I asked to see the actual data. What I was shown was a calculation based on the number of people who had left minus those who had been hired—this is how the agency defined "attrition." These people were not trying to fool anyone—someone, some time ago, for some reason had developed his or her own definition. I pointed out the obvious fact that attrition was the number of people who had left—period—which was a number of approximately 2,500 people per year. The total agency employment was approximately 20,000 at this point. I then told my staff that we would start our reduction program by not automatically replacing anyone who left. *That* got their attention!

"You can't do that!"

"We have to carry out the laws that Congress has passed—you will be defying the Congress!"

"Who will do their work? We all are already working flat out."

Again, these were real and sincere concerns of my career staff. It quickly became clear that they had never had to reassess the work they did, how they did it, or how it could be done more efficiently—things that well-run, surviving institutions outside the government have to do on a continuous basis. When I told them that there was some good news associated with this plan— because it would provide for significant promotional opportunities for the people in the agency—they looked at me as though I had just gone completely over the edge.

I explained that the process was not arbitrary or rigid. We would first analyze the specific situation created by the vacancy of the employee who left, answering such questions as: Was the work being done really needed? If so, could it be divided among others? If we found that the job was essential and must be filled— then we would do that. But the job would be filled by promotion from within the agency. I directed that no new outside hires could be made without my specific approval. We would then perform the same review of the position vacated by the promotion. Eventually we would find a position that did not need to be filled.

It didn't take long for these very intelligent, hardworking, career employees to enthusiastically embrace the approach. In fact it was this approach and the new "buyouts" program that we finally got passed by a reluctant Congress that resulted in the reduction of approximately 4,000 employees (down from approximately 20,000 when I arrived) by June of 1996, without any forced layoffs and with our "customers" (primarily other governmental agencies) saying that we were noticeably more effective. I am confident that had the political support for "reinventing" not all but disappeared by 1996, we could have similarly reduced at least another 4,000—with continued improvement in performance. Incidentally, I believe I received only two requests to hire outside of the agency over the next two years.

Although the GSA staff responded quite positively, other initiatives that I proposed or undertook as part of the broader reinventing programs outside of the GSA were not embraced at all. They were not only unfamiliar to the federal establishment, but they actually threatened the deeply embedded culture, which led to a series of personal attacks that continued throughout my stay in Washington. I'll go into more detail of these in ensuing chapters.

Fortunately I was tipped off early as to just how hard my job was going to be. Only a few weeks into my assignment, Janice and I were invited to a welcome cocktail party at the home of the agency's CFO Dennis Fischer, a very competent career employee. After a glass or two of wine, Dennis beckoned me to join a cluster of people gathered in a corner of the room. It turned out that this was a group of senior career officials of the GSA.

The CFO then said, "Mr. Administrator, I'd like to introduce you to the 'B' team."

I was caught off balance a bit but recovered quickly and demurred. "Oh no, I am very confident that this team is not second to anyone and will perform at an 'A' level."

The CFO, with a smile on his face, responded, "I don't think you understand. By 'B' team we mean that—we 'B' here when you came and we 'B' here when you leave!"

We all had a good laugh, but although my face was smiling, my head was hurting. However, as they say, forewarned is forearmed.

* * *

I also soon discovered that these issues were not partisan—resistance came from both Republicans and Democrats. It came from the executive and legislative branches and from individuals who were elected, appointed, or career professionals. The fact that the arrows were coming from all directions, although distressing and confusing in the beginning, in the long run helped me to realize that one characteristic common to each attacking group was that almost none of the people responsible for managing the government had any experience or formal training in the basic techniques of professional management. I came to realize that this was also not a surprise to most who study the issue. Unfortunately, I and others who have tried to modify the system have seen little meaningful improvement.

Further questioning and study led to the more fundamental conclusion that professional management is not a national policy issue, and because it is not a national policy issue there was and is no political constituency supporting good management. No one gets elected, appointed, or advances as a career employee because they are good at management. Equally, in most situations there are no political penalties for bad management. Professional management in government, or the lack of it, needs to become a national policy issue of equal importance with education, health care, and defense. In fact, its recognition as such may be prerequisite to meaningful progress in these and other major national policy issues. If for no other reason, there is the incentive that billions of dollars will be freed for better uses.

This book will attempt to make the case that:

(1) The need for making professional management in government a national priority is essential not only to save

or redirect billions of currently wasted dollars, but also, and even more important, to begin to reverse an ever-declining level of public confidence in governments.

(2) The underlying problem is not the quality of those in government, but rather that many if not most of those currently responsible are woefully untrained and inexperienced in the basics of professional management techniques.

(3) All of the professional management in the world won't make much of a difference unless sound management becomes politically important. It will need to become a national policy issue, with the same importance and visibility as education, welfare, and national defense.

To accomplish these objectives, including a major shift in how we determine political priorities, I will propose some new and probably controversial approaches to the governance process.

In this regard I do not propose to treat government as a business. As I noted earlier, both are quite different institutions. However, it doesn't mean that government shouldn't use appropriate versions of professionally proven techniques. The same is true for schools, hospitals, and orchestras—but they seem to be better at it than governments. Some argue that since nonprofits and governments have no "bottom line," they cannot be subject to the disciplines of professional management. Peter Drucker not only refutes that but counters as follows in his book *The Essential Drucker:*

> Twenty years ago management was a dirty word for those involved in non-profit organizations. Now most of them have learned that non-profits need management even more than business does, precisely because they lack the discipline of the bottom line. The non-profits are still dedicated to 'doing good.' But they also realize that good intentions are no substitute for organization and leadership, for accountability, performance and results.[8]

---

[8] Peter F. Drucker, *The Essential Drucker: The Best Sixty Years of Peter Drucker's Essential Writings on Management* (New York: HarperBusiness, 2001), pp. 39–42.

I suggest that this is no less true for governments. I will use both the research of a number of government management scholars as well as some of my own sometimes painful, sometimes humorous experiences to define this issue.

Simply identifying the problems is certainly not enough. We have seen that there has been no lack of problem identification in the past—but nothing seems to have changed. Therefore, I am offering some very specific recommendations that address such obvious questions as: How do we accomplish the needed training for both incumbents and those yet to enter government? What can we do in the short term? In the long term? And finally the most important question: How can we make "good" management a political priority? Because unless effective management is ingrained in the political process with penalties and rewards attached to successes and failures, nothing will change no matter how well trained those involved become.

Although the problems and solutions presented are applicable to state and local governments, this book deals primarily with the federal government. Having said that, the current massive budget problem in California would certainly benefit from professional management. I hope that Governor Arnold Schwarzenegger would consider some of the approaches outlined in the book. However, the primary reason for the federal focus is that the sheer mass and pervasive influence of the federal structure makes for a far greater impact than that of individual states and local governments. The Feds are already trying to solve some of their management problems through the federal government's own version of off-balance-sheet financing, called "unfunded mandates." Unfunded mandates are laws passed by the federal government ordering the states to do certain things, without providing the necessary funding. States also do the same things to counties and cities. The No Child Left Behind program is a good example.

This book will attempt to deal with all of these issues with the hope that at the very least, the lack of professional management in government will be taken much more seriously by readers who care more about taking action than merely refining our research on better defining the problems.

4

THE LACK OF PROFESSIONAL MANAGEMENT (IT'S A LOT MORE THAN THE WASTED MONEY!)

important? Who cares?

Peter Drucker, in his book *Management Challenges for the 21st Century,* describes government as having the greatest impact of the four growth segments of our economy in the 21st century (the four being government, health care, education, and leisure). He states: "The main economic function of government in a developed country is to redistribute 30%–50% of the country's national income. Therefore, nothing else has as great an impact on the shares of national income as changes in government policy."[9]

He continues: "Government in its traditional form, that is, as collector and redistributor of national income, is supposed to have stopped growing [though the figures so far, especially in the United States and the UK, do not support this belief]. But governments in all developing countries—despite 'privatization'—are rapidly acquiring new and very powerful tools to influence—if not

---

[9] Peter F. Drucker, *Management Challenges for the 21st Century* (New York: HarperBusiness, 1999), p. 52.

to control—the distribution of disposable income."[10] Examples include new regulations that control and redirect economic resources to new goals and regulatory actions that are directed at managing the environment.

Although we all know that federal spending is huge, it is still difficult for most of us, even those of us who have gone to Washington to help reinvent government, to grasp the magnitude of the issues.

★   ★   ★

One day I went to see Leon Panetta when he was still head of the Office of Management and Budget (OMB). (Leon Panetta was a long-term public servant, having started as a legislative assistant to U.S. Senator Thomas Henry Kuchel, R-Calif., in 1966. Panetta was first elected to Congress as a Democrat in 1977 and served there until he resigned in January 1993 to become Director of the OMB, and subsequently Clinton's Chief of Staff in 1994. He and his wife Sylvia now run the Leon and Sylvia Panetta Institute for Public Policy in California.) I began telling him how I thought the Administration could save millions of dollars just through efficient practices that were commonplace in the private sector.

I didn't get too far before he stopped me. "Roger," he said, "do this." Leon pursued his lips. I pursed my lips. "Now go, 'buh-buh-buh.'"

"What?"

"Now say, 'Buh-buh-buh-billions.' You keep saying *millions*."

"Yes, but . . ."

"Nobody is going to listen to you here if you keep saying millions. This town is made of buh-buh-buh-billions."

Like a third grader learning his multiplication tables, I repeated after him: "Buh-buh-buh-billions."

Leon grinned. "Very good," he said. "Now we can talk."

Even with Leon's elocution lesson and the fact that I had grown up in and directed some very large companies, it was still difficult for me to get my head around billions of dollars. Then I got lucky. One day I was looking though an edition of *Fortune* magazine that

---

[10] Drucker, *Management Challenges for the 21st Century*, p. 53.

carried its annual Fortune 500 list. I was eager to see where my old company, Western Digital, was placed. As I scanned through the list I eventually came to the various totals of different financial data at the end of the list. There it was—the number $61B—the total under the column "net earnings." In other words, *all* of the efforts of *all* of the 500 largest industrial companies in the nation had generated earnings equal to the size of the spending ($60B) that "my" GSA controlled! This figure not only put "billions" in perspective for me personally, but I was better able to communicate just how significant the work of the agency was. (Even at this level, GSA spending is modest in comparison to that of the Department of Defense. Only the funding of payment of the national debt, and entitlements such as Social Security and Medicare, outpace Defense.)

We are quite used to thinking of the cost of public policies as very large. An example is the cost of Medicare administration and distributions. However, we do not normally think of the costs in the macro sense as described by Drucker. I believe his observation that 30% to 50% of the national income is redistributed (more specific estimates for the U.S. are approximately one-third, or about 33%), with all of its ramifications, alone makes a clear case that professional management in government needs to be a major national policy issue. With one-third of our national income being redistributed (or reprioritized, depending on your political views) as a result of public policy decisions, even small problems with management not only waste billions of dollars, but could and do seriously jeopardize the policies themselves.

The fact that the lack of professional management costs money is easy to see but, in my view, the more important fact—that its absence also hurts otherwise excellent programs—is not as clear to the public. There was no better tragic evidence of this than the statement in the official Space Shuttle *Columbia* investigation report, which stated: "The NASA organizational culture had as much to do with this accident as the foam."[11] It was even more disturbing to see that the *Columbia* investigation time and time again

---

[11] Columbia Accident Investigation Board, *CAIB Report* (Washington, D.C.: Government Printing Office, 2003).

drew parallels to the *Challenger* disaster some seventeen years earlier. "For both accidents there were moments when management definitions of risk might have been reversed were it not for many missing signals—an absence of trend data, imagery data not obtained, concerns not voiced, information overlooked or dropped from briefings." The point is that the management problems were well known. Yet nothing changed in seventeen years. This is an issue that goes well beyond the money.

★ ★ ★

The televised hearings in April 2004 of the 9/11 Commission provide an excellent example of how the lack of professional management experience and skills has a far-reaching impact on all aspects of the governing process. The questions and testimony were almost all about management failings. The testimony of Condoleezza Rice was particularly revealing. Her comments and responses demonstrated a very passive approach to her responsibilities:

1. "The threat reporting . . . was not specific as to time nor place nor manner of attack."
2. "There was nothing actionable in this."
3. "If there was any reason to believe that I needed to do something . . . I would have . . . expected to be asked to do it. We were not asked to do it."
4. "In the memorandum that Dick Clarke sent me on January 25 he mentions sleeper cells. There is no mention or recommendation of anything that needs to be done about them."[12]

She clearly felt she had little or no responsibility to use her judgment to actively pursue the intelligence or recommendations she was getting or to follow up on what the agencies were doing about it.

Why should we be surprised? Rice has spent almost all of her career in government or academia. So, what about others in the Bush and Clinton Administrations? Who did feel or should have

---

[12] Testimony of Condoleezza Rice before the 9/11 Commission on, April 8, 2004, as recorded by the *New York Times* (retrieved online at http://www.nytimes.com/2004/04/08/politics/08RICE-TEXT.html).

felt responsible to take the obvious managerial actions of probing, urging, following up, or even "banging heads" if necessary to get cooperation from agencies or individuals who were, for one reason or another, not working together?

Every organization has people or structures that don't always share information or otherwise are not working in the best interests of the total organization. I agree that the federal government has turned not cooperating into an art form and that the final fix will require significant reorganization—but it doesn't mean it couldn't have been effectively addressed in parallel. This should have been particularly true when faced with the urgent set of national security issues being explored in the 9/11 Commission hearings. "Get this job done *together* or you'll each be gone!" I have found this simple statement by me to be very effective when two or more in the organization aren't pulling together. Why wasn't this said to the heads of the FBI and CIA by anyone in the Clinton or Bush Administrations? Why were they waiting for studies or strategic analysis of the "structural flaws"?

Why? Because no one felt responsibility. Why? Because no one had been assigned the responsibility. Why? Because no one had the prerequisite management experience or skills to apply.

It may be a long time before we hear "It's the management—Stupid!" as the rallying cry of a political campaign, but until we do, the country will continue to be at risk for a lot more than billions of wasted dollars.

★   ★   ★

The state of our national public education is another good example. I believe that every President in my lifetime, since Eisenhower, has at one time or another made education a central priority of his administration. I have no idea what the number would be if one were to add up the dollars government has spent on trying to significantly improve our public education system over the past fifty years. However, I doubt that I would get much of an argument that it would be at least multibillions. But what have we improved? Many say that our education system has been in a continuous decline. Can we even articulate what, specifically, was supposed to improve? We argue endlessly about how to "measure" education effectiveness. Once we define what "winning" looks like, how can we tell if we are achieving our goal? If we haven't made any progress, then who was/is responsible? These questions and many other similar ones should be an integral part of developing and implementing our policies. But they are not! The posing and answering of these questions, not after but in parallel with the policy definition and development phases, would be the natural outcome of having individuals who are professionally trained and experienced in basic management techniques actively engaged in the policy process.

In 2003 the Bush Administration asked certain questions about achieving goals in education, consulted experts in education policy, and created a rather simple metric for public education—measuring the schools by the improvement, or lack thereof, in the standardized (nationally) test scores of students. This may or may not be the key to improving public education; it certainly seems to be a crowd-pleaser. The verdict is still out as to whether or not this policy of imposing a performance requirement, without any accompanying substantial funding to help schools improve qualitatively as well as quantitatively, will result in substantial improvement of our public education. It may produce, at the very least, students who are more proficient at taking tests. It is also perhaps too early to tell if the policy of redirecting tax dollars to private schools (via vouchers and grants) will "encourage" public schools to improve—that is, to become more competitive in attracting "customers."

In the introduction to the 1993 report *Creating a Government That Works Better and Costs Less,*[13] a wide range of additional examples is cited. The Office of Management and Budget estimated that the Department of Defense owns $40 billion in unnecessary supplies. The Internal Revenue Service can't find people who owe us additional billions. A century after industry replaced farming as the nation's major business, the Department of Agriculture still operates 12,000 field service offices, an average of nearly four for every county in the nation—rural, urban, or suburban. We spend

---

[13] Vice President Albert Gore's National Performance Review (First Report), *From Red Tape to Results: Creating a Government That Works Better and Costs Less* (September 1993).

approximately $25 billion a year on welfare, $27 billion a year on food stamps, and $13 billion a year on housing—yet more Americans fall into poverty every year.

The report cites a Brookings Institute study that maintains we are suffering not only a budget deficit crisis but also a performance deficit. Public opinion experts argue that we are also suffering from a very deep crisis in faith in government. In past crises—such as Watergate, Vietnam, Monica Lewinsky—Americans doubted their leaders on moral and ideological grounds. They felt that their government was deceiving them or failing to represent their values. Today's crisis is different: People simply feel that government doesn't work. In Washington, however, the debate rarely concerns the *performance of government*—all of the attention is on developing or revising national policies.

We suffer much more from poor implementation of good policies and programs than we do from policies and programs that are inherently bad. However, as well intended as the reinventing initiatives of the 1990s were, and even though they did achieve significant success in changing some of the government's most egregious management failures, too many of the changes stagnated or disappeared after the deficit crisis abated. Why was this? Even with the President of the United States and his Vice President personally and publicly committed, why did political support disappear?

I have come to believe that the answer is quite simple: Professional management and government performance are *not* national policy issues and therefore are treated as episodic tonics to be administered only when a significant illness arises. When the aches and pains go away—so does the need for the medicine. There is no political will for ongoing, preventive actions and, even if there were, there are few in government who would know how to carry out such programs. Although the answer seems quite simple, the road to a solution can be complex and daunting. I hope this book will raise the attention level of the problem and then offer some very practical, not too complex approaches to begin solving the problem.

One of the most prominent themes that runs through the writing and teachings of Peter Drucker is that management should be considered a "liberal art . . . liberal because it deals with the fundamentals of knowledge, self-knowledge, wisdom and leadership; and art because it is also concerned with practice and application."[14] This view and its implications should help the cynic as he or she tries to come to grips with management's essential role as it is currently practiced in government. Additionally, professional management is not an "add on"—it is a mind-set, a way of thinking that needs to stand side by side with each function of any enterprise. For example, in a private company an engineer must be concerned with product cost, reliability, and manufacturability as well as with form and function. The members of a sales force must be concerned with customer service as well as competitive pricing and the size of their commission checks. The music director of a symphony must be concerned with audience receptivity to the program selection as well as with the artistic value of the performance. The hospital director must be concerned with the effective utilization of the equipment and facilities as well as with the quality of medical care provided to the patients. Every institution except the federal government (and a few states without a balanced budget requirement) must concern itself with professional management or it will not thrive—or survive! Unfortunately, those responsible for the federal government's finances can always run deficits whenever their spending exceeds their income. In fact, there is an argument made by some that deficits don't even matter! Various attempts at balanced budget amendments have been made from time to time, but those few that did succeed were quickly abandoned as soon as more money was needed.

If the federal government does not need to balance its accounts *and* (as the current administration believes) deficits are not that important anyway, it is easy to see why there is very little political appetite for giving professional management a high priority. But, even if there is a need for short-term flexibility vis-à-vis the ability to run deficits, long-term financial responsibility is as much a necessity for the government as it is for you and me. I believe there is a direct connection between the lack of sound management and

---

[14] Peter F. Drucker, *The Essential Drucker: The Best Sixty Years of Peter Drucker's Essential Writings on Management* (New York: HarperBusiness, 2001), pp. 12–13.

today's significant deterioration of Americans' faith and participation in the democratic process. No major developed country has
voter turnout as low as that of the United States.

What accounts for the electorate's declining levels of participation, confidence, and trust in their government? (Lest we all forget, the government of the United States derives its authority and
legitimacy from the consent of the governed. But active and
informed consent must not be confused with passive or indiffer-
ent acquiescence.) An often-quoted statistic is that in 1963 when
Americans were asked by pollsters if they expected the government to do the right thing, 75% responded "Yes." When asked the
same question in 1993, only 17% said "Yes." David Osborne and Ted
Gaebler, in their milestone book *Reinventing Government,* cite some
less-quoted statistics:

> By the late 1980's only 5% of Americans surveyed said they would
> choose government service as their preferred career. Only 13% of
> top federal officials said they would recommend a career in gov-
> ernment service. Nearly three out of four Americans said they
> believed Washington delivered less value for the dollar than it had
> ten years before.[15]

Once again we may ask: "Who cares?" Wasn't our country
founded with a healthy dose of government mistrust embedded
in the Constitution? Isn't it a good thing that Americans are skep-
tical about their government? As with many issues of this nature,
the answer is "yes, but"—and the "but" has to do with the degree
of mistrust. It has to do with healthy skepticism turning into
unhealthy cynicism. So, what happens when the balance shifts?
How do we know we're approaching dangerous ground?

In the book *Why People Don't Trust Government,* Joseph Nye Jr.,
dean of the Kennedy School of Public Policy at Harvard University,
says that the consequences include (1) the willingness of the public
to provide such critical resources as tax dollars, (2) the willingness
of bright young people to go into government, and (3) the voluntary
compliance with laws by all citizens. He continues by saying,

---

[15] David Osborne and Ted Gaebler, *Reinventing Government: How the Entrepreneurial
Spirit Is Transforming the Public Sector* (Reading, Mass.: Addison-Wesley, 1992), pp. 1–2.

If people believe that government is incompetent and can not be trusted, they are less likely to provide these resources. Without critical resources, government cannot perform well, and if government can't perform, people will become more dissatisfied and distrustful of it. Such a downward spiral could erode support for democracy as a form of government.[16]

He concludes with, "Even if government cuts back significantly from its current one third of GDP [gross domestic product] to something like a quarter, there is still a large part of our common life to be poorly administered."[17] It is interesting to note that Joe Nye and his contributors continue in the balance of their book to analyze a variety of possible causes for the disaffection, but, as Nye says, "It is not the intent of the book to offer solutions."[18]

Indeed, solutions are elusive! But I will still try to offer some that I believe can make a difference.

In another chapter of the same book, Gary Orren, a professor of public policy at the Kennedy School, cites a 1994 study: "Today's public cynicism cuts across all categories—black and white, male and female, rich and poor. Loss of faith in government has attached itself to every population group."[19]

Speaking more broadly, but in words relevant to this issue, Abraham Lincoln said during one of the Lincoln-Douglas debates on July 31, 1858, "With public sentiment nothing can fail; without it nothing can succeed. Consequently, he who molds public sentiment goes deeper than he who enacts statutes and pronounces decisions."

In *Managing in the Next Society,* Peter Drucker uses a question-and-answer format to make a statement regarding nonprofits. He begins: "But, so many people in business are leery of nonprofits because they see them as nonprofessional." He answers the point

---

[16] Joseph S. Nye Jr., "Introduction: The Decline of Confidence in Government," in Joseph S. Nye Jr., Philip D. Zelikow, and David C. King (Eds.), *Why People Don't Trust Government* (Cambridge, Mass.: Harvard University Press, 1997), pp. 2–5.

[17] Nye, "Introduction," p. 5.

[18] Nye, "Introduction," p. 5.

[19] Gary Orren, "Fall from Grace: The Public's Loss of Faith in Government," in Nye, Zelikow, and King (Eds.), *Why People Don't Trust Government,* p. 84.

by saying, "And they are both right and wrong. They're right because far too many nonprofits are either mismanaged or not managed at all. But they are wrong because nonprofits are not businesses and should be run differently." In what way? "They need more not less management, precisely because they don't have a bottom line. Both their mission and their 'product' have to be clearly defined and continually assessed. And most have to learn how to attract and hold volunteers whose satisfaction is measured in responsibility and accomplishment, not wages."[20]

What about innovation and management in government? Drucker continues:

> That's probably our most important challenge. Look, no government in any major country really works anymore. The United States, the United Kingdom, Germany, France, Japan—none has a government that citizens respect or trust. In every country there is a cry for leadership. But it is a wrong cry. When you have a malfunction across a spectrum, you don't have a people problem, you have a systems problem.[21]

He closes with the opinion, "Government—not business or nonprofits—is going to be the most important area of entrepreneurship and innovation over the next twenty-five years."

If one takes Drucker's point, one must recognize that, in some respects, people like me—experienced business executives—may well be a part of the problem. Our constant mantra, "Government should be run like a business," is not only wrong, but makes us look either naive or, at best, uninformed to people in government. The result is that we have been dismissed over time as not being able to contribute very much to the process. Consequently, each time a few of us do make it "into the system" we are met with an ingrained mistrust or even open hostility. Many have given up during the confirmation process. Of course, many have no interest in even being considered for public service. So the solutions suggested later in this book will deal not only with changing attitudes of those in government, but also the need to change the attitudes

[20] Drucker, *Managing in the Next Society*, p. 109.

[21] Drucker, *Managing in the Next Society*, p. 109.

of those in the private sector so that they can be an accepted and useful source for some of the solutions.

In my own case, I started out with the cooperation of a wide variety of people and the hope that I could make a difference, but ended up with the system closing ranks and attacking. For example, the most visible and controversial department of the GSA is the Public Buildings Service. This is the part of the agency responsible for the design and building of courthouses as well as the construction, leasing, and maintenance of government buildings. Its activities and the money it controls are of great interest to the nation's real estate industry.[22]

Almost from the first day the President announced my nomination, I was buried in calls and letters critical of poor management in the buildings program. The usual charges ranged from incompetence to fraud and illegal collusion. More serious charges, some in anonymous letters, came from federal employees as well as government suppliers. One congressional aide took the trouble to come to California to warn me personally that "powerful people" inside and outside the agency didn't want "an outsider" coming in and "screwing up" their "nice little operation."

It was clear that a broad but reasonably quick review of the federal buildings program would be necessary if I hoped to get to the bottom of the accusations. Reviewing one project at a time would take too long and wouldn't get the job done. (In early 1993 there were about 200 major building projects in progress around the country, with total costs on the order of $8 billion.) So, before moving to Washington, I began to think that declaring a moratorium on all the projects for a period long enough to conduct a useful review might be the best approach.

During the confirmation process—in both the formal public hearings and the ritual round of private meetings with individual Senators and Congressmen—I said that one of my first acts would be to call for a "time out and review" of all 200 projects. The projects included federal courthouses, office buildings, and facilities such as border stations and scientific laboratories. Surprisingly, no

---

[22] See Appendix 7: Jean O. Pasco, "GSA's Roger Johnson Castigates Washington for Plethora of Red Tape," *Orange County Register,* January 21, 1994.

one seemed to object. However, Senator John Warner (R-Va.) shed some light on why, when he called me aside after the hearing and said, "You know, Mr. Johnson, no one in my memory has ever stopped a federal building—but, I have to admit, that no one has ever tried to stop *all* of them. It will be very interesting to see how it works out."

How it "worked out" was going to be more than "interesting."

I asked the building service to answer a few basic questions about each project: Can the need for the facility be justified? If so, is the current scope of the project consistent with the need? Is the current project plan the most cost-effective available? If not, what recommendations would you make to reduce the cost and still carry out the mission of the facility?

We expected the review to take from six to nine months; it was actually completed in four. The results showed that the GSA could reduce the planned expenditure for these buildings by $1.2 billion and deliver better facilities. Most of the savings came from bringing the size of the projects into line with the needs. The federal process can take an astonishing three to six years for defining needs, developing plans, and getting congressional approval. It was easy to see how needs could change significantly during the process itself. Unless there was a method for constant review and reconciliation—which there wasn't—a project could fall significantly out of line with needs by the time on the project actually began.

Another savings involved the renegotiation of contracts in cases where we found material errors or contracting procedures that had not been properly followed. The most significant was a federal complex in Atlanta, which was reduced from a planned cost of more than $700 million to $450 million; because the savings principally came from contract renegotiations, the reduction in expenditures did not reduce the project's scope. But the most volatile part of our review involved a handful of courthouses that might not be needed at all.

This was my first exposure to the convoluted planning process for federal courthouses. What the GSA review committee had found was that either the original requirements driving the need could not be verified or that data justifying the requirements somehow couldn't be found at all. There were also several questions concerning the timing of when the courthouses would be needed. One of the more fascinating discoveries was that federal judges have extraordinary life spans. Key to the process were the projections of the number of judges' offices that would be needed going forward. The future office needs were calculated by forecasting not only the projected caseload of the district but also the number of offices needed for retired judges. (Judges are provided with offices for life.) As I looked at some of the detailed calculations, I began to notice that almost all of the current seated judges would still be requiring office space through the planning period—twenty to thirty years into the future. We then looked at the age of the current judges. Simple arithmetic disclosed that U.S. federal judges were expected to live for many years more than thee or me. Several would be living to be 100 or more and still going strong, according to these projections. Needless to say, their life expectancies were revised. This reduced the number of judges who were expected to need offices over time (shorter time), which in turn reduced or eliminated the need for expansion. Pretty sophisticated stuff, huh?

The committee's review made clear that five or six courthouses being planned or in the process of being built by the GSA were not needed then or, possibly, ever. Following my practice of thirty-five years in the private sector, I felt that the best approach to the problem would be direct: I would call the Senators and Representatives who had sponsored these courthouses. I'm not sure whether the GSA career staff believed I really would make the calls. They just said: "This is going to be interesting."

Late one afternoon I began calling Senators, beginning with Robert Kerrey of Nebraska and ending with Robert Byrd of West Virginia. My pitch went something like this: "As you know, Senator, we've been conducting a review of federal building projects in recent months, and I'm pleased to tell you that we believe we can make some considerable savings."

The response went something like this: "Admirable. Very admirable. I'm glad to see you're getting that agency to act responsibly. Now what can I do for you?"

"Well, it seems, Senator, that your courthouse"—in Omaha or Wheeling—"doesn't seem to be justified. I'm planning on recommending it for rescission of the appropriated money."

I never experienced such a quick change of tone in my entire career, during which I frequently had to deliver some fairly bad news to a variety of people.

"Well, Mr. Administrator, that's quite a statement," Senator Kerrey said. "I assume you can back it up because I've spent years of my life getting that project approved, and if you think you're coming in here and embarrassing me, you have another thought coming."

Senator Byrd's reaction came to four words: "We'll see about that."

I don't think all the calls took more than half an hour. The Senators had all been professionally informed, and now we could proceed with the formal requests for rescission. Or so I thought.

Not more than an hour later, George Stephanopoulos, Special Assistant to the President, was on the phone. "What are you doing with these courthouses, Roger? My phone has been ringing off the wall."

"Just trying to save money, George. That's what the President asked me to do."

"He doesn't want you to save it *that* way. These Senators are all calling and saying they're going to pull their support for NAFTA (the North American Free Trade Agreement, a very contentious but key part of President Clinton's early economic recovery program), not to mention a few other programs the President wants. He wishes you could find a way to reconsider. You wouldn't want to be responsible for the defeat of his programs, would you?"

"Of course not," I said, shocked at the thought.

"See what you can come up with. He's counting on you."

I'd been in more than a few tough confrontations before over unpopular decisions. But this was the President, the person I'd come to Washington to help. So with George's words still ringing in my ears, I called my staff together. They weren't as surprised as I thought they'd be. In fact, they seemed to have a solution ready before I posed the problem: We wouldn't actually call for rescinding the money; we could simply delay the projects until they could be better justified. Therefore, we could still show some planned savings, but we wouldn't embarrass the Senators by canceling their appropriations. It sure sounded good to me, especially since I could avoid being blamed for single-handedly defeating NAFTA.

I called the White House and told George that we had "solved" the problem—and thereby saved NAFTA, if not the presidency. George duly commended me with the assurance that "he" would be greatly relieved.

We pulled that one out if the fire, I thought.

Not quite!

The next morning I got a call from Senator Howard Metzenbaum of Ohio. I had met him some years earlier and again during the confirmation process. Among his great charms was that he didn't have a subtle bone in his body. In his formal remarks at my confirmation hearing, for instance, he said, "Mr. Johnson, I hope you realize that you are about to take over the worst pigsty in Washington." Despite the opinion of my Republican friends, who regarded Metzenbaum as one of the leaders of the Democratic forces of darkness and evil, I'd found myself all through the confirmation process beginning to like this crusty, straightforward man of boundless common sense. So it was with good humor that I picked up the phone.

"Good morning, Senator."

"I just read in this morning's *Washington Post* that you backed off rescinding those courthouses," he growled.[23] "You didn't really do that, did you?"

"Well, yes, Senator, but—"

"You wimp!" he cut me off. "I thought you were different. You're just like the other jerks we've put over there. No guts!" Without stopping, but with noticeable rise in the decibel level, he added, "Now what in hell happened?"

I related my story of the White House call, and how I had probably saved NAFTA and the presidency."

"You idiot!" he bellowed. "Did you talk to the President directly?"

---

[23] See Appendix 5: Al Kamen, "Starting the Body Count," *Washington Post*, December 17, 1993.

"No, not directly. But George said—"

"I don't give a damn what he said! The fact is that the President probably doesn't even know about the courthouses and never got a call from anyone. Some staffer over there is paying off a debt to some Senator. The next time those children at the White House call you and tell you, 'The President says,' you tell them to put him on the phone or go straight to hell!'"

His voice dropped again. In measured tones, he said, "Look, Roger. I'm told you're really okay. Even though I haven't seen evidence yet, I'd like you to get over here in the next week or so, and I'll try to give you some help with this town."

"Thanks for the offer, Senator. I can use it."

"No kidding," he replied, and hung up.

It seemed that within less than twenty-four hours, I had almost screwed up President Clinton's first term, and then saved it, and then was called a wimp and an idiot by a very senior U.S. Senator who had now offered to salvage what he could of my stay in Washington. It was not the kind of day a CEO, let alone an only child, likes to have. I went to see the Senator the next day and he became a valuable mentor and friend for the rest of my Washington stay.

The point of this story is that although there was a clear reason to stop these courthouses, there was no political appetite to do it. In fact, there were heavy political incentives *not* to do it. Did George Stephanopoulos and Senator Byrd want to waste money? Of course not! But the political rewards of taking that action were completely overwhelmed by the political penalties of cancelling the projects. Finding ways to change the political risk/reward ratio in Washington is essential, but undoubtedly the most difficult problem, and will take the longest to address. However, it seems to me that the mismanagement of one-third of our GDP combined with the serious consequences of the accompanying deterioration of public confidence cries for attention. Perhaps I can offer a few solutions— some reasonable and modest (but not wimpy!) course corrections that might eventually, slowly, alter the direction in which the super-tanker of government is plowing ahead. The real problem is that the engine powering the ship of state is very powerful, the inertia massive, and the rudder frozen in position.

With First Lady Hillary Rodham Clinton, at
the Art in Architecture awards luncheon in
March 1995.

At a GSA warehouse in Virginia: Vice President Al Gore, President Bill Clinton, and I
are speaking about the Reinventing Government initiatives. We found a better way to
obtain all those supplies!

September 1993: In a "green room" with President Bill Clinton and Vice President Al Gore, while staff members wait. We're preparing for a Reinventing Government event.

Golf at Pebble Beach, Labor Day weekend 1995: At the first tee with President Bill Clinton and his friend and advisor, Truman Arnold.

In the Vice President's White House office in March 1993, with Al Gore and his senior advisor Elaine Kamarck, discussing a Reinventing Government report. Is anyone listening?

5

THE DYSFUNCTIONAL ORGANIZATION

THE GSA WAS CREATED ON JULY 1, 1949, BY PRESIDENT Harry Truman, to "simplify the procurement, utilization and distribution of government property, to reorganize certain agencies of the federal government, and for other purposes." Over the next fifty years the "other purposes" had spread to cover almost every aspect of the government's day-to-day operations. These included procuring nondefense materials and services—from computers to ash trays, from airline contracts to janitorial services, from the government's communications contracts to food services—managing and maintaining the federal fleet of automobiles, establishing and maintaining day care centers for children of federal workers across the country, and of course acting as the builder, landlord, and maintainer of federal courthouses and office buildings around the country.

The agency's headquarters were at 18th and F streets in Washington, D.C. (just two blocks from the White House), but the majority of the employees, as noted earlier, are spread among ten regions in Boston, New York, Philadelphia, Atlanta, Chicago, Fort Worth, Kansas City, San Francisco, and Seattle, as well as a D.C. region separate from the headquarters operation in Washington. The original concept, resulting from the post–World War II Hoover Commission's work on restructuring the government, was to establish one central organization that would provide effective and efficient services and supplies to the agencies throughout the government. Prior to 1949 these functions were performed by each agency operating independently. In 1949 the concept of centralizing common tasks had just come into vogue and was reasonably logical at the time. However, the large centralized government organizations have not changed in more than fifty years, even though almost every other factor affecting government operations has changed several times. Moreover, organizational philosophies and approaches have undergone dramatic changes in most nongovernmental institutions. Evolution has always been necessary for survival in the private sector (with a nod to Charles Darwin), but no such imperative was acknowledged in the federal government.

In his book *Thickening Government,* Paul C. Light of the Brookings Institute noted that from 1930 to 1937 federal employment grew from 600,000 to 900,000.[24] Sixty new agencies were added to the executive branch. These new agencies widened the government's base, while new management layers increased its height. Into this "thickening" of organizations stepped a small group of scholars like Adolf A. Berle—the "brain trust" whose confidence in the science of management would shape the government hierarchy into the very present. Their goal was a tightly rationalized bureaucracy, led by a fully informed President. However over the years their management principles may have created exactly the opposite outcome: a wildly towering hierarchy in which accountability is diffused at best, and the President is sometimes the last to know. The original group of management scholars is long gone but the organizational structure of government has continued to thicken and spread, until today the structure itself is a major barrier to change.

Another effect of the unique federal organization is described by Dr. Martha S. Feldman in her book *Order Without Design.* In the first chapter she recounts her experience as an observer and analyst in the policy office of the Department of Energy, stating:

---

[24] Paul C. Light, *Thickening Government: Federal Hierarchy and the Diffusion of Accountability* (Washington, D.C.: Brookings Institution, 1995).

When I explained to the members of the office that I was interested in how the policy office produced information and how it
was used, I was met time and again with the response that the
information is not used. The analysts told me story after story
about papers that they had written that had never been read by the
policy makers who were currently concerned with the issues those
papers discussed.

Yet at the same time, I saw these analysts working hard to produce the information they claimed would be ignored. They
worked late nights and weekends. They poured energy into delib-
erations and negotiations with analysts in other offices. They spent
hours gathering information and analyzing it. They became angry
when their contributions to a report were overlooked by those in
charge of producing the report.[25]

The analysts told her, "It won't be used for one of the following reasons—either it won't be done in time, or it won't be good
enough, or the person who wanted it done will have left and no
one will know what to do with it, or the issue will no longer
exist."[26]

Later in the chapter Feldman concludes, "The process of producing information in this setting, in fact, mitigates against the production of clear and concise analyses that are decision relevant."[27]
In other words, even the policy development process itself was
hampered by a lack of clear goals. One can rightly argue, as does
Feldman later, that there is a real need and value for unconstrained
research and analysis. If all research was goal-oriented then the
world would be without a whole host of major discoveries and
insights. On the other hand, at some point, an organizational
structure, whether it be a government dealing with education or
a symphony orchestra dealing with artistic content, must have a
mechanism that allows for synthesis, summaries, and conclusions.
The structure must be such that responsibility for decision making, even with less than complete data, is clearly assigned and that

---

[25] Martha S. Feldman, *Order Without Design: Information Production and Policy Making*
(Stanford, Calif.: Stanford University Press, 1989), pp. 1–2.

[26] Feldman, *Order Without Design*, p. 2.

[27] Feldman, *Order Without Design*, p. 10.

those asked to contribute to that process have an equally clear channel for communicating about and contributing to the process.

Feldman's book continues to explore the work bureaucratic analysts do, and the way organizational constraints and the structure of their work influence what they do, and the possible effects they may have. Although her text deals primarily with the effective implementation of government operations and policies, the book provides a very detailed look at the results that poor or completely missing professional management disciplines can have on policy development itself. It is a very good reminder that the process of policy and operational procedure development must be done in conjunction with management considerations. Thinking of these as two separate activities does not work very well.

★ ★ ★

One of my own first personal encounters with the practical impact of this structure was when I realized that, on the organization chart, nearly forty agencies and individuals "reported" to the President. You don't have to have an MBA to know that this is an impossible situation in any organization, let alone for the most complex institution on earth. Invariably, informal structures take over. In the federal government what happens is that each agency secretary "reports" to dozens of people and organizations, depending on the issue. For example, in my case, as Administrator of the GSA, although the chart showed me reporting directly to the President, I was told that for budget issues I reported to the Office of Management and Budget, for personnel issues I needed approval from the Office of Personnel Management, and for "reinventing" issues I took direction from the Vice President (or one of his staff, depending on the subject). But that was just for the executive branch. In parallel there were six congressional committees and subcommittees that had "oversight" responsibility of the agency!

This diffusion of responsibility and accountability is equally a problem in other agencies. Therefore, with all of these different people and organizations having a piece of responsibility, the practical fact is that nobody *really* has responsibility—or, effectively, accountability. Any one of these people finds it very easy to point to someone else as the culprit when a problem arises. When things go well, then lots of people can take credit. For example, in my Senate confirmation hearing before the Government Operations Committee, not only did Senator Howard Metzenbaum make the "pigsty" comment but Senator John Glenn, the Chairman of the committee, told me that for years the agency had been the brunt of serious accusations of waste, fraud, and abuse, and that he hoped I would use my obviously pertinent background to turn that perception around. My response was the politically correct, "I hope I find that your characterization is a bit extreme, but I have had a great deal of experience with improving troubled operations that I hope will serve me well in this assignment."

"Well, I have every confidence that you can get it fixed," barked the Senator.

Although my response was politically correct I was quietly thinking that if the Senate has had oversight responsibility since 1949—and if the GSA is really a pigsty—don't the Senators bear some responsibility? Just what does oversight mean anyway? I found that it means a lot of different things to a lot of Senators, Congressmen, and their staffs—but being responsible for *anything* was not one of them.

Avoiding accountability and responsibility has been turned into an art form in Washington. Most of us have heard the term "deniability," which, in Washington's dictionary, means "Make sure the boss knows what we're doing, but do it in such a way that he can deny he knew anything about it in the future." In the rest of the nation's dictionaries the definition would read "Make sure the boss can lie about his knowledge without getting caught!" Accountability avoidance runs rampant throughout the federal system. It starts with the poorly structured organizations discussed above.

★   ★   ★

On April 4, 2004, an exchange on NBC's *Meet the Press* between host Tim Russert and the 9/11 Commission Chairman and Vice Chair—former Governor Thomas Kean (R-N.J.) and former Congressman Lee Hamilton (D-Ind.), respectively—further emphasized the impact of this pervasive lack of professional management skills and disciplines in government.

"I'm amazed that no one has been fired in the FBI and other law enforcement agencies. The commission has a lot of evidence the officials were not doing their jobs," said Chairman Kean.

Russert then asked Lee Hamilton: "Are you surprised that no one has been fired?"

He replied, "Not really. Government is not very good at holding anyone responsible!"

Failing to have trained management professionals and practices cuts across all areas of government, including national security. Thinking only in financial terms misses the fact that good management practices are essential in every phase of public policy development, analysis and implementation.

★   ★   ★

The task of organizing is one of the fundamental jobs of a professional manager. It is basically a matter of grouping the work to be done into smaller packages (organizational units) so that it can be accomplished more effectively. Simply stated, the goals of the organizer are to ensure that similar or related kinds of activities are grouped together; that the amount of work in a particular group is compatible with the group's ability to be managed; that there are no gaps and overlaps of work between the groups; that the results/outcomes of the work in each package can be clearly defined (versus the other packages); and that the results can therefore be measured. There are a variety of other challenges the professional organizer faces, but if these basic objectives are not met the rest become irrelevant.

The work to be done always involves a number of different activities. The trick is to organize these activities in a way that can best achieve the desired results/outcomes. Since the end objective is to achieve a specific result, it is generally desirable to organize around results as far down the organization as possible (e.g., assigning specific sales goals by product to each individual salesman vs. having one large sales goal for the whole sales office). However, many times the work involves a number of activities that can best be accomplished if they are grouped together—in which case the end result of the organization would be assigned at a higher level.

The problem with the federal organizational structure is that the people responsible for activities necessary to accomplish a particular result are not given real control over the resources (money and people) necessary to achieve that result. For example, although each agency submits a budget, it is the Office of Management and Budget (OMB) that finally decides not only the total budgeted number but also the specific amounts in each line item that is submitted to Congress. This means that from the outset the funding details may not be aligned with the operating plans and objectives.

In my case, for example, I set the priorities of spending by account that were consistent with the objectives we had set for the GSA. OMB just as consistently changed them, for whatever reason, which meant the GSA's financial resources were allocated to areas that didn't need it and not allocated to others that did. The problem was further aggravated because once line items were submitted, reallocating monies from one line item to another was virtually impossible. Therefore the agency's management loses all flexibility to change resource allocation in order to respond to an inevitably changing environment.

On another front, most changes in organizational structure had to be approved by the "M" part of the Office of Management and Budget. This, in spite of the fact that there was no one I could find in that department who had any significant experience in management, to say nothing of the fact that no one had responsibility for the operating results of the GSA. Additionally, most personnel matters had to be approved by the Office of Personnel Management, another multithousand-employee agency. It should be clear that the net result of this—multiplied thousands of times across the government—was, once more, that no one could be held responsible for anything—let alone specific results. How could I be responsible for operating problems in my agency if I didn't have a budget consistent with the organization's goals or the proper people to carry out the tasks? OMB and the Office of Personnel Management weren't responsible because they were not managing the agency on a day-to-day basis. Big jobs, with little or no responsibility. As the old saying goes, "What a country!"

In an effort to "fix" the problem, Congress tossed another ingredient into this nonmanagement stew with the passage of the

Government Performance and Results Act of 1994. This legislation, with the full support of the reinventing government group, mandated that each agency must provide a list of measurable results for each year. It is ironic that it took an act of Congress, some 198 years after the founding fathers gave us a republic, to point out that government should be held accountable for something. We all dutifully turned in our lists but, as far as I can tell, there has never been any follow-up—good or bad—on the actual performance versus the commitments.

The point of all this is that the organizational structures that are in operation every day in Washington, well out of sight of most of our citizens, are structurally flawed. No matter how well intended, trained, or experienced our people are, they eventually just comply with this grinding, senseless system. In any successful organization, with responsibility comes a reasonable measure of the control or autonomy necessary to meet your responsibility, to achieve your goal. No manager of any part of any institution would accept the kind of process to which responsible people in the federal government are subjected.

That goes for "support" departments or functions as well as "line" or "operating" departments and functions. In fact, it is vital for support organizations (like the GSA or a human resources or purchasing department) to have a "seat at the table" with all other departments or divisions. The auditors who "keep score" for the operations you support should not be in a position of determining what resources are allocated to you or setting the internal rules of charge-backs or other accounting metrics. Ultimately those matters are hammered out between the managers of different operations, managers who report to senior management. Conflicts and disputes are resolved, as necessary, by those in senior management who are both referees and the ones who ultimately define purpose and vision for the entire enterprise—the "big picture." In Washington it is difficult to tell referees from players.

★ ★ ★

These were all insights I acquired after the fact, so at the time and with Senator Metzenbaum's admonition still ringing in my ears, I set out to "make the needed changes."

No one likes to change! This is particularly true of bureaucracies whose processes are so highly dependent on hierarchies of laws, rules, and regulations. But before I appear to be dumping only on government people, I say that making meaningful, lasting change in any organization—public or private—is a daunting task.

At least, as I began my government assignment, I had been forewarned. As you may remember, I had been warned at the "B team" cocktail party that change wasn't going to be easy. In some respects, however, the opposition of the federal workforce was easier to deal with than opposition I had faced in the private sector. In the private sector when I informed my managers that we were going to change a particular process or program, too often they would say in a meeting such things as "That sounds good" or "Okay, boss, we're right behind you." They would then leave the meeting and say to each other "He's out of his mind" or "It'll never happen." I wouldn't know of the opposition or where it was coming from for a long time. In Washington this was not a problem. They would tell me to my face, right in the same meeting where I had proposed a change: "No, I don't think we'll do that."

Not all of the opposition was up front of course, because in Washington saying one thing and then doing the exact opposite was an accepted practice. Lying was also an accepted practice—but if you catch someone, God help you if you call it lying. There are "misunderstandings," or "misinterpretations," or perhaps one "may not have had all the facts," but even the most blatant misrepresentations are never called what they are—lies! After one particularly convoluted discussion I told my wife that although the people in Washington seemed to speak English, they used a completely different dictionary, and until I found a copy I was going to be in deep trouble.

In any event, it became very clear that in an atmosphere of open opposition on the one hand and covert sabotage on the other, changing the GSA or any other part of the federal structure—no matter how sensible it may have seemed—was going to take a lot of energy.

But once again I was surprised, this time favorably. I used some of the time-tested approaches to initiating and managing change that I had employed in the private sector. Once I explained what I was trying to achieve openly and honestly, the typical federal worker responded very well. What we were able to accomplish was certainly not because I had some magic approach. Rather, it was because no one had ever explained "how" to go about the change process. Once a proposal was explained openly and honestly, most of the GSA workforce enthusiastically embraced the approach. It was they who made the changes, saved the money, and improved our customer service. All I had to do was to show them how to do it. This may not seem important on the surface, but I believe that it is very encouraging. It is one of the main reasons I have confidence that if we can find a way to just get the basics of professional management into the system, the people who today are unfairly criticized for dumb management will quickly learn and implement professional practices. All they need is the training and an atmosphere where it becomes "politically" correct. For a brief period in the beginning of Bill Clinton's first term we had both. Although this climate of cooperation lasted only about a year and a half, it was sufficient time to show that meaningful improvements can be made.

*   *   *

So, specifically what did I do? What are some of these "professional management" techniques I'm talking about? My first task was to change how the employees thought about change. There are several well-known barriers to meaningful change that had to be addressed before I could even start.

The first barrier usually is with the senior management itself. Too often the senior management believes that the need for change is obvious. They can see the need—so it is assumed that everyone else sees it. This is usually not true. For example, let's say that the problem in a private company is that it is losing market share to a competitor. An obvious problem? Sure! But what are the specific causes of this drop in market share? There are probably myriad contributing factors, so each organization in the company will have to make changes to regain the competitive edge. The logical next step would seem to be for the CEO to bring together all the line and support managers, explain the overall problem, and call for each organization to review its operations and make the necessary improvements. Some of the areas to be reviewed seem obvious—we have fewer features than our competitor and our products are coming out late, obvious engineering issues. In addition, our quality is sub-par or our costs are out of line, leading to noncompetitive pricing. Manufacturing—go to work on these issues! The sales force is just getting outsold, and they don't seem to have the proper product training. Sales, get on top of these issues!

An obvious way to proceed? "Sure," says the engineer, "but not in my area—it's those idiots in marketing—we designed just what they asked for—if there are features missing it's their problem."

"Great plan" says the manufacturing manager, "but the real problem is not in my area. Those engineers hand me designs that are not checked out—no wonder we're having cost and quality problems."

And, of course when they all get together later they agree that the real culprit is the overpaid CEO who changes his mind and the company's direction every other day! To make meaningful change each person must be convinced that there is a need for him or her to change. The assumption that they will come to this conclusion automatically will usually doom any significant change program to an early death.

There are two fundamentals needed: One, be sure that the organization recognizes that the problem threatens the whole organization—no one can "win" if the total organization loses. Second, acknowledge that most problems are interrelated—no one is all wrong or all right.

This takes a lot of work and time up front in the process. What we did at the GSA was to spend the first several months going out into the regions—all of them—and meeting with as many employees as possible. We held "open to all" town meetings in each of the regions—explaining a couple of simple facts. First, the President had run on a platform of reinventing government, and the Vice President had been personally charged to make that happen. Therefore, GSA was going to change—the only question was who was going to make the changes. I explained to them that it appeared they had only two choices—either sit back and oppose change, in which case the White House and the Congress would decide what changes would be made, or they could take control of the change process themselves. I said that if it were me, I'd much rather control my own destiny than be at the mercy of the political structure. Still further, I suggested that if they chose to take the process into their own hands I would get them the tools and the time to do it right. Further, I would take whatever political arrows came their way during the process. Although it took a while to gain their confidence, eventually they took the latter course and made major changes in their own departments.

A second common barrier is that no matter how objective you are, when someone suggests that you need to "change" you can't help but feel that you must have done something "wrong." Otherwise why would you be asked to change? Who likes to be wrong? Nobody I know, particularly me! So the second task of a change maker is to try to reduce that guilty feeling. One approach I like is to hit the issue head-on—tell people that I realize they may have that reaction, but the reason for change is more that circumstances have changed, that past practices were quite good for the circumstances that existed at the time, but the *environment* has changed and, therefore, so must our reaction to it. It's not a question of being right or wrong; it's an issue of adjusting to the ever-changing environment in which we all work. During my career I was very fortunate to work for several very wise and caring people—many in my young years at General Electric. One of them once said to me: "Johnson, it's never wrong to be wrong—just don't stay wrong!" A wonderful message to remember when asking someone to change.

Another obstacle to change is that too often an organization has to endure the "plan of the month," which changes every other month. Changes that are dictated by senior management usually won't work, because the management does not really know what needs to be changed. They are too far removed from the operations of the organization to have a grasp of the details. The age-old adage of "seldom right, but never in doubt" too often describes management's approach.

To try to keep out of this trap I made sure that the process would be driven by the employees at the first and second levels of the organizations—not by their managers. The management would set broad targets for reduced head count, reduced expenses, and, most importantly, improved customer service, but the employees—not the management—would decide how to get there. This was fairly easy because I really had no idea of what needed or could be streamlined and I sure didn't have the time to learn. (It is harder to "let go" when you think you know what is needed.) As a result, across the country in small and big offices, GSA employees met in small groups and identified areas that they knew could be improved. Most of the employees saw the high turnover rate as an easy way to reduce expenses without having to lay people off. Improvement ideas began to pour in, ranging from elimination of paperwork to whole new procurement systems, from lower cost and better quality building maintenance programs to cutting months off the office/building leasing cycle.

Naturally, everything didn't go perfectly. I caught more political hell than I could have ever imagined—and for trying to make government cost less and work better! Some of our employees fought the process and quietly fed all sorts of misinformation to political enemies while the press predicted the "dire consequences" that would result from this "reckless Republican's" actions. The federal unions were always suspicious, but in the main were supportive as long as I kept them fully informed of our plans. The point of this recitation of GSA changes is not to cry about the problems or to show how smart I was, but to demonstrate that (1) meaningful improvement can be made using simple professional management techniques, and (2) federal workers are quite able and willing to put these techniques into effect. All they need is some training and political support.

Hundreds of other even bigger improvements were made across the other agencies as a result of the reinventing initiatives led by Vice President Gore and a dedicated staff. Unfortunately, a bipartisan political assault with the active participation of the press combined to trivialize and politicize the improvements over time. I have concluded that this is just another demonstration of the sad fact that if the political infrastructure doesn't understand something or can't control something, it will close ranks to destroy it. Sending people with my background to Washington once in awhile can make some differences, but until there is a major change in the political importance of good management, the improvements will be episodic and probably temporary.

It seems that we should be getting better results from the one-third of the national's earnings that are being spent. Achieving real progress in most of our nation's critical problems—health care, education, poverty, and energy—will only result from installing professional management into our governance process. In fact, achieving savings per se is probably not a realistic political motivator. However, convincing politicians that they can fund more successful programs from the savings that accrue from good management could be a big motivator. More about that later.

6

THE BUDGETING PROCESS (HOW 30% TO 50% OF THE NATIONAL INCOME GETS REDISTRIBUTED)

THE FEDERAL BUDGETING PROCESS IS SO COMPLEX, convoluted, and intellectually corrupt that it defies analysis or understanding by anyone other than the handful of career budget experts in the OMB or the Congressional Budget Office. Therefore, rather than try to tackle the total process, I believe we can use the GSA budget process as a case in point. This microcosm of the federal behemoth can then serve as an illustrative example as we look at how professional management practices would improve this mother of all reallocation systems.

My years of experience in managing large organizations in both the for-profit and not-for-profit areas taught me to always begin with a clear understanding of the financial condition of the organization. At the GSA this led me to meet with the agency's CFO, Dennis Fischer, and his key people soon after arriving in Washington. Fischer, who had worked for the federal government for more than twenty years, is a good example of the dedicated, honest, smart federal worker that is all but unknown to those not in government. The budgeting process was really a year-long task that just kept going month after month, year after year. This never-ending process was periodically interrupted by submissions to OMB, returned directives from OMB, followed by arguments with OMB, followed by resubmissions, and so on. This was being repeated all across the government as OMB prepared the President's annual submissions to Congress. This, of course, merely began another series of arguments between the White House and Congress and within the Congress itself, which then yielded a series of approved budgets whose priorities bore little resemblance to those that the agencies had submitted. But, let's get back to the GSA to see if we can get some buh-buh-billion-dollar examples that are easier to understand than the trillions at the higher levels.

"What's our budget this year?" I asked.

"Do you mean what we asked Congress for?" Dennis replied.

"OK, let's start with that."

"That would be about $250 million," he said.

Even though I had trouble keeping my millions, billions, and trillions straight—I knew something was wrong with that number. "Wait a minute, how can that be, we have about 20,000 people and even if their average salary was only $25,000—that would be $500 million—and that's not counting all the stuff we buy, buildings we build, and services contracts we let. How can the budget be only $250 million?"

"I see your concern, but we probably don't do the budget the way you are used to," he said rather sheepishly. "You see, the money we ask Congress for is only that money that we need *after* we subtract all the money the other agencies pay us." He went on to explain that GSA charges rent for the space the other agencies occupy, GSA bills the other agencies for the products the GSA buys and for the other services the GSA provides, so the "budget" is the difference—which is why it's such a small number. Almost all of the money the GSA spends is charged out to other federal agencies and is in the other agencies' budgets.

On the surface, and if properly done, this approach of "cross charging" is a good way to hold *both* organizations responsible when one is the user and the other is the provider of goods and services. However, it requires an additional level of budgeting and controls—otherwise you end up with *neither* organization being responsible or accountable. As I dug a little deeper it became apparent that we had the latter situation. I started by getting a better understanding of just how much the GSA really spent and therefore how much we "charged" to other agencies. Fortunately, Dennis Fischer quickly understood what I wanted, and in fact was eager to bring this issue to the forefront. He had long ago realized the fallacy of the approach, but had encountered no one in the organization who understood the issues, much less anyone willing to take them on.

It took a couple of weeks to get the results of the analysis. What it showed was that although we were budgeted for only $250 million, we actually were responsible for spending about $59 buh-buh-*billion* that year and approximately $61 buh-buh-*billion* the next year! After my first meeting with Dennis Fischer I knew the number would be a lot larger than $250 million, but I had not expected that big a difference. The real problem, however, was that because of the way the cross charging was managed there were no incentives to control or reduce the spending. In fact there were incentives to spend more—because whatever was spent would be charged to another agency and that agency had little recourse but to accept whatever was charged!

Another problem with this treatment of GSA's financial responsibilities was that the GSA employees had no concept of how much money they actually controlled. The fact that they have an impact on the federal budget was not evident to them because their "budget" was only a paltry $250 million. Additionally, the $250 million was so small in terms of Washington dollars that the employees of the GSA didn't believe what they did was very important. I was able to counter this attitude not only by showing them that they really controlled $60 billion, but also by using the Fortune 500 example to put the $60 billion in perspective.

It became apparent that the other agencies were being overcharged not only for services, but also for the GSA's own overhead. It was one of the reasons that one of my colleagues from the Department of Education told me one day that many other government workers called my agency the GA rather than GSA—because there was no S(ervice)! The only recourse that agencies had was to complain that the GSA was not efficient and that they (the agencies) could get better products and services at lower costs doing it themselves. Their complaints usually fell on deaf ears—because the GSA would argue that they were indeed efficient—that the cost of doing business, given the federal rules and regulations, was much more than the agencies realized, and therefore they were lucky it wasn't even more. It turned out both were right. And besides, the GSA had, by law, a monopoly on supplying most of the goods and services, so they could complain all they want, but it wouldn't do any good anyway!

In the months that followed I came to realize that the GSA, particularly the Federal Supply Service (the agency's purchasing arm), had been valiantly trying to open up the purchasing process, to eliminate the GSA's monopoly and allow the agencies to compete directly with other sources of supply. They had some limited success, but it was always a tough fight. But again I found government employees in the procurement process—led by Commissioner Roger D. Daniero and his successor, Commissioner Frank P. Pugliese Jr.—who were ready and able to take the lead in major reform as I gave them more management tools and got more political support. At that time in the autumn of 1993, however, no one had any idea of how efficient or inefficient the GSA was, because very little was being measured—no standards of performance had been set for what products or services should cost.

As I went further into the budget analysis that Dennis Fischer had prepared, some other numbers jumped out. There was a line item called "Real Estate Rent Use Charge"—$4.8 billion. But the "costs" of these rents, the actual rent (including the cost of services and real estate taxes) that we pay nongovernment landlords, as well as our own actual costs to operate federally owned buildings, was only $2.3 billion—that's more than a 50% profit margin. The "margins" for purchased products including computers were smaller, about 20%, but not bad. "Why are we charging agencies prices higher than our costs? I thought government was a nonprofit," I asked.

He explained that there were a couple of reasons: First, the margins for purchased products went to cover the expenses of GSA employees who are working in the Federal Supply Service organization. Some of the margins in the rent area serve a similar function, but most of these dollars went into the "building fund."

"What's the building fund?" I asked.

He explained that the fund had been built up over the years so that Congress could use the money to fund new buildings when there wasn't enough money in a particular year's budget.

I wasn't sure I heard him correctly, so I asked, rather stunned, "You mean this is some kind of slush fund that can be tapped in addition to the annual budget funding?"

"I'm not sure I'd call it a 'slush' fund," countered Dennis defensively—"but I guess, otherwise, you're correct."

"How much is in the fund as of today?" I asked.

"About six billion," he replied.

"Who knows about this?" I asked.

"I guess those people directly involved with federal buildings know about it—but I don't think many others do."

So here was a process, buried in the bowels of the GSA accounting system, that allowed a small special interest group—those connected one way or another to federal real estate activities—to circumvent the federal budget process. Of course it was only $6 billion—so who would notice!

Once again naive Roger picked up his lance and charged the windmill. This time it was two people: Congressman James Traficant (D-Ohio), Chairman of the House Subcommittee on Public Buildings and Grounds, and Eleanor Holmes Norton (D-D.C.), the delegate from the District of Columbia. Delegate Norton had taken a special interest in the GSA's public building program because of its major impact on her district. Congressman Traficant, as Chairman of the subcommittee, ran the meeting. I challenged the concept of the fund as inappropriate and suggested that the practice of marking up agency rents be stopped and the surplus balance be turned back to OMB! An alternative, one that I still believe was proper and appropriate, was to reassign the $6 billion to be used for annual maintenance. At that time we had a large amount of needed maintenance that had been deferred for lack of funding, and understandably, politicians would much rather spend the limited funds on new buildings for their states and districts than for maintenance. Therefore each year the proposed maintenance budget was cut in favor of new construction. I believe that charging some extra rent to ensure that needed maintenance would be done could be justified. I argued that in addition to circumventing the budget process, the excessive rents being charged served to make the rest of the government unfairly critical of the GSA for inefficient operations. Those agencies knew competitive rents were much lower and the GSA knew it was overcharging. But those involved wouldn't reveal the real reason, probably because they knew powerful people could put their careers at risk.

By this time I knew that I shouldn't expect my proposal to be welcomed with open arms, but the response was more aggressive than I had anticipated. First I was told by Delegate Norton, essentially, to back off—this was her territory—and I would do as I was told. Who was I to be challenging the Congress of the United States? Moreover, my staff was told that the GSA's total budget would be severely cut if I persisted—starting with my own salary. There were also threats through third parties that "my days in Washington were numbered." I raised the issue with OMB, and they promised to investigate—but nothing changed. I believe the practice is still in place today.

At the same time that Norton was attacking, Traficant was taking a less aggressive—but also clearly unfriendly—approach to my policies. I learned sometime later that many of the problems I was having with Delegate Norton and Congressman Traficant, as well as with Congressman Jack Brooks (D-Tex.), were being generated by a midlevel subcommittee staffer. My staff informed me that in previous GSA administrations, this person had a significant influence on the agency and its Administrator—particularly in the area of the public buildings program, but not limited to it. The person had become something of a self-appointed overseer of the agency. In fact, it appeared that the past Administrator was actually taking direction from this person. This obviously gave the individual a role in the programs and policies of the GSA that were quite disproportionate with the responsibilities of a subcommittee staffer. Unaware of this history, and trained to be sensitive to organizational structures, my personal dealings were directly with committee chairmen, Senators, Congressmen, and the appropriate officials at the White House. I was aware of the important role of staff, but did not usually deal with them directly, for what I felt was a very good reason. My own career staff were much more familiar with, and competent to handle, the detailed issues that usually surrounded staff work. But this approach was obviously very unpopular with this subcommittee staffer. I had unwittingly cut off the staffer's power base. Not a good thing to happen to you in Washington.

Before I realized, or was told, what was going on, this staff person had forged alliances with the people publishing *Crosswind,* an anonymous two- to four-page flyer that first appeared shortly after my nomination was announced and continued to appear every few weeks for my entire term. Its stated purpose was to keep track of Republican Johnson's activities by "concerned" Democrats. In reality it was a "hit" piece that contained a wide range of outrageous allegations. In addition to the attacks by *Crosswind,* there was stiff resistance from others within the GSA who opposed my changes. The congressional staffer apparently fed a continuous stream of "bad Johnson" stories to key Congressmen and Congresswomen. Since the staffer had their ear a lot more than I did, and was operating behind the scenes, it was several months before I figured out what was going on. Once I understood the situation, I was able to counter the campaign and regain the confidence of most of those *Crosswind* was trying to subvert—in particular, the zany, cockeyed, toupee-wearing Ohio Congressman, James Traficant. Traficant, in fact, eventually became one of my strongest supporters—although he was later convicted of completely unrelated federal charges and at this writing is serving time in prison. I'm not sure what conclusion should be drawn from that—but that's the fact.

The point of this little story, however, is that the almost complete lack of clear lines of authority and responsibility allows—even encourages—staffers and others to step into the void and cause all kinds of trouble. I was told by my colleagues in other agencies that there were people like this all through the government. Men and women with professional management skills won't eliminate the problem, but there would be far fewer issues with authority and responsibility.

I should point out here that I never saw anything to suggest that anyone was using the building fund for his or her own personal gain. As was the case with almost all of what I consider to be bad management practices, the congressional and OMB people involved believed they were doing the right thing. I never saw any evidence that anyone was acting for his or her own benefit. They felt they were protecting the federal buildings program from being annually "raped" by other higher priorities. The problem, of course, is that the approach they chose was devious at best. Another reason why we need professional management skills in government is that the lack of them leads good, but frustrated, men and women either to give up or turn to questionable practices.

*   *   *

Although there were obvious problems within the Public Buildings Service, I do not want the reader to conclude that everything was a problem. In fact, in the main, these were well-administered (if not well-managed) projects that provided not only excellent buildings but also often contributed great architecture and art to the country.

One little known but very valuable and well-run portion of the Public Buildings Service was the Art in Architecture initiative, which was begun in 1962 in response to a report from President John F. Kennedy's Ad Hoc Committee on Federal Office Space. The report was called "Guiding Principles for Federal Architecture," and these guidelines, although revised several times, are still the essence of a program that allocates 0.5% of the cost of each new or renovated federal building to "the creation of publicly scaled and permanently installed artworks that are appropriate to the diverse uses and architectural vocabularies of Federal Buildings and Courthouses." As a result of the 0.5% allocation, some of the nation's most important artworks can be seen in and around federal office buildings and courthouses. Some of the most well known of the dozens of major artists commissioned by the GSA include Alexander Calder, Sam Gilliam, Maya Lin, Frank Stella, and Eric Orr. There also is an Art in Architecture awards event each year to celebrate exceptional accomplishments.

Also in 1962, a young man who would become a legendary Senator from New York became a quiet but very effective champion of great federal buildings and architecture. Senator Daniel Patrick Moynihan (D-N.Y.) spent much of his career ensuring that the federal building program produced high-quality results. He was also a constant source of support to me. We were always under attack by someone for "excessive" or even "ugly" buildings and art—but Senator Moynihan was always there to defend the long-range view. One afternoon in his office, after offering advice on how to counter attacks on what would become the Ronald Reagan Federal Office Building, he told me how he first became interested and then passionate about federal buildings. In 1962, walking in the Inauguration Day parade as an aide to the newly elected President Kennedy, he recalled what a blighted mess Pennsylvania Avenue was with decaying buildings including the historic but vacant Willard Hotel, auto repairs shops, littered empty lots, and more than a couple of brothels. The President had also seen the same thing and at the end of the parade commented that something needed to be done. There was no further discussion, however, until that day in November 1963, just before the President left for Dallas. In a passing comment that morning, the President said to Moynihan—in effect—"Pat, the nation's Main Street is a disgrace and I'd like you to figure out what to do about it." These were the last words that Moynihan had with JFK, and he told me that upon learning of his assassination he became determined to carry out the young President's assignment. He spent a good part of his long, illustrious career doing just that. As a result we have a beautiful stretch of Pennsylvania Avenue that includes the graceful lines of the Canadian embassy, a saved then restored old Post Office, the renovated Willard Hotel, as well as the 1 million square-foot Ronald Reagan Federal Office Building—possibly the last major federal building to be built in the District of Columbia.

The point of this little diversion is that, although we have some very big problems in governmental management, there are also many programs that are well run by dedicated federal workers that fly under the political radar screen and thereby escape the daily search for "scandals" and are out of sight of those who would do them harm.

★   ★   ★

Returning to the overall GSA budget—there was no way to compare the costs with any standards even if they had set them up. This was not because the people in the GSA or in the agencies were dumb or lazy. They were intelligent people caught in a mind-numbing system that defied common sense, but the system was so embedded in the culture and the laws that these people eventually just threw up their hands and did "whatever it took to get the job done the best way I can." In some cases I found that government career employees, at significant personal and professional risk, would circumvent some regulations when those regulations stood in the way of what was obviously a more common-sense approach.

An example of a regulation that certainly would have been a candidate for circumventing was reported by Bob Stone, a former Deputy Assistant Secretary of Defense who had been responsible for military base installations, and a leader in the Vice President's reinventing office. In Osborne and Gaebler's book *Reinventing Government*, he talks about a simple steam trap that costs $100. "When it leaks," he explains, "it leaks $50 worth of steam a week."[28] So obviously it should be replaced quickly. Until the process was changed it took a year to get a replacement valve because the required procurement procedures were all aimed at ensuring the absolute lowest priced steam trap. In this case the government saved $2 but lost $3,000. The rules left no room for judgment even when quick replacement was obviously more important than getting the very lowest price.

Another example of an inane budgeting rule is the one that says the responsible manager cannot move budgeted dollars from one account to another when circumstances warrant without the permission of the OMB. Well-managed institutions—including non-profits—understand this and provide room for executives to make adjustments as circumstances change. To forbid moving budgeted dollars from one account to another, as long as the total doesn't change, flies in the face of any common-sense approach. Allowing requests to change to be made only after OMB approval adds insult to injury. The time it takes to prepare the request, submit, and then explain and argue the issue with someone buried in the bureaucracy isn't worth the time or frustration.

★ ★ ★

---

[28] David Osborne and Ted Gaebler, *Reinventing Government: How the Entrepreneurial Spirit Is Transforming the Public Sector* (Reading, Mass.: Addison-Wesley, 1992), p. 10.

Although these issues are not monumental issues in their own right, they are representative of thousands of situations whose total effect is monumental. For example in early 2003 the Congress refused to give the Bush Administration added flexibility over the supplemental budget approved for the war on Iraq. If there was ever a need for flexibility it would certainly be in the unpredictable prosecution of a war. Why do otherwise intelligent people act this way? They surely didn't want to hurt the war effort. To get an insight into this mind-set we must understand that the objectives of most of the laws and their ensuing regulations covering the operation of government are based on the premise that the laws and regulations should try to prevent *anything* from ever going wrong. To accomplish this, regulations are intended to minimize or eliminate the use of judgment in their implementation. The net result is that the "law of unintended consequences" runs rampant. Intelligent, well-intended federal workers are at first frustrated and eventually numbed into a state of compliance because they are impotent to change the system.

Although the web of rules and regulations appears very complex on the surface, they would not be hard to change if basic professional management concepts that defined desired outcomes and assigned responsibility and accountability for those outcomes were a part of the law-writing and subsequent regulation-drafting processes. This would, of course, require that individuals with knowledge and training in these areas of professional management would have to be in the executive branch agencies as well as the congressional committee structures. The plot thickens!

You Want to Sell What?

Some of the problems with the budgeting process are more subtle—but they can also be more lethal—literally.

The word "Uzi" jumped off the page at me.[29] The document said: "U.S. Marshals Service. Quantity: 85. Type: Uzi." I scanned a list two pages long. There were quantities of handguns, rifles,

---

[29] See Appendix 6: Letter from Roger Johnson to Attorney General Janet Reno (Re: Guns).

shotguns, and automatic assault weapons, along with the names of various federal agencies: Federal Bureau of Investigation, 9,600; Customs Service, 15,000; Internal Revenue Service, 4,000; Immigration and Naturalization Service, 19,000.

It was a Thursday morning and, as it happened, on most Thursdays the Commissioner of the Federal Supply Service was in my office overlooking the east entrance to the White House. He had all kinds of documents for me to sign. He always did. We were going through a large stack of them.

"What's this?" I asked, showing him the list of weapons.

"A waiver," he said.

"And why am I signing it?"

"It's a waiver we've been signing for the last ten years," he said.

"I see."

"It allows the federal agencies to resell firearms they no longer need. They count on this money to help with their budgets."

"I'm not going to waive the law."

The Commissioner sat back in his chair, rather stunned. "We have to," he said.

"If I'm not mistaken, this Administration is breaking its tail trying to get gun control passed. We're taking all kinds of heat for that. If you think I'm going to sign a document that allows us to resell—"

"But—"

"Wait a minute. When you say resell, what are you talking about?"

"We resell them to federally authorized gun dealers."

"You mean the guy on the street downtown selling all kinds of stuff on the used market?"

"Yeah," he said. "I guess so."

"No way."

"Well," he said, "we're going to get into big trouble."

"Why is that?"

"They will swarm all over you, Mr. Johnson, because this is about $10 million for different budgets."

"These guns have not been sold yet, have they?"

"No, no. Not until you sign the waiver."

"Are these all the guns we have?"

"No, we have others," he said. "Waivers were signed just before you got here. I'm not sure if they've been sold or not."

"I want to know how many weapons were sold," I said, "and how many are still in inventory waiting to be sold."

The information he brought back amazed me. Since 1982 under the Reagan and Bush Administrations, the federal government had sold 61,901 guns on the street, the bulk of them in the three previous years. We had another 36,855 already approved, waiting to be sold. How many lives would *they* claim?

I picked up the phone and called the Attorney General. Janet Reno came right on. "Do you have any knowledge of this?" I asked, explaining the situation.

"I've never heard of such a thing."

"I'm not going to do it. Is this something I'm legally required to do?"

"Don't do *anything.* Let me call Louie Freeh. I'll get back to you."

That night I had just arrived home when the phone rang. It was Louis Freeh, Director of the FBI.

"Thank God you caught this," he said. "Don't let it go through. We'll back you all the way."

The next day I wrote a formal letter to the Attorney General, confirming our conversations, and as the head of the General Services Administration I issued a directive stopping the gun sales. The government may have lost millions of dollars in revenue but we saved lives and untold misery. We had the weapons melted down. They were destroyed even before Congress passed the Brady Bill antigun legislation. And I never signed a weapons waiver in my term as GSA Administrator.

The point of the story is not that the federal government is run by evil individuals out to sell weapons and kill people. It is that good, intelligent people, people with common sense who want to do good things like balance the budget, are so bound up in an absurd process that it controls them instead of the other way around. They know it's ridiculous. We know it's ridiculous. But that's how it is.

★ ★ ★

Another dimension of the budgeting process, which never surfaces publicly, is a set of rules generically called the "scoring" rules. I first ran into them in a meeting attended by a rather large number of people (thirty or so).

This was the Reinventing Government status meeting chaired by Vice President Al Gore. I had just been in my job a few weeks and this was my first time at this particular meeting. Its purpose was to have each of the agencies present a summary of their projects highlighting successes as well as any problems they were facing. The meeting was proceeding quite nicely with several agencies each in turn presenting progress and issues. When problems were identified, the Vice President would make sure that there was a course of action determined and that someone was clearly assigned responsibility to deal with the problem. I was impressed that the Vice President was not only staying for the meeting, but was also actively engaged and obviously in charge.

About a half-hour into the meeting Gore called on the person who was heading the task force dealing with federal real estate. Although I had not yet met him, he was from the GSA's Public Buildings Service—David Bibb, I believe currently Deputy Administrator of the GSA and a respected expert on federal buildings. He reported the following problem. The government had been renting a large office building in Virginia on a fifteen-year lease, which had ten years yet to run. The real estate market was in bad shape in 1993, as was most of the economy, and the owner of the building was having financial problems. He had approached the GSA with a proposal, as follows: "The owner is willing to cut our annual rent by one-third if we would be willing to start the fifteen-year term over. Additionally if we would re-up the lease for fifteen years we would own the building at the end of the fifteen years."

I thought to myself—that's great—cut our rent by a third and own the building at the end of the period! The Vice President obviously thought the same thing. "Great," he said, "So what's the problem?"

"OMB won't let us accept his offer because they say it will break this year's budget," replied Bibb.

"I must have missed something," said Gore. "How can a one-third reduction in rent be a budget problem?"

"I think you'd better ask OMB, Mr. Vice President. I don't think I can explain it to you."

All of the heads then turned to the OMB representative, who stood, rather slowly, and began quite a long explanation. In essence he explained that since the government was making a commitment to own the building in the future, and since that building would have a value at that time, the budget "scoring" rules required that the estimated value of the building be expensed at the time the commitment was made to own it. Since the building is estimated to have a value of several million dollars—much more than the annual rent savings—the budget impact was a large unbudgeted expenditure this year, which would increase the deficit and violate the Budget Enforcement Act of 1992 being sponsored by the Administration.

I couldn't believe my ears. Here was a clear cash savings of several thousands of dollars a month—with a "free" building at the end of the term—but something called a "scoring" rule was preventing us from taking the deal. I guess I forgot where I was for the moment, because before I knew it I was on my feet blurting out, "That's bullshit!"

Most of the people in the room didn't know who I was and I suddenly realized that I was probably on thin ice—so I held my breath and sort of wilted back into my chair as all the heads turned to the Vice President. Luckily, he got this big grin on his face and said, "I agree with our new GSA Administrator. Roger, would you please take responsibility and fix this?"

With a big sigh of relief I said, "Yes, sir!"

The air returned to the room and the meeting went on. I remember sitting there and thinking, "Not bad—my first week here and the Vice President gives me a direct assignment to 'fix' something that I can probably do in less then a week. Then I can start 'fixing' some really big things!"

Was I ever wrong! Although I worked on this issue for the better part of the next year, not only did I never "fix" it, but in following the twists and turns of the underlying philosophy, laws, and regulations I crossed swords with Senators, congressional committee chairs, as well as the all-powerful gnomes of the OMB. I think the final score was Washington 15, Roger 2. Although we didn't get much changed in this area, I believe the process I discovered will serve as a good example of the huge management problems—ones still to be confronted—that continuously fly below the public radar, partly because good management is not a high political priority and partly because those involved in the process have a vested interest in keeping it out of sight.

As I began to try to unravel the seemingly illogical "scoring" rule I quickly ran headlong into a subtle but huge budgeting issue. The federal government has no capital budget. Therefore, there are no normal accounting rules for dealing with fixed assets such as buildings. If there had been a capital budget and anything resembling a government balance sheet, the building brought to our attention by David Bibb could have been booked into the balance sheet fixed asset account at whatever value OMB decided, but the amount charged to any year's expense/operating budget would be only the annual depreciation—not the whole value of the building. (The fact that, if the deal had gone forward—which it didn't—we would be putting it on the books fifteen years before we owned it, and that it was free, were issues for which I never did get a satisfactory explanation. Except this: "We've committed to do it—therefore we own it!") I think that in normal public accounting conventions this would be booked as a "deferred liability"—but I never got far enough to even discuss that side of the problem.

So why is this a problem that anyone other than an academic accountant should worry about? Who cares if the government doesn't have a balance sheet? Aren't there bigger issues to worry about? Does Johnson want to make "accounting" a national policy issue? Good questions—let's go a little deeper.

First of all, accounting has been a national policy issue for many years. We just don't think of it that way. In 2002, the corporate scandals sent almost every Senator and Congressman to the nearest TV camera, where they opined at length about the horrors of corporate greed, immoral and criminal behavior, and the need to return integrity to the boardrooms of America.

The result was the Sarbanes-Oxley Act, which injected the U.S. Congress into the middle of establishing accounting standards for the nation's private sector. The impact of the resulting regulations that have been pouring out of the Securities and Exchange Commission almost hourly since the law's passage is not yet clear. Many, however, forecast that the unintended consequences of these rules will at least equal the positive impact.

The point here is certainly not to defend the immoral and criminal acts of those involved—I am confident that our justice system will take care of them. And I am not arguing that new regulations are not needed—they are—because unethical but intelligent men contrived schemes that either circumvented existing laws or escaped exposure until it was too late. Closing these gaps is a good thing. What I am concerned about is that the "let's write laws that will make sure this never happens again" mentality will generate about as many new problems as it solves. This does not have to happen and wouldn't have happened if the congressional and agency staffs had much broader experience in professional management. Yes, they had good accounting counsel and of course good legal counsel, but if that's all that was necessary then we should see most organizations run by accountants and lawyers. We do not, because a perspective embracing all the aspects of an institution must be considered—not just accounting and law. Remember, it was many of these same people who, just a few years earlier, had advocated stock option awards as the best way to incent CEOs on a pay-for-performance basis. Oops!

More specific evidence of how "accounting" issues directly impact us is covered in Federal Reserve Chairman Alan Greenspan's comments to a congressional committee in February 2003. He said that the federal deficit would have been $365 billion in 2002—twice as big as the reported $158 billion deficit—if the government had used the accounting method preferred by Greenspan and used by most institutions. The larger figure is based on the method of accounting in which expenses are recorded when they are incurred. But the method used by the government records expenses only when they are paid. The former is called "accrual" accounting and the latter is called "cash" accounting. Greenspan said, "Accrual-based accounts would lay out more clearly the true costs and benefits of changes to various taxes and outlay programs and facilitate the development of a broad budget strategy." He continued,

"In doing so these accounts should help shift the national dialogue and consensus toward a more realistic view of the limits of our national resources."[30]

In other words, it would be like you and me ignoring the fact that our credit card charges totaled $5,000 and were growing, only being concerned with the $150 we had to pay this month. Moreover, by following this approach, we might keep on charging $300 per month even after our salary dropped by 10%. That's just what a lot of people do, you say. Of course they do—that's why many go bankrupt. As my grandchildren would say: Duh!

"Oops—we're off by $70 billion!"

"Who cares—we'll just pretend the tax cuts will stop a year or so earlier."

The financial shenanigans surrounding George W. Bush's 2003 tax cut plan would make even the Enron accountants blush. The President first asked for a tax cut of about $750 billion over ten years. The "prudent" Senate said that was way too much—and approved "only" $350 billion. "Teensy-weensy," decried the President. The House—showing more partisan support—approved $520 billion. The halls of Congress, the White House, and the weekly talking head TV shows were consumed for weeks with high-sounding debates over the absolute size, the types of cuts, who would benefit more, the impact on the economy, and on and on. Finally, a $350 billion cut was approved. But here—as Paul Harvey says on his radio broadcasts—is "the rest on the story":

On May 21, 2002, the Associated Press ran a story (buried deep inside most newspapers) that said the congressional tax experts had underestimated the cost of the cut in dividend taxes by $70 billion. So the real cost of the Senate bill was $420 billion—not $350 billion. The "problem" that resulted from the fact that the language in the bill covered accumulated dividends rather than just this year's dividends—the latter being the intent of the Republicans—could be easily fixed. Democrats, however, saw an opportunity to make the Republicans look bad and refused to allow the

---

[30] Alan Greenspan, testifying before Congress, as reported in the *Los Angeles Times*, February 15, 2003.

correction to be made! (Another example of the fact that bad management is a bipartisan affliction.)

Why didn't we hear more about this? Even in the land of billions, $70 billion should be noticeable. After all, it represents a 20% increase over the "approved" $350 billion. We didn't hear much about it because it didn't really make any difference anyway. Congress was busily finding ways to give the President even more than he asked for, while still having it look like only $350 billion. The Washington arithmetic rules just took over. A shopping list of tax cuts that would equal nearly $1 *trillion* over ten years was eventually enacted into law. The way they got the number back to $350 was to "sunset" (a term that describes a tactic sometimes used by lawmakers to set a date in the future when a particular law will cease to be effective) many of the cuts in two to five years, thereby technically limiting the cost to only the effective years. One might be a little skeptical about the sunsets for two reasons. One, Congress hardly ever lets the sunset provisions in any law go into effect. And two, the day after the bill was passed, Tom DeLay (R-Tex.), the Chairman of the House Finance Committee, said that not only would he be opposed to allowing the sunsets to stand, but that the Administration would soon introduce *more* proposed tax cuts. President Bush's 2004 State of the Union Address confirmed that direction.

Two points here. One—these issues are a bipartisan disease. Any current claims by one party or the other that they are the party of good government management is a complete fabrication. The second point is although the shams are despicable enough, the real problem is that the country doesn't get to debate the real issues. The hard decisions over whether tax cuts are good for the economy or not, the critical issues of "fairness," to say nothing of clearly understanding what are the real costs of the alternatives— all of these critical issues are buried or deferred for another day.

Finally, one of the most frightening aspects of the lack of intellectual integrity in our budgeting process came to light publicly in a 2003 *Wall Street Journal* article by David Wessel. The story covered an interview with Barry Anderson, who had recently retired as the number two man in the Congressional Budget Office. Anderson described what he called a "demographic time bomb" ticking beneath our fiscal house. In his analysis he divides the federal budget into three pieces—interest on the national debt; the cost of Social Security, Medicare, and Medicaid; and all the rest. He told the *Journal* that it was fairly common knowledge inside the Budget Office that the cost of Social Security, Medicare, and Medicaid will double over the next thirty years. As the baby boom generation gets grayer, the government will spend more and more on retirees and their health care. He maintained that "unless we have a substantially larger government than we've ever had in our history, everything else is going to be decimated." He also pointed out that "Social Security, Medicare, and Medicaid already eat up 15.3% of wages; 80% of taxpayers pay more in those payroll taxes (including taxes paid by both employer and employee) than in income taxes."[31]

When asked what politicians were doing about the issue, he said, "Ignoring it!" In fact, he says that although the problem is recognized by both Republicans and Democrats, neither side is dealing with it "honestly." Barry Anderson speaks with a great deal of authority; he has wrestled with these budget issues since the Carter Administration, serving in both the White House Office of Management and Budget under nine Directors and, more recently, in the Congressional Budget Office. I have to respect a man whose favorite T-shirt—given to him in the Clinton years—reads: "I Balanced the Budget and All I Got Was This Lousy T-shirt."

The inevitable collision of demographics and the budget is getting closer. The leading edge of the baby boomers turned 57 in 2003. Hopefully, we can get some men and women into the process soon who not only recognize the problem, but can also do something about it!

So, this seemingly arcane issue of federal "accounting" is not so arcane after all. It all too often allows our political leaders to abdicate their responsibilities. Many times it doesn't let those responsible have visibility into serious financial problems—and when the

---

[31] David Wessel, "Budget Nearsightedness Hastens Collision," *Wall Street Journal*, May 8, 2003.

problems surface anyway, it provides a whole series of ways to hide or at least defer needed action.

The Washington arithmetic rules also have a direct effect on how we manage our private sector. Are the people responsible for the financial aspects of our nation stupid? Are they crooks?

No, of course not—they are doing the best they can with the knowledge they have and with a political environment that has its own motivations. Incidentally, the comment by Greenspan showed up in a small box on page 4 of the *Los Angeles Times,* and coverage of the budget shenanigans was "stuffed" on the inside pages of most national media, while the Wessel article ran on page 2 of the second section of the *Wall Street Journal.* I wonder where they would have run if it had been about GE's or IBM's accounting methods.

While we're on the subject of scandals and accounting issues, in 1994 the GSA and the Small Business Administration were the only two agencies to get a "clean" opinion from the government's auditors at the time—Arthur Andersen. My CFO, Dennis Fischer, was quite proud of his accomplishment because the GSA had gotten a "clean" opinion for several years. Are you having the same problems with these statements that I had when I first heard them? Well, it seems that Congress, seeking to establish more credibility, passed a law in the late 1980s requiring that each agency have independently audited statements. This had not been the case up until then. Here it was 1994, and two of us had passed an independent audit. Dozens of other agencies had failed to pass and many others had not even started the process! No wonder Dennis was proud! (It might be of interest to some readers that the Department of Defense had its appropriations audit requirement *waived* because it had a "small" problem accounting for just where a trillion dollars had been spent. The Senate and House Armed Services Committees agreed to allow the Pentagon to skip these annual audits in their authorization bills. Look at the footnotes in the annual reports of companies in which you have invested. I doubt you will find any mention of audits being "waived." It would make the SEC distinctly unhappy. It would make *you* unhappy also, I assume.)

Very intelligent people, who lack experience in financial planning frequently fall into another trap when trying to deal with a variety of budget issues. For example, I'm sure that I added to my "outsider" status in an early Cabinet meeting when Bill Clinton's Secretary of Defense was decrying the President's proposed "radical" cuts in the defense budget. I believe the cuts being proposed were 4% or 5%. There was a chart in our briefing book that showed the department's budgets for the preceding five years—but the Secretary was only using the most recent year's budget when comparing to this year's proposal. Using the data in the book I asked, "It seems like the proposal, although below last year, is still 20% higher than it was five years ago, and about equal to the budget of just two years ago. Why can't we return to the spending levels of just two years ago?" The room was silent, no one said anything, after what seemed like an eternity, but probably only a few seconds, the Secretary just shook his head (a little like the AFLAC duck's reaction to Yogi Berra in the 2003 TV ad) and went on with his presentation. In his mind my question didn't even deserve an answer.

I was really mad at what I felt was an unnecessary insult but I now realize my line of thinking was so different from his that he really couldn't think of a suitable response. This thinking is not limited to the federal system. The recent 2003 California state budget problems found agency after agency condemning the draconian "cuts" even though most of the reduced budgets were still well above the 2000 budget. This was particularly true of the education budgets. Most other institutions—nonprofits included—start with a zero base and build their budgets from scratch. This forces a reassessment of all spending and avoids the assumption that all of last year's spending continues to be needed and anything new must therefore be added to that. Again, these are not complex concepts, and I believe they would become quickly adopted if we gave federal workers the proper tools and political support.

In summary, accounting information has many uses, but basically it is a retrospective account of financial activity. However, any professional manager, whether he or she is with a private company or a not-for-profit, will tell you that financial data must also be useful in helping to make decisions affecting future activity—not just recording the past. Therefore, when determining how to construct and present the data, its usefulness to management for making future decisions must be equally as important as accurately recording the transaction. Failing to do both can lead to very bad decisions.

For example: Let's pretend that you are the CFO of an orchestra and you are preparing a financial report for next week's board meeting. You are halfway through the year and your six-month results are as follows:

	6-Month Budget	6-Month Actual	Variance
Revenues	$2,500,000	$2,300,000	$(200,000)
Expenses	$2,000,000	$2,100,000	$(100,000)
6-Month Operations Net Income	$500,000	$200,000	$(300,000)
Fund-raising	$600,000	$900,000	$300,000
Results	$1,100,000	$1,100,000	$0

Therefore, the six-months' operations income was $300,000 more than budget. The fund-raising budget was $600K but had already come in at $900K. Reporting only these numbers—all factual—would show that revenues were down by $200K, expenses were up by $100K but fund-raising was up by $300K. So through six months you are still "on budget."

These are factual numbers and everything looks okay. However, as you look a little deeper you see that although revenues were $200K worse than the year-to-date budget, the amount recorded included advanced ticket sales of $100K that were budgeted in the second half. In reality the orchestra is really behind by $300,000 for the first six months.

The expenses for the six months included an early payment of $50,000 for concert hall rent that was budgeted in the second half. Fund-raising benefited from a $500K gift that was planned but actually received in the first half. So looking forward you would see that revenues benefited from the $100K advance—so the second half would be lower. If nothing else happened, expenses were really only down $50K when you take out the early rent payment, but fund-raising was off by $200K—because the $500K gift came in early. Although the first set of data was technically accurate and would lead the orchestra's board to believe everything was okay, on closer examination it looks like the orchestra has a ticket sales problem—as well as a fairly serious fund-raising problem. The orchestra was really down $250K for the first six months. As you see, very different decisions affecting the future could be made using the same data, but those decisions would be based on different presentations of the data.

This may be too simple an example, but I believe that it points out a way to understand that many things we *assume* are happening in our government's management systems are not happening. It also demonstrates that it wouldn't take a room full of Peter Druckers to make a big difference in how we conduct our nation's affairs. It is possible to change. There is hope.

The issues surrounding "accounting"—whether in the planning/budgeting process, recording what we're committed to spend, or ensuring that our accounts are accurate and properly reflect our financial conditions—are indications that the practices and processes, measurements and controls of the federal government are woefully inadequate. "We the people," to whom government is accountable, are given an accounting that is far removed from anything approaching reality. Alan Greenspan was right in 1996 when he warned that "irrational exuberance" can unduly escalate asset values,[32] and he is also on target about the government's "usual and accepted" accounting practices.

---

[32] Alan Greenspan, "The Challenge of Central Banking in a Democratic Society" (Speech given at the annual dinner and Francis Boyer Lecture of the American Enterprise Institute for Public Policy Research), Washington, D.C., December 5, 1996.

7

STANDARDS AND MEASUREMENTS (THEY'LL JUST CRITICIZE US ANYWAY—SO WHY BOTHER?)

ONE OF THE REASONS THAT WE LACKED STANDARDS and measurements in the GSA was because the agency employees had been attacked by congressional committees, other agencies, and the press for so long that they had developed a culture of trying to be invisible. As one senior staff member put it, "We try very hard to stay out of the line of fire, because we always seem to be the ones that get hit." This meant that they tried to keep out of sight any results, performance data, or anything else that could (and in their judgment would) be used against them. They felt that the best way to accomplish this was to have as few measurements as possible. There were other more structural reasons why many agencies didn't have standards or measurements—and that I'll go into later—but let's start with this one.

One problem surfaced when I received a letter from Congressman Ralph Regula (R-Ohio), Chairman of the House Committee for Government Operations, complaining about the GSA's management of the federal fleet program. The GSA was responsible for the procurement, scheduling, and maintenance of all federal vehicles except for those in the Department of Defense. When I called the Commissioner of the Federal Supply Service, who was responsible for the fleet program, he said, "Oh yeah, we get that letter every year. We just show up at the hearing, let him blast away at us, and then go about our business."

"What does he 'blast' you about?"

"He thinks we should outsource or privatize this whole operation to Hertz or Avis or someone like that, because he feels that the private sector can always do things better than the government."

"Is he right?" I asked.

"No, of course not. I've done a lot of studying on this and he is dead wrong."

"Have you presented your studies to the committee?"

"Yes, a couple of years ago—but they didn't believe us—they just kept blasting away—so I stopped trying to convince them. It's easier to just go up there each year and take their pounding. All the Congressmen want is the press coverage they get by showing they're 'taking on' the bureaucracy," the Commissioner said.

"Don't they ever follow up—force you to go to Hertz or someone like that?" I asked.

"No, they just holler once a year, get their press, and on we go."

Later I reviewed the studies he had mentioned and found them to be very enlightening and reflecting a lot of effort, but they were not well organized or documented. So, I asked that we do a formal comparison. We developed a very complete description of the tasks involved in managing the federal fleet of vehicles and then sent out requests for proposals from the better known car rental agencies and others who were in the business of wholesale car purchasing and maintenance.

The responses showed the following:

- The government has operations and people needing cars almost everywhere in the country. However, none of the rental companies had operations in all these locations. In fact, it wasn't even close—the best could only serve about 70% of the locations.
- Finding locations for maintenance and service was even more of a problem. (Incidentally, the Federal Supply

Service was already subcontracting all auto maintenance to private repair shops all over the country. These
contracts were competed each year and the costs were
well in line. The turn-around times were, by contract,
better than what you and I can expect when we bring
our car in for service or repairs. This stood as an example as a job well done and, equally desirable, as an indi-
cation of what might be done in the future.)

- Surprisingly to me, the quotes showed that the various
companies' costs to purchase the cars were 20% to 30%
higher than the purchase prices the GSA was getting.
The cost of gas and oil showed the same thing.

"How can that be?" I asked. "I know we buy in volume, but so
do the private sector companies."

"Oh, it's not the volumes," the commissioner said, "it's the fact
that by law, the government is the only organization that can buy
direct from the car manufacturers—the private companies must
buy from dealers. We skip that channel and their markup—plus we
pay no taxes on purchases of vehicles or gas. That's what causes
most of the gas price differences."

Therefore, to level this playing field, Congress would have to
start regulating auto distribution agreements between the manufacturers and their dealers and/or forgive gasoline sales taxes for
selected leasing companies. It didn't seem likely that Congress
would be willing to so.

It seemed to me that we had quite a compelling story—so,
reluctantly, the Commissioner agreed to put it together on some
simple charts. Up we went to Capitol Hill to the hearing. In addition to our determination not to be defensive about our performance, we took the offensive at the end of the presentation and told
the committee that there were other parts of the government that
were not using our service, and we thought we could save them
money. Even I didn't expect the reaction of the committee: The
GSA was complimented by the chairman and most of the committee members and directed to aggressively pursue purchasing
arrangements with other agencies that were not using our "very
efficient and effective" program.

I used this example and some others we developed over the next months to convince GSA employees that measurements were not only good management—they were also our only defense against erroneous attacks. I suggested that if you can't tell people how you are doing, in some factual way, and compare your performance to others doing the same or similar work, then you are vulnerable to anyone who wants to attack you. The detractors can say anything they want about your performance and you will have no defense. In the political atmosphere of the federal government you would be particularly vulnerable.

Another subtle but equally important outcome of this strategy was to begin to restore a sense of pride in our employees. No one wants to work in an organization that is constantly criticized, particularly publicly. Our people began to hold their heads up and be a little more likely to tell people they worked for the GSA, rather than shrinking into a corner.

★   ★   ★

As with many of the areas of professional management, the practitioner approaches the issues of standards and measurements not only with a set of specific tools—but equally important, with a particular state of mind that thinks about measurements and standards in concert with analyzing possible solutions. Failing to have this mental set in most government employees shows itself in a wide variety of ways.

For example, we set up several small working groups in the Public Buildings Service to identify areas for improvement. Early on I met with the leaders of each of these groups to see how they were doing and to determine what I could do to help. One of the areas they had decided to tackle was the result of fairly universal criticism from other agencies that it took much too long to "deliver" new rented office space to the agencies. On an average it took the GSA nine to twelve months from the time the need was identified to the time space was available. However, they were having a big problem describing what "good" performance would be. They knew why it took this long, but they had no reference point that could be used to compare their performance.

"It seems that we should have two different sets of compar-isons," I suggested. "One should be of other governments, such as state governments that have their own GSA equivalents, or other national governments—possibly the United Kingdom or Canada. The other set of data could be from large private corporations that have their own real estate operations, such as General Electric or General Motors."

These seemingly obvious suggestions were greeted with facial expressions ranging from blank stares to looks of concern.

"What's the problem?" I asked. There was a rather uncomfort-able silence from the ten or twelve seated around the table. "Come on," I said, "How can I help if I don't even know the problem?"

Finally a hand went up, and one of the group said, "Well, there are a couple of problems. First we don't know how to get the data you suggest and, of more concern, just asking for it would put our jobs at risk."

The first problem was understandable—since they didn't have a mind-set of establishing standards and then measuring progress. They had never dealt with the problem of finding others who per-formed the same or nearly the same functions, to help set some standards. I had an answer for that. But the second problem com-pletely took me aback.

"How can finding out how others do their office renting process possibly put your jobs at risk?" I asked.

"Well it will put us into the 'A-76' process, which says that if the comparisons show that someone else does it for less money, we automatically have to outsource what we do."

Further discussion led to the knowledge that there was a law passed some years ago (before reinventing) with the intent of finding less expensive ways to conduct government activities. A part of the well intended, but very poorly executed, outsourcing craze had started in the Reagan years and continued during our own reinventing initiatives. The regulations resulting from this law yielded a federal form designated A-76—which had now taken on its own meaning. "We don't want to be A-76'd," said the employee.

It turned out that the regulation was very prescriptive and forced a rigid dollar comparison between a task performed by a federal agency and the same or similar task performed by another entity—usually a private company. There was no room for discussion of the dozens of other factors that should be considered in making an outsource decision—such as the quality of the service, the time to deliver the service, or the different regulatory requirements involved in the process. Therefore federal workers put themselves at risk with this rigid formula even if they merely tried to find a meaningful standard of performance. No wonder they didn't seek outside comparisons!

Accordingly, before we could go any further, I had to back up my promise to run interference for our employees and take the political heat. Fortunately, one of the most effective tools that the reinventing staff had been able to put in place was a process whereby an agency could request a temporary waiver from a specific law or regulation. This waiver would allow an agency to conduct a pilot test of a process or procedure that would otherwise be banned. I asked for and got a waiver from the A-76 rule so that we could gather the needed comparison data.

With permission in hand we now could begin to find sources for the needed data. Getting information from other governments was not too hard. The reinventing staff had already developed good relations with the United Kingdom, Canada, and Australia. Our own GSA people had plenty of contacts within the states. Soon, data began to flow in.

The outside private comparisons were another matter. Our auditor at the time was Arthur Andersen. I had met their Washington office people when I discovered that our audited financial data only went back to 1987. It is relevant to mention that in the 1990s Arthur Andersen was riding high and enjoyed status as one of the top accounting firms in the United States—indeed, the world. No one could have imagined that less than a decade later the company would become embroiled in the Enron accounting and securities scandal, and would collapse (in a scenario that played out in the private sector, and had nothing to do with the federal government).

In our case in the early 1990s, the auditors from Arthur Andersen agreed that they would contact their private sector offices and see if they could gather answers to a long list of questions we had developed concerning rental office planning and acquisition processes. The responses that would be taken from specific company data would be anonymous to GSA, as the company names would be known only to the audit firm.

During this process the GSA employees were able to analyze the "best practices" of several other government organizations as well as those from the private sector, and incorporate those that were appropriate. They also gained confidence from the fact that, in many areas, they already had the "best practices."

The net result was that the GSA staff studied a lot of useful data from other governments (especially Canada, which had real estate markets that closely resembled ours) and the private sector. Changes were made, and the GSA was able to accomplish a significant (two or three months) reduction in the leasing cycle. However, we couldn't reduce the delivery time to be equivalent to the private sector's overall "best practices" because the federal process mandated, by law, certain procedures that the private sector did not have to follow. Most of these procedures related to the actual contracting process and were quite necessary. Even this issue was beneficial, though, because it allowed the agency to explain logically to critics why our process, although improved, still "took too long."

The point is that we again see federal workers responding very well once they are given access to professional management tools and realize that the political system is going to be supportive or at least, as in this case, not negative. We publicized this experience throughout the agency to demonstrate that in the process of setting meaningful standards and measurements, the Public Buildings Service people found ways to improve their operating procedures and also ways to defend themselves against common unwarranted criticisms.

The lack of experience in setting standards and meaningful measurements has led to extremes on both ends. In the one extreme, they don't exist. In the other, the standards are so detailed as to be laughable to most people. For example: Steve Kelman—a professor at Harvard's Kennedy School of Public Policy and chief of procurement reform in the Clinton Administration from 1993 to l999—in his paper "Remaking Federal Procurement," cites ridiculous specifications for "everyday items, ranging from ketchup to troop underwear to chocolate chip cookie mix."[33] The government publication *From Red Tape to Results: Creating a Government That Works Better and Costs Less* includes a report from Vice President Al Gore on the National Performance Review, and records what were no doubt intended to be very useful descriptions and specifications for ashtrays. These nine pages told procurement officials how ashtrays—better known to the GSA as "ash receivers, tobacco (desk type)"—should be constructed. Specifications and drawings gave the precise dimensions, color, polish, and markings required for simple glass ashtrays that would pass U.S. government standards. Samples, as provided by Vice President Gore:

> A Type I, glass, square, 4½ inch (114.3 mm) ash receiver must include several features: "A minimum of four cigarette rests spaced equidistant around the periphery and aimed at the center of the receiver, molded into the top. The cigarette rests shall be sloped toward the center of the ash receiver. The rests shall be parallel to the outside top edge of the receiver or in each corner, at the manufacturer's option. All surfaces shall be smooth."
>
> Government ashtrays must be sturdy too. To guard against the purchase of defective ash receivers, the GSA required that all ashtrays be tested. "The test shall be made by placing the specimen on its base upon a solid support (a 1¾ inch, 44.5 mm maple plank), placing a steel center punch (point ground to a 60-degree included angle) in contact with the center of the inside surface of the bottom and striking with a hammer in successive blows of increasing severity until breakage occurs."
>
> Then, according to paragraph 4.5.2., "The specimen should break into a small number of irregular shaped pieces not greater in number than 35, and it must not dice." What does "dice" mean? The paragraph goes on to explain: "Any piece ¼ inch (6.4 mm) or more on any three of its adjacent edges (excluding the thickness dimension) shall be included in the number counted. Smaller frag-

---

[33] Steven Kelman, "Remaking Federal Procurement" (Working Paper No. 3), from *Visions of Governance in the 21st Century* (Harvard University, January 2003), p. 19.

ments shall not be counted." *Regulation AA-A-710E, (superseding Regulation AA-A-710D).*[34]

Vice President Al Gore even used the ashtray test procedure to lampoon the specifications on a highly publicized 1993 television appearance on *Late Night with David Letterman.*

By any definition this is a ludicrous description of an ashtray—it must have been written by idiots! Wrong—it was written, over time, by competent people who were caught up in a system that, by legislation, was trying to ensure that they met the buy-from-the-cheapest-bidder rule. As explained in Kelman's paper:

> To buy the low bid, the government needed to specify what it was buying, so it could choose among comparable offers. Whenever the government discovered that a previous low bidder had "cut a corner" in such a way as to make the product less costly, a new element was added to the specification to "tighten" it. Over time, some element of the growingly complicated spec would appear that commercial vendors could not meet. Unwilling to adapt their products solely for government, which was a tiny part of their business, these vendors exited the bidding. The unintended negative consequence was that eventually the only firms bidding on these items became ones with no commercial marketplace presence, who had come into existence solely to bid on government spec items, and that generally meant higher costs and poor customer responsiveness.

The effects of this thinking had also infected the Department of Defense specifications for "milstandards," where common electronic components had such rigid requirements that many successful high-tech companies exited the process, leaving the business to specialized firms with much higher cost structures. It was also this mind-set that eventually led me into another of my battles with the Washington culture.

★ ★ ★

[34] Vice President Albert Gore's National Performance Review (First Report), *From Red Tape to Results: Creating a Government That Works Better and Costs Less,* Chapter 1, "Cutting Red Tape, Part II" (September 1993).

As I mentioned earlier, many companies (those not happily, deeply, and inextricably embedded in the military-industrial complex) deal with the federal government through an arm's-length relationship, through divisions specifically tasked with the onerous burden of dealing with the government and its perplexing ways of buying any kind of good or service and keeping the government from "infecting" or screwing up the company's core businesses. Or they would sell to value-added resellers that had been specifically set up to do direct business with the government.

The purpose of each of these different structures, as noted, was to isolate the primary business from a variety of unintended consequences of government rules and regulations. In addition to the spec issues outlined above, there were other big issues. One of these was the Truth in Negotiations Act, a well-intended law passed in 1995 whose intent was to prevent fraudulent costs from being presented to the government. (Now really, who could be against truth?)

In effect, however, because the law was interpreted to apply to all products, a company could have been required to submit confidential cost data that their competitors would love to get. Additionally, most of the pricing of these otherwise commercial products was a result of competitive forces in the marketplace, and therefore "competitive bids" were not only not necessary, but also served to significantly reduce the number of competitors! Finally, it doesn't take a CPA to understand that the definition of "product costs" will, legitimately, vary widely depending on how the data are to be used. Flexibility is not one of the characteristics of federal regulations. One of the specific results of this, says Kelman, was that

> five of the country's ten largest semiconductor firms refused to accept Defense Department contracts requiring provision of such cost data. . . . The unintended negative consequence was to limit participation to significant parts of defense contracting, even at the subcontractor level, to firms bidding only on government business that were often more expensive and less innovative.[35]

---

[35] Kelman, "Remaking Federal Procurement," p. 20.

Companies or divisions of companies devoted solely to government contracting are not limited to defense work. Scores of computer and computer-related companies surround Washington. My first run-in with the commercial purchasing implications of all of this occurred when I saw a purchase order for new desktop computers being ordered for the GSA for approximately $10,000 each! At the time I could have purchased a similar unit at Computerland ten minutes away for $2,500. I was also surprised by the brand of computers being offered because it was not one of the major suppliers.

"Why are we paying so much for a PC that I can buy for a fraction of that today at any number of stores in the DC area?" I asked the federal supply officer.

"We can't buy from just *anybody*, we have rules to follow," he said.

Why wasn't I surprised? "What rules?" I asked.

"Well, a lot of them, but mainly the Brooks Act," he said with some confidence. It turned out the Brooks Act, named for Congressman Jack Brooks (D-Tex.), was written when the computer industry was in its infancy and was dominated by IBM. At that time there was no such thing as a desktop unit and computers were anything but *personal*. Even though the industry and the products had changed almost every year since then, the provisions of the act had remained essentially intact. Among many of its obsolete provisions was one that required competitive bidding in situations where the market had long ago rendered such bidding unnecessary. Consequently, many computer companies had left the government playing field, leaving the business to others who were not as competitive or responsive but knew how to navigate the federal procurement system.

The American computer industry had been making huge leaps in performance, in combination with lower and lower prices for years, but the government was being prevented from enjoying these advances by a very old law. Although others in the government, and Steve Kelman in particular, agreed that major changes in the law were necessary, it was the GSA administrator (me) who found himself in the crosshairs of Jack Brooks's Texas six-shooter.

With major help from Senator William Cohen (R-Maine, who would eventually become Clinton's Secretary of Defense) and Steve Kelman, we were finally able to make major changes in the law, these being embodied in the Federal Acquisition Reform Act of 1995. However, not before Jack Brooks and others extracted their pound of flesh from my hide.

Brooks's attack reached a new level of ferocity one morning in March of 1994. I had been called to testify before the House Sub-committee on Government Operations, chaired by Congressman John Conyers (D-Mich.). There was already an atmosphere of apprehension in the hearing room because an interview with my wife about our days in Washington had just run on the front page of the *Los Angeles Times* Sunday edition.[36] Among other com-ments, Janice was quoted as saying that she was so upset by the antics of certain politicians in Congress that they should "go jump in the Potomac!" My legislative assistant, former Connecticut Congressman Bill Ratchford, was obviously quite shaken as I entered the hearing room, as he whispered to me, "There's a copy of your wife's interview on each of the committee members' desks!"

I said, "Great—I hope they ask me about it!" That clearly was-n't the response he wanted to hear, as he slumped back into his chair.

As it turned out, no one said a word about the article—and in fact, Janice received a lot of support for her bold comments, even from members of Congress. One of the strongest notes of support came from First Lady Hillary Clinton.[37] Janice's relationship with Hillary Rodham Clinton started on the campaign trail in 1992 and continues through today. On September 17 of that election year, Janice helped put together an event for Hillary at the Westin Hotel in Costa Mesa in Orange County. The Los Angeles campaign committee had underestimated Hillary's drawing power, and

---

[36] See Appendix 9: Ann Conway, "From O.C. to D.C., It's Downhill All the Way," *Los Angeles Times*, March 20, 1994. Also see Appendix 12: Letter from President Clinton to Janice Johnson (Re: *Los Angeles Times* article).

[37] See Appendix 13: Letter from Hillary Rodham Clinton to Janice and Roger Johnson (Re: *Los Angeles Times* article).

while they hurriedly rounded up additional seating for the overflow crowd Janice and Hillary waited and talked in the hotel kitchen. Janice commented on how well the campaign was going, and for the first time, at least to either of us, Hillary replied, "You know we entered the race not thinking that we could do it the first time around but, you know, I believe we are going to win!"

After we arrived in Washington, President Clinton appointed Janice to the Committee for the Preservation of the White House, of which Hillary was honorary chair. Unlike many such committees this one met regularly and did some significant work, including the first renovation of the East Room (the State Dining Room) since the Kennedy years. Hillary attended the meetings and was an active participant. During this time she also created the "Twentieth Century American Sculpture at the White House" exhibit, which featured the work of American artists displayed in the Jackie Kennedy garden just outside the East Wing of the White House. She also brought into the White House collection the first work by an American female artist, Georgia O'Keefe.

I saw another dimension of the relationship between Hillary Clinton and Janice on the evening of the day that the Monica Lewinsky story first broke in the *Washington Post*. Janice and I had been invited to a White House dinner, which was recognizing the White House Endowment Committee. This committee had, in less than three years, raised approximately $20 million in private donations for the White House endowment. The endowment had been started by Barbara Bush when she was First Lady to help pay for the day-to-day wear and tear that the White House suffered from the more than 1 million visitors each year. Many don't realize that much of the physical care of the White House must be paid for by private funds. Approximately $12 million had been raised when the Clintons arrived. So in less than three years the fund had gone over its goal of $30 million, which would provide the approximately $1 million each year needed for the maintenance. In any event, as we entered the White House that night not knowing what to expect, one of Hillary's assistants pulled me aside and said, "Mrs. Clinton would like Janice to sit next to the President tonight at the head table." I went off to another table and Janice did well in her role of a trusted friend.

But back in the congressional hearing room, we had all just settled in awaiting the traditional opening remarks by Chairman
Conyers, when a buzz ran through the people seated behind me.
I turned to see Jack Brooks making his way to the front of the
room. His appearance made Bill Ratchford's concerns about my
wife's article seem to pale, as Bill said something to the effect of,
"Uh-oh, now we're really in for it."

"What's he doing here?" I asked Bill.

"I'm not sure, but you can bet it won't be good for us," he said.

As Brooks, obviously enjoying the response to his grand
entrance, made the rounds shaking the hands of the Chairman and
others on the committee, Ratchford whispered, "There's a tradition of congressional courtesy that says if another Congressman
wants to appear at any hearing, he can just show up and the Chairman will yield him whatever time he needs to make his comments."

Very quickly, the hearing was called to order and Conyers
immediately recognized the "distinguished Congressman from
Texas." Brooks, relishing the stage and the surprise of his appearance, opened slowly in an exaggerated Texas drawl: "Mr. Chairman, I have spent over forty years in this House serving the
American people . . ."

After about ten minutes of relating his accomplishments, which
were not insignificant, he finally got to the meat of his comments.
He began by describing how the government had or could be
cheated by unscrupulous companies in the computer industry, and
how his Brooks Act had defended the American taxpayer from
these depredations for all these years. Now his good efforts were
being sabotaged by a certain Republican computer business executive who had come to Washington with the sole purpose of turning control of the federal procurement process back to these
culprits.

I had become used to these attacks and was quite prepared to
counter them point by point if given the chance. What followed,
however, was quite unexpected. "Mr. Chairman," Brooks continued still quite slowly, letting the words crawl out his mouth, "you
and I remember another Orange County California Republican

who came to this town about twenty years ago." His delivery became more staccato. "And I know you remember what happened to him!" I'd been called a lot of things, but never compared to Richard Nixon—at least until now! "We sent him packing back to California!" he said rather triumphantly. "Today we have another Orange County Republican who doesn't belong here and we're going to send him back also," he said with fire in his eyes. "But there will be one difference, Mr. Chairman: President Nixon was able to fly in a fancy government plane back home—but not Mr. Johnson. No big plane for him, I'm going to make sure that he has to ride back on a bicycle without a seat!" he sneered.

Even John Conyers, who in his career had seen just about everything, seemed to be taken aback by the downright nasty nature of the delivery. For some reason, it struck me as being kind of funny. It was so bad, so improbable, that in a way it was hilarious. For several years after that, I had dreams of riding this seatless bicycle. I was always going up some mountain—one of the Rockies, I suppose—I was out of breath and out of strength, but I couldn't get off—I had to sit down. Fortunately I always woke up before that happened![38]

I'm not sure that having professional management more ensconced in the federal government would have helped this situation much—but it did leave me with a valuable lesson. Never attack a law that is named after a living and still sitting Congressman! Dumb, dumb! In Washington it seemed that everyone except me knew that when logic collided with politics, logic was the loser.

Ironically, Jack Brooks was defeated in the 1994 Republican surge. Although I didn't even know who was running against him, I was accused in the anonymous *Crosswind* newsletter of having funded the Republican's campaign in an act of vengeance. My last encounter with this longtime public servant was several weeks after the election, at the annual Christmas party given at the Chevy Chase Club by Washington lawyer and former ambassador to the Dominican Republic, Chuck Manatt. Janice and I were

[38] See, for example, Appendix 11: Richard Tennant, "Pandora's 'GSA Reorg.' Box" [Cartoon], *Federal Computer Week*, April 11, 1994.

standing in a group talking when Brooks suddenly appeared at my side. (He was still in office until January.) "I'll bet you're the only one in the room that is happy I'm not coming back," he said with a slight twinkle.

"Not true, Congressman," I said. "Now I won't have the chance to get you straightened out." He looked a little surprised for a second, but then started laughing. His wife gave me a wink and was laughing harder than Jack.

Jack Brooks had come to Washington when Dwight Eisenhower was president; he was called by Lyndon Johnson in Dallas on that fateful November day in 1963, to join him on Air Force One for the flight back to Washington with our fallen President, John Kennedy. He served with great distinction for many years. Although my encounter with him was not a high point in the annals of gentlemanly behavior, this story points out another example of the lack of professional management thinking in Washington. It also is equally an example of how someone not experienced in the political realities of Washington can engender resistance and outright hostility. I should have shown much more respect for Jack Brooks and his accomplishments and his obvious defensiveness over attacks on "his" law.

Although I had had two private meetings with him (prior to the subcommittee hearing) that were supposed to have cleared the air, as it turned out I had backed him into a corner, and he had shown his teeth. Changing attitudes and gaining acceptance for professional management processes will require educating professional managers about Washington's political processes and social amenities, just as much as the political entities need to be educated about management processes.[39]

---

[39] See Appendix 14: Thomas R. Temin, "Credit Where It's Due" [Editorial], *Government Computer News*, August 8, 1994.

8

IT CAN BE FIXED!

PROBABLY THE MOST CONCERTED EFFORT TO fundamentally change the culture, process, and procedures of the United States government since Roosevelt's New Deal occurred with the Reinventing Government initiatives of the Clinton-Gore first term (1993–1997). I am using this period and its activities as examples for that reason. The issues that I am addressing are not partisan. The nonmanagement of government is a bipartisan failure and has been for some time. Therefore, the reader should not impute any political bias or message to my selection of data. I use these references simply because this period witnessed a broadly based focus on the symptoms of nonmanagement. Even though there may be disagreement as to the degree of success of the Reinventing Government initiatives, I believe that analysis of the activities can yield some valuable lessons. They can be drawn largely from the achievements documented in the Reinventing Government progress reports submitted annually between l993 and 1996, under various titles, as part of Vice President Al Gore's National Performance Review.

Now to begin. In 1787 James Madison, in the *Federalist Papers* (No. 40), said, "In framing a government . . . you must first enable [it] to control the governed: and in the next place oblige it to control itself."

In the 20th century, Americans did a much better job of the former versus the latter. In May 1932 at a speech at Oglethorpe

University in Atlanta, Franklin D. Roosevelt said, "It is common sense to take a method and try it; if it fails, admit it frankly and try again. But above all, try something." This is just as true today as it was in the depths of the Depression. Innovation and creativity are just as important in managing the affairs of government as they are a cornerstone of our economic institutions. However, we need a political atmosphere that will encourage it, and people who know how to do it.

Beginning with the motto "Works better and costs less," the Reinventing Government initiatives targeted some of the most fundamental concepts and processes needing change. One of the most subtle, but most significant, barriers to positive sustainable change is the zero-sum mental set. This concept assumes that in any situation there is a fixed set of outcomes, and that any change in one of these will automatically cause an equal change in the other. For example, this zero-sum thinking would conclude that the total amount of trade between Mexico and the United States is fixed, and that any gains in one will be offset by an equal reduction in the other. The main opposition to the Clinton Administration's proposed North American Free Trade Agreement (NAFTA) was based on the argument that the elimination of tariffs on Mexican imports would automatically reduce jobs in the United States. Organized labor has promoted this concept for some time and has fought against many, in my judgment, sensible free trade initiatives that would, in the final analysis, create more U.S. jobs. It is the same logic that now has politicians rushing to condemn the treaty as an example of why we're losing jobs. Not true—but that is another book.

Zero-sum thinking also assumes that the total budget for a governmental agency is exactly what is needed to provide the services of that department. How many times have you heard that a reduction in a department's budget will cause a commensurate reduction in the services the department offers? Cut the Sanitation Department's budget and you get reduced trash collection services; cut the education budget and you get fewer teachers; cut the police budget and you get fewer police on the street.[40]

---

[40] See Appendix 20: Letter from Roger Johnson to President Bill Clinton (Re: Balanced budget).

IT CAN BE FIXED!   101

This assumption is not only an issue in government, but is also a problem in many private companies as well as other institutions. Try to cut the engineering budget in a for-profit company and the engineering management asks, "What projects do you want to cut?" The underlying assumption is, of course, that costs and performance are in constant balance and that no improvements can be made in either. The fact that most businesses and many state and local governments have made major improvements in the way they run their sanitation departments, their schools, and their law enforcement organizations is ignored by those trying to protect their turf.

Likewise, another reality ignored by those trying to protect their own special interest areas is the fact that the total output and jobs in the nations involved in reciprocal tariff elimination / reduction has historically gone up. Zero-sum thinking produces false choices that are then used to threaten the public with reduced services. Unfortunately, it is quite a successful tactic because there is little or no "push back" from governmental management. When confronted with this logic, professional managers would simply tell their staff to go back and start their budgeting process from zero and justify all proposed spending. Additionally, these false choices are usually reinforced with vigorous support from affected special interest groups. Therefore, "Works better and costs less" was a lot more than just a cute slogan—it directly attacked this embedded cultural assumption and tactic.

Another fact: Productivity in the private sector has improved 1.5% to 3.5% per year for most of the past ten to fifteen years. However, this concept, which means getting more output with the same resources, or getting the same output with fewer resources, is hardly ever a subject of governmental budgeting. Although there are many other factors involved, simple math would suggest that government should be doing 25% to 30% more work with the same resources they had ten to fifteen years ago! Although most of the private sectors have done far better, this fundamental concept isn't even on the radar screen of governments. It also seems to escape the attention of educational institutions—particularly state-run universities.

I am confident that federal and state employment levels could be frozen at current levels for at least three to four years without limiting the ability to expand programs. Alternatively, in a budget crisis—such as the current one in California—state employment could be reduced by 20% without any services being reduced.

Once again, however, we find that it is one thing to recognize the issue and yet quite another to successfully address it. How to make something "work better and cost less" requires skills that have to be learned. It is the result of honing those management skills through extensive experience. Zero-sum thinking, on the other hand, is an easy sell and comes much more naturally to most of us.

I found out early on that zero-sum thinking was not the only barrier to change. Soon after my confirmation as head of the General Services Administration, I began a round of customary courtesy calls on Congressmen and Senators in leadership positions or who had some responsibility for the GSA—a surprisingly long list that I will discuss later.

Among the first I visited was Speaker of the House Tom Foley (D-Wash.). When I entered his office he grunted a greeting but seemed to continue working with some papers on his desk. Undeterred, I launched into a summary I had prepared of the issues facing the GSA as well as some of those broader issues on the Reinventing Government agenda. He still kept on working. I was getting a little irritated but concluded with a brief statement of my own background and something to the effect that I looked forward to working with him on these issues.

I had hardly gotten the last word out of my mouth when he looked up from the papers. "You didn't have to go through all that stuff," he said, "I know exactly who you are and what you're up to, and if you think that some rich Republican businessman and those children at the White House are going to tell me or the Congress how to run our affairs, you have another think coming! I run the House, and the sooner you and Gore understand the separation of powers, the better off you'll be. Thank you for the visit."

I remember thinking, "I guess he was listening after all." Foley represented the feelings not only of many legislators, but also of many career and appointed people. However, most were not as aggressively negative—they tended to be more passive while making their thoughts clear. In contrast, some legislators were quite supportive, Senators John Glenn (D-Ohio) and William Cohen (R-Maine) in particular. The bottom line was, however, that the only reason why any progress was made was that there was strong political support from both the President and the Vice President that helped nullify the opposition—at least for awhile.

It was in this atmosphere that the relatively small number of change-minded men and women on the Reinventing Government team started their work. Remarkably, however, in spite of the lack of general political support and the lack of management-experienced people in the process, significant changes were made. Admittedly, those improvements represented rather small bites of the federal elephant (or donkey if you prefer) but there *were* bites! The fact that the federal beast threw off most of its tormentors does not mean that it wasn't seriously tormented. The fact that the Washington political press (probably the group least trained or qualified to understand professional management) trivialized the efforts and closed ranks with the other defenders of the status quo doesn't mean that the status quo was not shaken. Looking back, rather than despairing, I am very encouraged because major improvements in the management of the affairs of government were made.

Changes take time and a lot of concerted effort. For those who read this book and take its thesis to heart, I hope to dispel the age-old barrier to change that goes: "Why bother, I can't do anything about it anyway!" What I saw in the 1990s in the Reinventing Government initiatives was a federal workforce that responded with enthusiasm and competence. I could cite many examples of what can get done when good ideas got political support. Let's take a look at some of the specific results of these efforts. I believe that most of the readers of this book will be surprised!

★   ★   ★

You could almost hear the "insiders" snicker and guffaw when the President and Vice President posed for photographers on the South Lawn of the White House with several large front-loader vehicles filled with regulations that had been eliminated. They knew that this photo op represented only a drop in the bucket of the billions of pages of rules and regulations that gave them job comfort and security. They were safe. But, not quite as safe as they were before, because behind this photo op were some *real* changes that hopefully were just the beginning.

For example, some years earlier someone had decided that doctors should be required to fill out and sign an "attestation form"—sort of a truth oath—swearing to the accuracy of the information they provided to the hospital when they discharged a Medicare patient. It didn't matter that the doctors had already provided all the information when the patient was released. They just have to do it all over again, on a longer form, essentially confirming that the information they had just given was indeed true. It added nothing to the patients' care, did not create any useful new information, and in fact spawned 11 million new pieces of paper and took up 200,000 physician hours. Under the Reinventing Government initiatives, the redundant forms were eliminated.

You'll remember the GSA specification for ashtrays I mentioned in the last chapter. Ensuring we have proper ashtrays is important, as David Letterman and others are now aware. However, once the "ashtray problem" was conquered, there were other challenges. Protecting the federal workforce from "bad grits" must have been deemed critical by someone at some time because we clearly defined what we wanted and how to prove we got it. Here's the spec that protected them:

> Grits, corn grits, hominy grits is the food prepared by so grinding and sifting clean, white corn, with removal of corn bran and germ, that on a moisture-free basis, its crude fiber content is not more than 1.2 percent and its fat content is not more than 2.25 percent and when tested by the method prescribed in Paragraph (b)(2) of this section, not less than 95 percent passes through a #10 sieve, but not more than 20 percent through a #25 sieve.

Now here comes the really interesting part: It tells how to prevent sub-par grits from entering the government "food chain":

> Attach bottom pan to a #25 sieve. Fit the #10 sieve into the #25 sieve. Pour 100 grams of sample into the #10 sieve, attach cover, and hold assembly in a slightly inclined position, shake the sieve by striking the sides against one hand with an upward stroke, at the

rate of about 150 times per minute. Turn the sieve about one-sixth of a revolution, each time in the same direction, after 25 strokes. . . . The percent of sample passing through a #10 sieve shall be determined by subtracting from 100 percent the percent remaining in the #10 sieve. The percent of material in the pan shall be considered as the percent passing through the #25 sieve. (21 CFR Sec. 137.230)[41]

In reading the above, I am reasonably sure that any graduate engineer from Stanford or MIT could, indeed, prepare grits in the proper manner! These specs were eliminated along with the 2,700-word description of french fries, dozens of pages on how to tell whether fish is fresh, dozens more to describe a camp lantern, and on and on.

When Jay Leno and David Letterman used these specifications as fodder on their late-night television shows we all laughed and shook our heads in disbelief. But just behind the humor is the sobering fact that the process that led to these specs forced federal procurement people to buy from specialized suppliers, at outrageous prices, products and services that could have been obtained at the local grocery, computer store, or office supply house for a fraction of the cost and a fraction of the overhead.

But how could intelligent people do this? They must really be stupid—or maybe in cahoots with the specialty suppliers getting a kickback for each ashtray or bag of grits that is purchased!

Not so.

To have some understanding of how the buying of grits could be turned into a federal case, we need to go back and take another look at the basis of federal procurement laws and regulations. Professor Steve Kelman, in his paper "Remaking Federal Procurement," observed:

Government procurement, like much of the organization of government in general, was traditionally characterized by high levels of rules, hierarchical signoffs, and what may be called "objectification"

---

[41] Vice President Albert Gore's National Performance Review (Third Report), *Common Sense Government: Works Better and Costs Less,* Chapter 2, "Getting Results" (September 1995).

in decision-making. Rules tell people what to do. Hierarchical signoffs require people to get approvals at higher levels of their chain
of command when no rule tells them what to do.[42]

Kelman explains his newly coined word "objectification" to
mean that the regulating culture will go to great lengths to try to
eliminate human judgment in decision making, and if words
won't suffice to define a regulation, then numbers or some quan-
tification would be substituted.

He continues: "The procurement system, again like much of
government, has tended to become ever-more rulebound, signoff-
ridden, and objectified over time."[43] This approach, with its atten-
dant regulations, is intended to take all human judgment out of the
decision making process.

There is another deeply rooted concept that permeates the regulatory process: the unspoken but very real assumption that
almost everyone involved in a process is either stupid or crooked
or both! Therefore, the regulations are written by people who are
trying to prevent government workers from ever making a mistake—covert or overt. The impact also spills over into the private
sector because the same thought process is followed when people
write regulations that apply to business. The fact that it is impossible to cover all aspects of human decision making—or that even
attempting to do so adds needless complications, costs, and time to
a process—is not recognized. Why? Because those involved have
had no experience with any other system for guiding human
behavior. Additionally, those involved see that every "mistake"—
no matter how small or infrequent—is treated the same by the
press and the political process and they are given no room for
error.

In this environment it is very difficult to get those involved in
the regulating process to consider the approach used by the management of most other institutions: setting regulations that "rule
by exception." Regulations that allow human judgment and com-

---

[42] Steven Kelman, "Remaking Federal Procurement" (Working Paper No. 3), from
Visions of Governance in the 21st Century (Harvard University, January 2003), p. 3.

[43] Kelman, "Remaking Federal Procurement," p. 3.

mon sense would, by definition, accept some degree of error. The "rule by exception" concept accepts as a trade-off that some mistakes will be made, but that the cost of trying to prevent *all* errors greatly outweighs the cost, direct and unintended, of the few errors that are made. This approach is second nature to those trained and experienced in professional management, but completely alien to the federal system.

Kelman continues to add backdrop to the procurement process: "As of the early 1990's two major statutes established procurement rules." He describes the first of these statutes as follows:

> The Competition in Contracting Act of 1984 established rules for choosing suppliers based on the policy of "full and open competition" (procurements should be widely advertised, open to all, and evaluated strictly on criteria announced in advance).[44]

Curiously enough, national security considerations were cited in the Bush Administration's award, without any prior competitive bidding, of massive contracts to Halliburton for reconstruction of Iraq's infrastructure and oil industry. Apparently the rule of exception can be invoked when desired by the executive branch. The public was reassured that the substantial funding involved will "trickle down" to subcontractors—who will, no doubt, be subjected by Halliburton to the rigors of competitive bidding and other criteria.

The other statute involved the disclosure of cost information and is described by Kelman as follows:

> The Truth in Negotiations Act of 1962 established rules for disclosure by bidders of cost information, which government could use to negotiate prices and that also served as a basis for audits and legal action against firms failing to disclose "accurate, current, and complete" cost data. The system's regulations were codified in the 1,900-odd page Federal Acquisition Regulation (FAR), as well as in agency "supplements" to the FAR. (The Defense Department FAR Supplement was itself over 1,800 pages, and each of the military services in turn had service-specific supplements!) Many common

---

[44] Kelman, "Remaking Federal Procurement," p. 3.

(although not universally followed) practices—such as buying from
the low bidder or giving no consideration to a supplier's past performance in awarding new contracts—were not rules at all in that
they did not form part of any law or regulation. Rather, they were
informal "rules" reflecting the spirit of a system that [imposes
rules and eliminates as much judgment] as possible.[45]

I found this to be quite common. Federal employees told me
that they sincerely thought some processes couldn't be changed
without an "act of Congress." I learned to challenge all such allegations. "Show me the law" was a question that they soon came
to expect. In several cases there were no laws to be found.

Some of the set procedures in the traditional system were
what Kelman calls "decision rules" such as "Award to the low bidder" or "Do not reimburse contractors for entertainment
expenses." Most, however, were about what process needed to be
followed in making a decision, including dictums like "Allow every
interested business to bid," "Allow bidders at least 30 days to
respond to a solicitation," "Evaluate proposals only based on the
evaluation criteria in the solicitation," "Do not accept late proposals," or "Negotiate only about price and about what elements
of a bidder's proposal do not comply with the government's
requirements."

Even with all of this history and the numerous barriers encountered, the Reinventing Government team was able to achieve
what Kelman calls a "trend break" in which "rules, objectification,
and hierarchy were all scaled back."[46] With significant support
from Senator William Cohen (R-Maine) and his staff, two pieces
of reform legislation were passed—the Federal Acquisition
Streamlining Act (FASA) of 1994 and the Federal Acquisition
Reform Act of 1995.[47]

Two major changes were made in the FAR. First, a statement
of "guiding principles" for the system was added to Part 1, which
set a primary goal of satisfying the customer "in terms of cost,

[45] Kelman, "Remaking Federal Procurement," pp. 3–4.

[46] Kelman, "Remaking Federal Procurement," p. 4.

[47] For instance, see Appendix 8: Gary H. Anthes, "Procurement Horror Stories Draw
Feds' Scrutiny," *Computerworld*, February 21, 1994.

quality, and timeliness of the delivered product or service," and added that those in procurement should "exercise personal initiative and sound business judgment in providing the best value product or service to meet the customer's needs." The guiding principles further stated that "in exercising initiative, Government members of the Acquisition Team may assume if a specific strategy, practice, policy or procedure is in the best interests of the Government and is not addressed in the FAR, nor prohibited by law (statute or case law), Executive order or other regulation, that the strategy, practice, policy or procedure is a permissible exercise of authority."[48] It is interesting to note that the use of judgment had to be written into the laws.

The second change, as noted by Kelman, came in 1998 when "a rewrite of Part 15 of the FAR, dealing with source selection procedures for large buys, was adopted. By the end of the decade, the system looked quite different" from the way it had been when the reinventing government effort got under way. In total, of the estimated 87,000 pages of federal regulations, the Reinventing Government initiatives eliminated 16,000 pages and simplified or revised another 31,000 pages. Significant improvements can be made!

Not all of the changes were to specific regulations. Many of the biggest gains came from just asking a federal worker what he or she thought should be changed.

The Occupational Safety and Health Administration (OSHA), one of the most controversial and despised of the alphabet agencies, had a policy of rating its inspectors on the number of violations they found. For decades they would sweep into a company and start writing up violations—big ones, little ones, important ones, and petty ones—often for things the employers had never even heard of and sometimes for things that had nothing to do with safety. One of the most aggravating practices was for the inspector to look for the OSHA compliance poster. If it wasn't up or was in the wrong place—an automatic $400 fine.

The problem was somewhat similar to that created when a police department instructs its officers to hand out a certain num-

---

[48] Kelman, "Remaking Federal Procurement," p. 5.

ber of speeding tickets (something law enforcement management insists never happens—well, rarely, anyhow). The emphasis was on finding violations—and the easiest ones to find and deal with were more minor than major. Not surprisingly, members of the business community, particularly small businesses, were furious. There was little correlation between the number of violations and improved safety of the workers.

For example, one of the largest privately held manufacturing concerns in the United States has a horrific record of workers killed and maimed in its plants over many decades, arguably because management (and the owners) allow nothing (defective machinery, equipment either obsolete or badly in need of repair, insufficient manning of machinery, and very demanding production quotas) to get in the way of production. OSHA cited numerous flagrant violations and fined the company on a number of occasions. But the punishment was hardly equal to the crime.

Many times an employer would challenge OSHA's findings in court. But in general, employers had little incentive to change any of their practices, if they were unsafe but profitable, because it took several months for all of the paperwork to be filed and the litigation settled. The entire scenario was nonproductive, both in terms of OSHA's relationship with employers and its ability to accomplish its goals.

The Reinventing Government team turned this process on its head. Instead of rewarding inspectors on the number of violations, they got rewarded if the companies in their region had very good or improving safety records. The approach they took quickly turned from a "gotcha" mentality to one of "how may I help you?" They even carried extra OSHA compliance posters with them and helped select the best locations—no fines! They offered consulting on how others were reducing the number and severity of on-the-job injuries.

All this came about simply by employing the proven management axiom that one should measure outcomes, not inputs. As soon as the measurements were changed, the behavior changed. President Clinton observed in January 1995, "If government rewards writing citations and levying fines more than safety, then there's a good chance that what you get is more citations, more fines and no more safety."[49] This principle was applied with equal success to other enforcement agencies such as the Customs Service and the Environmental Protection Agency (EPA). I believe that some have slipped back into their old practices, but the changes that were made demonstrate that major improvements are clearly possible.

Not all of the improvements needed serious analysis—some in fact just needed a little creativity. The Vice President's third annual report on the Reinventing Government initiatives gave us the following example:

> Harley is a potbellied pig. He also happens to be very good at sniffing out drugs. In fact, the police in Portland, Oregon, think he is even better than a dog in tracking down narcotics on the city's streets. And, he sure is a great mascot for anti-drug programs aimed at school kids. The kids love Harley.
>
> Harley has been such a success that the Portland police wanted to buy some more potbellies, and to train them to detect guns as well as drugs. The whole project would cost about $25,000. But . . . they haven't found any federal anti-drug money available for training pigs. Dogs, yes. Pigs, no. Never mind that Harley gets the right results—that he finds the drugs and charms the kids.
>
> When the White House found out that Harley was denied training funds because he was a pig, it acted swiftly—and designated Harley an honorary dog. It was a comical response to a ludicrous problem.[50]

But it got us a new "soldier" for the war on drugs and another example of common-sense government.

Another common-sense approach yielded more big changes in how the government worked. It doesn't take an MBA to know that customers comprise the cornerstone of any successful enterprise. Unless an orchestra is serving its audiences, a university is serving its students, a hospital is serving its patients, or a business is serving those who buy its products—it will not last long. Even though

---

[49] Vice President Gore's National Performance Review, *Common Sense Government*, Chapter 2, "Getting Results" (September 1995).

[50] Vice President Gore's National Performance Review, *Common Sense Government*, Chapter 2, "Getting Results" (September 1995).

the federal government, in almost all cases, is a legal monopoly, that doesn't mean it can treat its "customers" poorly and not pay a penalty. The federal "customer" certainly does not have the alternatives that are available to private sector institutions and businesses—but over time the public can withhold resources (such as taxes) and also make the federal workers' lives very unpleasant by treating them with indifference, contempt, or even hostility.

One of the few positive outcomes of the outsourcing craze that sweeps through the government periodically is that it does place an element of threat that the monopoly could be broken if effective service is not given. However, my experience showed that the hostile work environment was a much bigger motivator for the federal worker to improve customer service than the threat of outsourcing. The OSHA inspectors certainly didn't enjoy being disliked. No one likes to feel that his or her work is not respected or that they are perceived to be doing a bad job. The federal worker is no different from the rest of us in that regard. The main problem was that no one in governmental management ever made customer service an important priority. There were no standards of performance—there were no measurements. There were no rewards for good customer service. There's an old management saw that says "If you don't measure it, you can't manage it." This attitude is as true in government as it is anywhere.

Therefore, another theme of the Reinventing Government initiatives was "Putting customers first." Did it work? You decide.

The May 29, 1995, issue of *Business Week* asked, "Who'd have guessed that the Social Security folks give better customer service on the phone than Corporate America's role models?"[51] The article reported that when researchers from Dalbar Financial Services, North America's biggest financial news publisher, went looking for the best 800-number customer in their "World Class Benchmark survey," they found that the Social Security Administration ranked *number one*. It topped such service-oriented private companies as Southwest Airlines, Nordstrom, L. L Bean, Disney, Federal Express, and others.

---

[51] Cited in Vice President Gore's National Performance Review, *Common Sense Government*, Chapter 3, "Putting Customers First" (September 1995).

The survey rated each organization on attitude, helpfulness, knowledge, the time it took to answer the phone, and the time it took to reach a customer service representative. While the SSA lagged behind the others on the time it took to answer the phone, once the agency staff came on the line they were tops in the nation for being "courteous, knowledgeable, and efficient." How could this be? A fluke? Not really. Let's see how it came about.

It all began when the reinventors asked each agency to do two simple things. One, don't assume that you know what your customers want. Ask them. And two, set up customer service standards and a way to measure the agency's performance against them. So that's just what the SSA did. It recognized that in the past the agency had been blasted by its customers. People who had been paying into the system all their lives didn't think they should have to work even harder to get their money out than they did to put it in! With these responses in hand, the agency then asked its front line workers, who served these customers every day, how they would redesign their system if they had the chance. They also studied the best practices of the best customer service companies in the country. The result was a streamlined approach that was based on what customers wanted—not what the agency felt they should get. They took the best of the best from other organizations. Everyone won—the customers, the federal employees, and the taxpayer.

The SSA wasn't alone. The Internal Revenue Service received about 96 million calls each year in the 1990s and got very bad grades for almost all areas, but particularly for not giving out the right information. The reinventors made changes. Tops among the IRS's new goals was "The right answer the first time." Subsequent measurements showed that they had improved the right answer to 91% of the time—but still below their self-imposed standard.

The Department of Veterans Affairs assumed that its patients didn't mind sitting around in waiting rooms because they "enjoyed the chance to swap old war stories." But when they finally asked the patients, they found that veterans didn't like waiting around any more than anyone else did, so they set out to reduce the waiting time.

Here's another example. The Miami International Airport was notorious for long waits to get through customs. It reached a crisis level on June 29, 1995, when things really fell apart. Incoming flights completely overloaded the Immigration and Naturalization Service (INS), which is responsible for checking passports and clearing passengers. As the wait approached three hours, fistfights broke out between weary passengers. Meanwhile, others had to wait in their seats on the planes before they even got into the long lines in the terminal. It was quite traditional for government agencies to blame each other in a crisis. But not this time. Representatives of the INS and the local Customs Service representative contacted their partners in the American Federation of Government Employees and the National Treasury Employees Union and brought together an emergency coalition of customers and officials to solve the problem. In just two weeks of brainstorming, the airlines, airport officials, and several government agencies worked out an entirely new passenger handling system. Two weeks later as the vacation season peaked, the waits were gone. In fact, the airlines had a new problem—the passengers were clearing so fast that they were reaching the baggage pickup before their bags had come down! The improvements were too good, better than excellent!

When an agency or any organization is free to respond to customers' concerns rather than having to live with rigid rules, it can break down the barriers and develop creative solutions to almost any problem. Too often, however, it doesn't work that way. Government workers who sign up to be public servants end up being regulation enforcers instead. As noted by the Reinventing Government initiatives, "The government has to shift from a restrictive culture to a responsive culture." This is not hard if the workers are given the tools and a positive political environment.

The word "trust" is not seen or even heard much in Washington. In fact most regulations and procedures assume that no one can be trusted. In a contrary move, the GSA held a competition with the major credit card issuers and awarded a contract to Visa for its IMPAC (International Merchant Purchase Authorization Card) plan—a credit card that federal employees could use to make small purchases rather than going through the long process of requisitions, competitions, and purchase order approvals. Additionally there were no fees, and the government even got rebates on certain purchases. No more $4 staplers with another $50 in paper-work. In 1994 the government made 18 million small-dollar pur-chases. If they had all been made with the IMPAC credit card, the savings would have been $250 million. I believe the savings in time and aggravation would have far exceeded the dollar savings. How-ever, a GAO report found that there were federal workers who were "abusing" the system. They were charging personal items to the cards and, although, they were paying for charges themselves, it was still a violation. Several Congressmen jumped all over the "scandal" and demanded that the cards be withdrawn. So much for a common-sense level of trust!

In summary, the Reinventing Government initiatives had resulted in a reduction in federal employment from its high in 1990 of 2.174 million workers to approximately 1.9 million by 1999, the smallest federal workforce since John F. Kennedy was president. The total savings were estimated to be in excess of $200 billion! But the biggest impact that I observed was the improvement in the atti-tude of federal workers and the compliments on improved gov-ernment services that came from the public.

And the improvements garnered many positive comments. For instance:

- A citizen, a typical American "out there," wrote a let-ter in May 1995: "What you have accomplished here [at the National Climate Control Data Center] is some-thing the average person believes could not occur. . . . You have changed my thinking about federal employ-ees. . . . I previously thought that the negative stereo-types were all correct."
- The *New York Times* called the reinventing initiatives a "quiet revolution."
- And *Information Week* magazine informed its readers: "Tell your CEO that the federal government may be outclassing your company. . . . For once the Federal Government is ahead of the private sector."

In general, however, the changes went unnoticed and unpubli-cized. The budget at first was shrunk, then balanced, and then, remarkably, turned to a surplus. The heat was off! The reinventors couldn't get more than a handful of reporters at a major news conference, although to Washington insiders the Reinventing Government team had in many areas accomplished what was believed to be impossible.[52] By all reason, this should have been exciting stuff. However, it is the negative that makes the news—a teenager caught in a terrible crime gets nationwide coverage, while another teenager who achieves scholastic or sports excellence is local news at best.

Thus, "next steps" for the continuing reinvention fell mostly on deaf political ears, and Washington returned to "normal." Well, not quite. The genie was out of the bottle. Using professional management techniques and common sense did make a difference. The federal worker found a new freedom and a new sense of accomplishment. I am convinced that the ground has been prepared for major, but this time more permanent, change. The potential for meaningful change is now latent in the halls and offices of Washington. It is just waiting for the tools to be made available and a political atmosphere that recognizes the importance of good management.[53]

---

[52] See, for instance, Appendix 24: Daniel B. Wood, "Mr. Fortune 500 Runs a Federal Agency," *Christian Science Monitor,* May 9, 1996.

[53] See Appendix 18: Letter from Roger Johnson to Vice President Al Gore (Re: 1996 budget); and Appendix 19: Performance Agreement Status Report to the President.

9

"JOHNSON, YOU'VE GOT A PROBLEM!"

THOUGH I HAD A FAST AND SOMETIMES PAINFUL education in the public sector, I was very naive in the ways of Washington when I first arrived. Although I had some understanding that Washington was "different," I had no idea of how different. Even so I was self-assured—probably a little too self-assured—that my experience in dealing with tough business problems would be directly transferable to the government assignment I was taking on along with a role in the reinvention of government—an effort to make federal processes more efficient, sensible, and user-friendly, while eliminating waste and unnecessary expense.

What I found was that almost nothing in my prior experience was directly transferable. Almost everything I knew had to be rethought, translated, or otherwise modified to fit into the "Washington way." Of course, it took a long time for me to gain this insight. I'm not sure I would have made it though without the very supportive and understanding help from my chief of staff Barbara Silby, and my special assistant Pamela Blass. Although as Pamela once said, "dealing with an only child, an ex-CEO, and a Republican from Orange County was not the easiest assignment," they did their very best to help me understand the ways of Washington. I only wish I had learned faster. In any event, although I would do it all over again, my tenure—which ended with my resignation in January 1996[54]—was anything but calm.

I soon had to confront what I think of as the "dark side" of Washington. In relating some of my personal experiences—as well as those of a few others—I am not seeking sympathy. What happened to me needs to be exposed because it is an aspect of life in Washington that most people don't know about, and it represents another major barrier to change. There has been some media exposure of this dark side of the culture, but usually as the result of some headline-grabbing scandal—a sensational event that seems so far removed from most of our daily lives as to make even the scandal seem irrelevant. Even so, a couple of examples are worth noting here, because they set a framework for the larger problem.

★   ★   ★

None of my problems could compare with the saga of Henry Cisneros, Secretary of Housing and Urban Development during Clinton's first term. The *Los Angeles Times* reported in April 2003 that the investigation of his alleged misstatement about how much he paid a former mistress had been going on for nine years and had cost nearly $19 million! The *Times* story noted that the judge who hired and fired special prosecutors had told David Barrett, the lawyer and lobbyist who was selected in 1995 to investigate Cisneros, to "wrap it up soon."[55] In an almost unbelievable display of insensitivity to the anguish that these long investigations inflicted on those being investigated and their families, Barrett was quoted as saying, "We're wrapping it up. . . . I will be the second happiest person around when this is finished. The happiest will be my wife."

What about Henry Cisneros, and his wife and family, to say nothing of the taxpayers, Mr. Barrett?

---

[54] See Appendix 21: Letter of resignation submitted to President Clinton; Appendix 22: President Clinton's reply; and Appendix 23: Letter from Vice President Gore to Roger Johnson. Also see Appendix 25: Jim Wood, "Mr. Johnson Returns from Washington" [Interview], *Orange County Register,* September 1996.

[55] David G. Savage, "It's Time to Finish Inquiry into Cisneros, Counsel Told," *Los Angeles Times,* April 11, 2003.

As expensive and drawn out as the Cisneros investigation was, it is less than the $25 million spent investigating Mike Espy, former Secretary of Agriculture, on charges that he accepted Super Bowl tickets and other favors from people who worked in the food business. In 1999 a jury quickly acquitted Espy of all charges.

This atmosphere in which personal character assassination has become a favorite political weapon is a cancer within our governing structure that impacts everyone associated with the process. These two high-profile cases are only the tip of a huge iceberg. Federal workers as well as elected officials and their staffs live daily with the specter of personal attacks that could ruin them professionally and financially—regardless of the outcome. I hope that discussing my experiences will show how this atmosphere has become not only a silent, powerful deterrent to change but also creates a debilitating work environment within the government.

What happened to me is more representative of what occurs on a day-to-day basis and has a very negative effect on all of those involved in the governing process. It will be no easier to change this poisonous climate than it will be to deal with the other issues I have discussed. But revising the system that fosters this subculture is a prerequisite to any meaningful change.

* * *

One day in 1993 Barbara Silby and I had just landed at Chicago's O'Hare Airport when her cell phone rang.

"What? Who said that? How could they know so soon?"

I listened to her staccato, obviously irritated responses. "What was that about?" I asked my chief of staff.

Rather shaken, she said, "You won't believe it but the IG [Inspector General] wants to meet with us as soon as we return to Washington. He said he has evidence that we flew first class on this flight in violation of federal regulations."

"That's ridiculous, you know we cleared first class travel with the White House—they said as long as the government doesn't pay for it, there is nothing wrong with going first class. United gave us a free upgrade in Washington—but he probably doesn't know that." I thought for a moment and then asked, "But how the heck did he know we even flew first class?—We just landed."

"I asked him, but he wouldn't even tell me who told him or where he got the information," she replied. "But it's obvious that those people who are after you are not going to give up!"

This was far from the first time I had been "reported" for doing something in "violation" of federal regulations, but it would become the incident that fueled a three-year investigation by the GSA Inspector General's Office, the FBI, and the Department of Justice of a whole range of my "improper" activities! I was at once stunned, amazed, dumbfounded, and perplexed! I could not think of *anything* that I had done that was improper, unethical, or illegal. Nothing I had done so far would be seen by those in the profit-oriented private sector as improper conduct by a CEO.

It took *three years* before I was informed, in a letter from the Justice Department, that there was no reason to pursue the matter any further.[56] The cost to me personally was more than $250,000. During this entire time I was never charged with a *single* violation, although dozens of press accounts of the investigation read as though I was already guilty of everything. The charges that triggered these investigations included expense account issues, improper use of federal employees, improper use of federal facilities, illegally accepting upgrades from airlines, illegal stock transactions, illegal conflicts of interest associated with my former employer, and a few other similar issues. My lawyers estimated that the dollar cost to the government was in the millions (although the government agencies involved officially have declined to state the costs when directly questioned by me). Whatever the amount, the cost to the agency employees and other federal workers and the taxpayers in terms of time wasted that should have been spent on making needed changes is also beyond calculation. *You* helped pay for this nonsense and, as you read these words, your tax dollars are paying for more of the same—in many different areas of government.

To understand just how pervasive and destructive this atmosphere has become, I need to take you back to the beginning of my own story.

---

[56] For instance, see Appendix 26: H. G. Reza, "Former GSA Chief Johnson Cleared in U.S. Ethics Inquiry," *Los Angeles Times*, May 2, 1997.

It began a few days after I was nominated to head the General Services Administration, but before I was confirmed. Even though I had jumped parties and actively campaigned for Clinton-Gore, there were Democrats who were angry that the President had nominated a Republican to head this agency. On August 4, 1997, the *Wall Street Journal,* while preparing a front page story on my days in Washington reported:

> Angry that the job wasn't going to a Democrat, members of the American Federation of Government Employees protested. Faxes and mailings were dispatched all over Washington saying Mr. Johnson was unfit for the position. "The White House wants to use GSA as a place to put or dump Republican Roger Johnson," wrote union official Bruce Williams, who organized much of the opposition, in a letter to fellow GSA workers.[57]

I remember getting a call from Dennis Fischer, the permanent CFO who was also the acting GSA Administrator during the transition period, telling me about the opposition, but dismissing it as nothing important and that if we ignored it, it would "go away." Accepting that advice turned out to be a major mistake on my part. However, the fact that it was given by an exceptionally talented and experienced federal official points to one of the reasons why the tactic of personal character attack has been able to grow day by day to the point where it is the political "weapon of choice," as Vince Foster said just before his suicide in 1993. Vincent W. Foster Jr. was the White House deputy counsel when he left his office one day in July 1993 and committed suicide in a Virginia park. He left a note that said, "The public will never believe the innocence of the Clintons and their loyal staff. . . . I was not meant for the job or the spotlight of public life in Washington. Here ruining people is considered sport."[58] I would later discover that the Washington deck was stacked in favor of the attacker and that any defense would usually just invite more and wider attacks and could spread to those who came to the defense of the one being attacked.

---

[57] Edward Felsenthal, "Johnson's Offenses Were Minor, but Investigation Took 3 Years," *Wall Street Journal,* August 4, 1997. (See Appendix 27.)

[58] Vincent W. Foster's suicide note, as cited, for instance, in Adam Nagourney and Judy Keen, "Foster Felt Betrayed by Washington," *USA Today,* August 11, 1993.

Why do the attackers have the advantage? First, the "anonymous" source is a way of life with the political press. There is even
a specific language assigned to this area. At one end of the
anonymity spectrum is the totally unidentified source ("a usually
reliable source" or "sources close to the investigation"). Then
there are off-the-record comments, which means that the person
quoted won't be named although his or her organization may be
cited ("a senior White House aide"). At the other end of the spectrum is an understanding of "deep cover." This means that if what
you tell the reporter is printed, it will appear buried in the body of
the story but not even identified as a quote and certainly not attrib-
uted to your position or organization. Most responsible publica-
tions and electronic news organizations require confirmation from
at least one other credible source for major stories. However,
there are a lot of papers and electronic media that, in the heat of
competition and under "news cycle" pressures, don't always hold
to that ethical standard. Problems uncovered in mid-2003 at the
Washington Post and the *New York Times* are flagrant examples. In
the latter instance, a reporter was found to have blatantly fabri-
cated dozens of news stories, a scandal that led to the resignation
of the paper's editor.

Although it was of no real importance, I had experienced the
same type of reporting soon after I arrived in Washington. I had a
large collection of all sorts of elephants—which had nothing to do
with the Republican symbolism—I just like elephants. In fact Governor Clinton had seen them when he visited my office at Western Digital during the 1992 campaign. I told him about the origin
of the collection, which began during my early days in the General Electric training program, when I used to characterize management as "elephants." (When they came out of their offices they
tromped all over everything, followed each other around with their
"noses" attached to the next one's tail, etc.) When I graduated
from the training program a friend gave me a crystal elephant with
the admonition: "Don't become one of these." You can imagine
my surprise when one morning the *Washington Post* carried a little story—in a box on the "federal page"—saying that the newly
arrived Republican GSA Administrator had a collection of elephants and that President Clinton had ordered that they be

removed. A complete fabrication. I even called Betty Currie, the President's secretary, and asked her to check it out. When she called back she said that the President had never talked to anyone about it—let alone wanted them removed. But she said he had a good laugh and hoped that this would be the worst erroneous story I would ever have to put up with. Nice wish!

In my case, although the early campaign had no effect on my appointment—I was confirmed *unanimously* by the Senate—my lack of response did not make the attacks "go away." In fact, as mentioned earlier in the book, I became the subject of the anonymously written newsletter *Crosswind* (subtitled *GSA News from a Democratic Perspective*).[59] The same *Wall Street Journal* article I previously cited reported that "a pattern developed: Allegations would be floated in *Crosswind*, picked up by the mainstream news media and then pursued by government investigators."[60] In its initial publication, *Crosswind* stated that its purpose was "to monitor and quickly publicize the activities of Republican Roger Johnson." The newsletter continued to come out every four to six weeks for the duration of my stay in Washington. It contained distortions, half-truths, and even out-and-out lies. At one time or another it reported that I had a "Republican" plan to fire all the Democrats in the agency, including the ones I had previously personally selected; that I was an "inside" stock trader; that I was secretly funding Republican candidates to run against incumbent Democrats who were opposing my attempts to "eliminate" the GSA.

These were complete fabrications. However, the writers found a willing accomplice in someone on the staff of the *New York Post*, who printed almost every allegation that *Crosswind* came up with. Although there was no independent verification, the *Post* stories would get picked up by radio or TV and then by other mainstream press—and suddenly these unfounded, untrue, and anonymous charges looked like they had enough substance, that they were facts! Soon, there was the "news" that the Inspector General of the GSA would start an independent investigation—which in and of

[59] For a sample of *Crosswind* content, see Appendix 10.

[60] Felsenthal, "Johnson's Offenses Were Minor, but Investigation Took 3 Years."

itself generated another story about "the embattled GSA head, the subject of an IG investigation."

And so it went—around and around—and I was helpless to stop it. At one point a *Washington Post* headline read "GSA's Embattled [they love that term] Chief Enlists a Friend as Lawyer."[61] The lawyer was Albert Beveridge of the firm Beveridge and Diamond. He and my wife Janice had met when they both were on the Board of Directors of the National Symphony, and he and his wife Madzy were and continue to be good friends. Albert's colleague David Krakoff handled the details of my case for three years, and I credit him with the very successful outcome.

When the *Washington Post* story ran, much to the dismay of my public relations person, Hap Connors, who was still operating under the principle of "keep a low profile," I fired off a fax to the author of the article:

> How can hiring a lawyer—in Washington, D.C. of all places—be news? *Not* having a lawyer for a year and a half [in this town]—now that *was* news. But I guess it is just an extension of the grossly distorted mind set in this town that chases fleas with great zeal while letting the elephants run wild. When are you going to move into some depth on the real story at GSA? I will warn you in advance, however, that you will probably discover one or two positive results. If you think you can handle that, please call me.[62]

I never got a reply—but I also never appeared in that particular column again either. So much for keeping a low profile!

And so it went. For three years. Newspaper articles, TV evening news items, more anonymous *Crosswind* pamphlets, and a constant swirl of rumors about what I would do or whether the White House was supporting me. One night, while I was working late, Janice called, obviously upset, to tell me that NBC's *Nightly News with Tom Brokaw* had just run a piece that said I was another of Clinton's Cabinet in deep trouble. It ran between reports about a

[61] Cindy Skrzycki, "GSA's Embattled Chief Enlists a Friend as Lawyer," *Washington Post*, October 28, 1994. (See Appendix 15.)

[62] Memo from Roger Johnson to Cindy Skrzycki (Re: October 28 column). (See Appendix 16.)

gang killing and the sensational O. J. Simpson case. Surprise! Surprise! The Justice Department's exoneration letter never made the evening news! (And, for the record, I did not hold an official *Cabinet* position, even though I was invited to attend all of the Cabinet meetings and did attend most of them.)

During the process I learned that employees of the federal government do not have the same civil rights as other citizens. Early on I asked to confront the person making the charges. I was told that not only would that not happen, but I didn't even have a right to question that person. If you think this is a scenario from a Franz Kafka novel of political tyranny, you are wrong. This was *your government,* in the land of the free, in the land where you and I are supposed to be innocent until proven guilty. *Two years* after I asked for it, invoking the Freedom of Information Act, I got a copy of what was supposed to be interviews with those accusing me. More than half of each page was edited out—sometimes whole pages—to the extent that not only could I not identify who was testifying, but I couldn't even make sense of what they had said! One morning, people from the IG's office swooped down on my office and took out, without any permission or authorizing documents, all of my personal files and those of my secretary and chief of staff. They were returned a few weeks later with many documents missing. They later showed up in long and contentious depositions with the IG and legal counsel. Again, you are not reading a novel set in an oppressive dictatorship, although the scenario isn't much different, it would seem.

A few years later I could sympathize with Richard Jewell, who happened to be in Atlanta, where he lived, and on the scene when someone set off a bomb in a park near the Olympic Games stadium. Somehow, Jewell was identified (partly by leaks from law enforcement agencies) as the dastardly perpetrator. Reporters and photographers clogged the street where he lived, and his face was featured on a billboard alerting people to keep abreast of the news about this "criminal." Finally, it was found that there was no basis in any fact to allege Jewell was even slightly involved. However, for many days he was the prime focal point on news shows nationwide.

It became very clear during one of my depositions that the IG investigators had very little understanding of what they were investigating. The kinds of questions they asked regarding "insider trading" and the stock options that I had received while chairman and CEO of Western Digital were so out of context that at one point I asked point-blank, "Please tell me what you mean by insider trading?"

I think the first response was something like, "We ask the questions here, not you." But I pressed on by telling them, quite truthfully, that I was having problems answering their questions because their questions didn't relate to either insider trading or options. When I saw that I wasn't getting anywhere, I asked if it would be helpful if I gave them my understanding of what constituted "insider trading" and how options were awarded and the whole process surrounding how they could or couldn't be exercised. They agreed. It was clear after my explanation that they did not have a clue about these fairly complex and technical financial issues, and were just acting on what they had read in *Crosswind* and newspaper articles.

I then suggested that those who were expert in these issues were at the Securities and Exchange Commission and that it might be useful if they asked the SEC to handle this part of their investigation. My lawyer was not happy with my helping to broaden the scope of my own investigation, but the IG people were relieved. Within a couple of days the SEC said there was nothing wrong with my actions.

The point here is that the people who populate the Inspector General offices of the various agencies throughout Washington— and there are several thousand of them—have come principally from places such as the Secret Service, other law enforcement organizations, or the military. Created as one of the responses to the Watergate era, they have a very broad charter including internal audit of the agencies' operations. Many of these men and women, although well intended, have absolutely no training or experience in the areas they are asked to audit. The laws and regulations say they *must* audit—so they do! They also operate with complete impunity. They do not report to the agency head. Neither I nor the secretary or administrator of any other department or agency can hire or fire IGs or their staff. When I pursued this further to find out whom they reported to, all I could learn was that periodically—I think every couple of years—they were supposed to have a peer review by IGs from outside of their department. Therefore, as far as I could tell, they reported to no one. To me, this was and is the very opposite of "government of the people, by the people, and for the people." Instead, it belongs in Machiavelli's *The Prince*—a guidebook on how to be an effective tyrant!

This was made very clear early in my tenure, before any of the investigations, when the GSA Inspector General came to me with a request to add several people to the approximately 400 people already on board. His request came at the beginning of the hiring freeze, and we were not even automatically replacing those who quit. I explained the plan to him and asked that he join in this effort and see if he could not find more effective ways to do the job. He politely told me that he was there only as a matter of courtesy, and that he could do whatever he wanted and didn't need my approval! At that point I was not aware of his unique status, but the agency legal counsel quickly confirmed that he was right. Although he had the right to do what he wanted, I told him that I would publicly oppose his actions as not being in the best interests of the Reinventing Government initiatives. He was not happy with that response.

I further endeared myself to him when I vigorously opposed an IG request to the Justice Department that their people be allowed to carry guns. I could see no need for people supposedly involved in audit functions to be carrying weapons, even when confronting nasty villains involved in "insider trading," whatever that is. I believed that they already represented enough of an intimidation to federal workers without adding firearms. I believe that some of them finally got their guns.

Although I have no specific evidence that these conflicts affected the IG's approach to the subsequent investigations, I'm sure they didn't help. Of course, as time passed all of the allegations—except one—gradually faded away as it became obvious that they had no basis. The single remaining allegation was the one related to my accepting first class air travel upgrades. It was also subsequently dismissed as having no basis, but only after two more years of investigations.

The broader point is that this powerful investigative structure is constantly hovering above the entire federal workforce, able any time and for any reason to move into their lives and put careers and financial well-being at risk. They can do this on a whim. Federal workers "under investigation" have their positions "frozen." They cannot get promotions or salary increases while the investigation is under way. They have no control over the process—which, in many cases, goes on for *years*. One may argue that there is nothing wrong with the concept behind the law that established the Inspector General offices. However, in a Washington atmosphere where attacks on individuals' ethics and integrity are an acceptable day-to-day tactic, the IG process offers a tempting vehicle for those with a personal or political agenda.

One example of this type of harassment came to my attention soon after I arrived in Washington. I was told of a career female employee with more than 20 years of excellent service, mostly in the purchasing function of the Federal Supply Service, who had a promotion as well as pay increases frozen for over two years because an IG auditor had said he found "discrepancies" in her documentation of a particular procurement. She could not find out what the "discrepancies" were during this period, and she was eventually cleared. Although never proven, she told her supervisor that she was singled out because she had been quite vocal about the fact that she was one of the few African American females in a senior position in the agency. Later on I discovered that although the agency employment was about 80% black, African Americans held fewer than 10% of senior positions, and there was an even lower percentage of females in senior positions. Career management positions were almost exclusively held by middle-aged white males.[63]

Another incident took place in one of the early "town hall" meetings I held—this time in Fort Worth, Texas. I had finished my comments and had asked for questions or comments. Near the end of the Q-and-A session a man who obviously had some appre-

---

[63] For further perspective on this issue, see Appendix 17: Letter from Roger Johnson to Vice President Albert Gore (Re: Affirmative action program for executives in government).

hensions asked if I knew anything about the insurance they were being encouraged to take out. I had no idea what he was talking about and said, "No, but I'd like to hear about it."

He began with something to the effect of "You probably don't realize how bad the situation is with IG investigations in the GSA." Then, gathering some confidence as others nodded their heads in support, he continued, "We are completely helpless and any time anyone has a beef against someone all they have to do is tell a friend in the IG's office and they find a reason to start an investigation. All of our increases are frozen and many of us, particularly in purchasing, have to hire a lawyer, which we can't afford."

I then asked the others in the room if they agreed with this man and they responded with a loud "Yeah—we sure do." I told them that I would certainly look into it and if I found any problems I'd do everything I could to correct the problem. I continued, having almost forgotten the original question, and asked, "What is this 'insurance' issue you mentioned?"

"Well," he said, "the union [the American Federation of Government Employees] has just issued a recommendation that we each get personal liability insurance to cover our legal expenses in case we are investigated by the IG."

Later I checked with Harry Dawson, the very responsible president of the union, who confirmed that this was true, and that the problem was serious and was not isolated to the GSA. I was just beginning to investigate the allegations when the Inspector General began his own investigation of me—which effectively left me impotent to pursue the matter any further.

Obviously there are issues of discrimination and politically inspired attacks in any institution. However, in most professionally managed organizations, there are built-in safeguards that help prevent and/or correct these abuses. The lack of such checks and balances—ironically in a federal structure that was founded on the basis of checks and balances—leaves the federal employee working in an atmosphere of fear and apprehension.

Even though a person who is caught in the crosshairs of the IG may not be guilty or even engaged in anything except activities of the highest ethical and moral standards, he or she must face the accusers and endure months or even years of humiliation. Faced with such despotic actions, some who had hoped to serve the government simply quit. There are other things in life to do. American citizens are the losers. Once again we see the logic of unintended consequences—the government set about dealing with certain problems (improper conduct, abuse of authority, etc.) and created another set of problems—and a potential for abuse of power.

The Inspector General function is one that has been employed in the military for a long time. The idea behind it is to authorize people in a given organization to investigate improper or illegal acts by members of that organization—including those who manage or administer it. In order to insulate IG personnel from interference or retribution from managers, administrators, or others in that organization, the investigators have autonomy, do not report to management, and are free to report their findings to any officials who have oversight over that particular department. At times the press is appealed to—generally through leaks. The whole idea is to prevent culpable officials from "stonewalling" or obstructing an internal investigation.

This is, on the face of it, a good and logical way to proceed. IGs have to be "independent and objective," just as accounting firms auditing a public or private company are supposed to report their findings without fear or favor. But one always comes back to the fact that such investigating or accounting is done by human beings. No matter what a particular statute or SEC regulation stipulates, people are subject to influence, bias, and agendas—objectivity is a great and perfect thing, but hard to maintain. Which brings us to the question Plato asked centuries ago: "Who will guard the guardians?" In the U.S. scheme of government, such "guarding" is done through constitutional checks and balances. The Congress is a check on the Executive; and the Judiciary, like the pathologist, often has the final word.

The whistle-blower process now mandated for public companies is a much more effective tool than the IG, minimizing the potential for both obstruction and investigative abuse of the sort described above. But the people, assisted by a fair, free, and objective press, are supposed to have the final, *final* word—and render their judgment through the ballot box or the right to petition against grievances. This may require a bit of time.

This balance of authority and monitoring is lovely in theory, but difficult to achieve in practice. We must go on trying to achieve it. But we should never forget that this system of checks and balances has inevitable imperfections—and abuses. So, again, it comes down to trust, just as it does in the case of the press.

Still, as recent corporate outrages remind us, the question remains: Who will or should audit the people doing the audit? And how does one build in protections for innocent people who end up in the path of the investigative and media juggernaut?

★   ★   ★

Although not generally used to attack individuals, the General Accounting Office (GAO) is another seemingly appropriate investigative body that has been used by people who want to attack or intimidate a government department. All it takes is a letter from a Congressman or Senator raising a question and asking for an investigation to begin a process that almost always ends up with something negative. It was my impression, however, that using the threat of a GAO investigation has, over time, lost some of its importance. There are so many negative GAO reports issued almost daily that their individual impact is muted.

A much blunter weapon is launched (and usually flies below the pubic radar screen) when a legislator threatens or actually cuts or reduces an agency's budget because the agency or its staff has disagreed with or holds a different view from the Congressman or Senator.

Sometimes it gets more specific: One Congressman threatened to eliminate my salary from the GSA budget. He was not happy when I told him to go ahead—I was so underpaid that it wouldn't make any difference to me! I still cherished the notion that Janice and I were making a contribution to American government, an effort to share with the Clinton Administration some of the knowledge and enthusiasm that had spelled success for us in our years in the private sector.

I believe it was this, and other similar comments I made, that led Senator Alan Simpson (R-Wyo.) to call me into his office one day. He had a big smile on his face as he said, "Johnson, I don't think you realize how dangerous you are to people in this town." Taken aback, I agreed and said that I couldn't think of why I *should* be considered dangerous. Simpson's response: "You don't need your job, you don't need your salary—in fact, you have no intention of making this a career—that's what makes you dangerous—they have nothing to threaten you with." Then he continued: "Right now you've got them off balance—but sooner or later they'll get you. But keep it up as long as you can—it's a lot of fun watching!"

The point here is that most people in the federal workforce need their job and need their salary. Fortunately for the country, many have decided to make public service their career. They are very valuable but unfortunately also very vulnerable! They need at least the same protections that you and I have in our lives outside of government service. It will not be possible to make significant improvements in government operations if most of those responsible are subject to these subtle, almost secret, intimidation tactics. I would like to be clear that the vast majority of those in Washington are trying to do the right thing and do not engage in these practices. However, these vehicles combined with the press and media's all-consuming appetite for scandals allow a small minority to have a large and disproportionate impact. Close your eyes for a moment and envision what might happen to *you* if you decided to volunteer your services as a leader and innovator in Washington. I wonder what would happen if a Sarbanes-Oxley Act (which attempts to legislate accounting practices for corporations) dedicated to the federal organizational structure should be enacted!

Beneath the surface of the visible governing structure is an informal web of attitudes and practices that further complicate and frustrate reform activities. Just imagine a procurement employee's dilemma if she knows that a particular regulation is preventing a common-sense decision, and if that common-sense decision is made it could bring an IG investigation that would side with the regulation—regardless of the results. Or the employee who knows that the boss is doing something improper, but also knows that if he comes forward, the boss could quickly ask the IG, a friend of the boss, to investigate and he would have no defense.

This side of Washington is probably the most difficult to understand for those who have not been directly involved, and therefore will be one of the most difficult to change. There are two major contributing factors. First, the ever-escalating partisan political atmosphere has continuously lowered the standards of what constitutes civil debate. The lowering of political discourse standards carries over to all other Washington activities, thereby granting a lower threshold for "gotcha" tactics across the board. Second, there has been a rapid increase in the investigatory mechanisms mostly spawned by Watergate. These new factors stem from the "investigative reporter" mentality of the press that has even turned our nation's sports pages into chronicles of athletes' transgressions. Additionally, the proliferation of thousands of Inspector Generals and other special investigators has infested the federal structure as a result of Watergate-related legislation. Each of these primary causal elements also tends to reinforce and enable the other— amplifying and accelerating the "meanness factor."

I can offer little that can affect the ultrapartisan nature of the current politics. I suspect this will only change when the leadership of each party is turned over to people who are problem solvers rather than ideological zealots. On the other hand, I believe that I can offer some realistic suggestions to at least mitigate the investigative mechanisms.

The offices of the Inspector General are too often used as implementation weapons. I am convinced that the good work they have done over the years is more than offset by their negative effect on government employees' performance and attitudes. Therefore, I see little downside to eliminating their operational auditing responsibilities. Because the IGs have, in general, very little knowledge and experience in either the operations or the auditing process, this internal audit responsibility is more appropriately assigned to the financial organization of the agency, where it is found in almost every other nonprofit and private company. The financial organization and the CFO have the primary responsibility for the integrity and accuracy of the financially related operational processes and procedures. Making an "external" audit mandatory would help dramatically. The restoration of that responsibility would not only put it in the hands of more capable people, but would also more clearly align responsibility with resources. What would be left for the IG would be the investigation of fraudulent activities. I believe this function could be carried out by no more than ten capable investigators in each agency. Many agencies could perform the task with far fewer people. The remaining IGs should report to the Legal Department of each agency. This would accomplish three important things. First, it is the logical place to put investigation of illegal acts. Second, it would ensure that the IGs had to account to someone. And third, it should help ensure that those being investigated would be guaranteed the same due process as any other citizen.

To me, this is a win-win situation. The government would save money and at the same time revise an investigation process that seems to be completely out of step with American freedoms. At the same time, talented people in all walks of life in the private sector—not just corporate CEOs—would be *attracted* to volunteer for government service.

10

HOW CAN WE FIX IT?

ALTHOUGH I BELIEVE WE SHOULD BRING A SIGNIFICANT number of people, experienced and trained in professional management, into the federal government, in absolute terms it will take relatively few people to make a big difference. The first task will be to open up the appointment and staffing process that, in its present form, is closed to almost every citizen who is not actively involved in supporting, in a meaningful way, one of the two major parties.

The "citizen government" envisioned and practiced by our founders has long ago been replaced by a government of those who have made politics their primary career. Adding to the problem is a thick layer of political operatives who hover around the "insiders" and who raise the money, take and analyze the polls, "manage" candidates and campaigns, and "consult" on a wide range of domestic and foreign issues. This circle of operatives also provides another layer of protection for the insiders and their jobs. Many of the "advisors" act not only as screeners for the potential officeholders, but also as sources of candidates for choice positions. Since they deal primarily with the thousands involved in the process, it is only natural that they go right back to that pool when it is time for recommendations. This group also helps keep track of those contributors who have been encouraged to believe that they will be given jobs if their candidate is elected.

Because the nominating process has become so complex, time-consuming, and contentious, there is a big temptation to nominate someone with prior Washington experience—someone who has been "through the mill" and is well known to the establishment. A Democratic insider will have much less trouble getting through the process, even with a Republican legislature, than an outsider—regardless of capabilities—and vice versa. This in-breeding is further facilitated by the fact that a large number of former officeholders and appointees never leave Washington—they take up positions with Washington law firms, lobbyists, think tanks, fund-raising groups, or party organizations, often biding their time until an offer is dropped in their lap. Therefore, there is a pool of known, "sound" people who just mill around the town between administrations. They are not only willing but also readily available because they are "just down the street." Even if they do leave Washington, the "in" group stays closely connected with other insiders and the political process. When an administration changes, they become just another source for the recycling process. (Note that a large number of people from the Carter Administration showed up twelve years later in the Clinton Administration, and also note that a large number of Bush I people came in with Bush II eight years later.) The architecture of this self-perpetuating, in-breeding structure will be hard to break down because there are enormous amounts of money and power invested in it. Those in control will not be easily dislodged. But, fortunately, as I indicated above, we won't have to displace them all to make a big difference. So, let's get to work.

Identifying and Defining the Jobs

The primary task is to identify the specific jobs that should be filled with men and women trained and experienced in professional management. Such people would make a big difference as heads of nonpolicy agencies whose missions are primarily operations management. For instance, let's begin with White House positions. Certainly the GSA would be one such agency. Additional agencies that I believe fall into this category would include the Small Business

Administration, the Federal Emergency Management Agency (FEMA), the Office of Personnel Management, the General Accounting Office, and several commissions. The White House staff position of Director of the Office of Management and Budget would certainly be another one.

I do not believe that Cabinet secretaries should necessarily fall into this category. Management-experienced people might be appointed, but these are political policy positions and the primary skills and experience needed by Cabinet-level secretaries should be political savvy. On the other hand, at least one senior deputy secretary in each agency should be management-experienced. More than one deputy may be appropriate for the larger, more complex agencies. These people would help ensure that management issues are considered, from policy development right through implementation. I further suggest that these deputies as well as the other management-trained executive branch people form a President's Management Council. The Clinton Administration had such a structure (I served on the council). It was chaired by Vice President Gore—and although it had only limited success, its meetings provided an excellent forum to review and discuss management issues across the government. The "limited" success was a result of several factors including the lack of significant professional management experience of most of the council members themselves, the deeply entrenched bureaucracy, and the lack of consistent political support from people outside the White House.

Institutionalizing the Vice President's role as a "chief operating officer" may also be worth serious consideration. One advantage would be that the presence of a senior political force should ensure that the necessary and inevitable political realities are also a part of the management thinking.

In addition to the senior positions in agencies and commissions, there are other appointed executive branch positions and career jobs that should be staffed by management-experienced people. Examples include chief financial officers, and real estate and purchasing specialists. Some agencies are already staffed by qualified people who just need some support to be effective.

Now let's turn to legislative positions. Improving the managerial skills in the executive branch will not yield optimum results unless it is accompanied by similar changes in the legislative structure. Hopefully, as good management becomes more politically important—I'll discuss this very important issue in Chapter 11—more candidates with management experience will be elected to Congress. However, even when that happens, the congressional staff will need a major infusion of trained and experienced people. In some respects these staff positions are at least as important as those of the legislators themselves because so much of the specific legislative language is developed by these people. Therefore, I suggest that at least one senior staffer of each Senator and Congressman have such experience. Additionally, internships filled by management graduate students could supplement their staffs. Each of the legislative committees should also have at least one such person with similar credentials, as should many of the subcommittees.

What would these professional managers do? Although they would work in a wide variety of policy organizations, the professional managerial positions would have very similar responsibilities. Some of the management problems would differ from agency to agency, of course, but the issues involving organizational structures, responsibility definitions and assignments, financial planning, and measuring functions would be quite similar. More importantly, the approach to management functions and issues would be much the same regardless of the subject matter. An additional, but subtle, advantage of this transferability of skills is that these people could be easily moved from one agency to another, thus adding a degree of flexibility not generally found among federal organizations at the present time.

How many do we need? If we add up all of the possible positions, we get approximately 800—executive branch, 100 people; Senate, 50 members plus approximately 20 committees and 70 subcommittees; House of Representatives, approximately 500 members, 20 committees, and 83 subcommittees. Therefore, fewer than 1,000 people out of the total federal employment would make a big difference in the effective management of government affairs.

How Do We Identify, Recruit, and Retain Qualified Candidates?

Open up the process. We must reopen the management of our government to our very capable citizens. It needs to start with the process itself. That will require a new approach to the way the government develops job specifications and then identifies, performs the vetting process, and confirms the qualifications of the candidates.

Again, my own experiences with the process should serve as a representative example of the problems.

In July of 1993, after filling out and amending what turned out to be three large file boxes of forms and incurring a lot of personal anguish as well as several thousand dollars of unreimbursed expenses and four months of "process," I was unanimously confirmed by the Senate. This grueling path was for a nominee that everyone said was "squeaky clean" and therefore a "slam dunk." I had bipartisan support during the confirmation hearing from Representative Christopher Cox (R-Calif.) and Senator Barbara Boxer (D-Calif.).

Even so, the process got so frustrating that, at one point, I walked out on a Senate confirmation staff meeting, telling them they "knew what they could do with their job." Looking back, the incident was more of the "last straw" variety. It arose over the amount of detail needed to fill in the section on financial assets. I had already redone the Senate version of the forms three times— each time giving more and more detail they had demanded regarding income, investments, and real estate. For example, I was required to list every investment and asset no matter how small. They even insisted that I list the stocks that were owned by a particular mutual fund! I told them that the whole idea of mutual funds was to invest in a diversified market basket of stocks chosen by professional fund managers, and that I didn't know, and really didn't care, what individual stocks the fund held. In addition, I had no control over what the fund bought or sold and therefore there wasn't any potential conflict of interest. But they had insisted, so I gave them a year-old report that I found, which listed the stocks held by the fund at the time. I don't know what good it did, but they were satisfied. During this period I had also responded to dozens of questions and revised forms time and time again, for the White House and my own agency, the GSA. I had traveled to Washington several times to meet with dozens of Congressmen, Senators, and their staffs for what was called obligatory "courtesy" meetings.

By this time the anonymous publication *Crosswind* had begun to appear, and I was told that Senator Slade Gorton (R-Wash.) was going to put a "hold" on my nomination unless I agreed to remove a software regulation that he felt was harmful to Microsoft, head-quartered in Seattle. (A hold is a very old Senate practice that allows any Senator to stop a nominee's confirmation process until the Senator releases the hold. All other Senators recognize the hold and will take no action until it is released. The holding Senator can invoke this privilege at any time, for any reason, and does not even have to disclose the reason. It is like a temporary—but sometimes very long—blackball.) I had never met Senator Gorton, nor discussed with anyone the issue he was raising. I had no idea what he was talking about. I later told the Senator that I would review any issues he had with the GSA after I was confirmed but that I would not precommit any actions prior to a complete review. Obviously I couldn't undertake any meaningful review until after I was in the job. I never heard from him again, but the hold was removed a few weeks later.

It was in this atmosphere that a "final" meeting was scheduled with certain members of the Senate staff (read *three lawyers*), me, and the GSA ethics officer. Everything was going well as they once again went through my responses to the dozens of questions on their forms. Then one of the lawyers said, "Mr. Johnson, we just need the details behind your listing of art and jewelry and we'll be finished." There was a space for "other assets" and I had listed a single figure for "art and jewelry." I asked what he meant and he said, "We need you to list the individual pieces of art and each piece of jewelry separately."

I blew my stack. Excluding expletives, I said something to the effect that I could see no reason why that detail would be relevant to the process and, additionally, since all of this information would be available to the public—I wasn't going to give every thief in Southern California a shopping list of the items in our home! I told him that I had had enough of this nonsense and walked out of the room—heading for the hotel and the airport. I hadn't reached the elevators when the GSA officer and another senior lawyer caught up with me and said that the lawyer who had challenged me had misinterpreted the regulations, and that I didn't have to provide any more detail on that issue or any others. In fact they were finished and would give a favorable recommendation to the committee chairman. I thanked them and agreed to continue with the process.

There are two points to be made here: One, the process is needlessly complex and intrusive, and two, it is so complex that it can be interpreted and used by any one of the people within the confirmation process to harass, discourage, or even discredit a candidate almost at will.

Another issue that is a problem for many is the personal cost of serving. Earlier I alluded to unreimbursed expenses. Under the current rules the only costs that are paid by the government are those directly related to the travel associated with the confirmation process and the moving of household goods, if the candidate is selected. There is no reimbursement for the legal or accounting costs associated with the required disclosures. Unlike the situation in the private sector and for government employees already on the payroll, there are no expense allowances for the cost of selling or buying a home or for lease cancellations or any other of the dozens of costs that one incurs when moving from one city to another. Most appointees who have been successful in the private sector realize that the salaries in Washington will be small, but when combined with the requirements to "divest" anything that may have even the appearance of a conflict of interest, the results in financial penalties and inconvenience become unreasonable for many.

Although my own experience may help to define some of the barriers to attracting qualified people into government, there are other problems that result from the current practices.

For example, in his book *Thickening Government,* Paul Light cites political scientist G. Calvin Mackenzie's study, which found that delays in both the nominating and confirming of the President's appointees have grown steadily over the past three decades. The time has lengthened from 2.4 months under Kennedy to 3.4 months under Nixon, 4.6 under Carter, 5.3 under Reagan, 8.1 under Bush (the elder), and 8.5 under Clinton. As of this writing, figures for the current Bush Administration are not yet complete. The delays are approaching 20% of a four-year administration, which not only creates the obvious problems of leadership vacuums, but also, in and of itself, constitutes a major deterrent for many qualified candidates.[64]

Additionally the average appointee stays on the job for only two years—with one-third leaving after only eighteen months. This would indicate that the process not only takes too long to attract appointees but also does not seem to do much to identify individuals who are willing to stay very long.

In 1999 the Bookings Institute undertook the Presidential Appointee Initiative funded by the Pew Charitable Trusts. This study, based largely on comments and suggestions from more than 200 former presidential appointees, advanced several significant reforms that comprise a proposed new piece of legislation, the Presidential Appointments Improvement Act (S. 765), introduced on April 2, 2003, by Senator George Voinovich (R-Ohio) and Senator Richard Lugar (R-Ind.). A companion bill (H.R. 1603) was introduced in the House by Representative Jo Ann Davis (R-Va.). Among the reforms suggested by the bill are the following:

- Provide all nominees awaiting clearance and confirmation with twice-monthly status reports.
- Provide all nominees with privacy and the right of "discovery" with respect to allegations concerning personal character, which may be raised in the course of Senate hearings. [If passed I would hope this would extend to the period that they are in office as well.]
- Provide all nominees with both a formal orientation to the federal government and an additional orientation to their respective agency.

---

[64] Paul C. Light, *Thickening Government: Federal Hierarchy and the Diffusion of Accountability* (Washington, D.C.: Brookings Institution, 1995), p. 67.

- Provide each nominee with adequate guidance through the appointment process.
- Receive assurance of an up-or-down vote within 45 days.
- Remove the burden of postemployment conflict-of-interest regulations.

Although these changes will be helpful, they do not address many of the major issues. The current political appointment process almost ensures that no one outside of the political establishment will even get considered. Or if they do somehow get to enter the process, there is a high likelihood that the process itself will discourage or destroy their candidacy. Therefore, as step one to bringing men and women with expertise and experience into professional management, I propose a perpetually maintained candidate pool, and a nonprofit consortium to administer it. Here's how it would work:

Breaking the Mold

We need to take a very different approach to identifying and selecting qualified candidates to serve in government—an approach that opens the process to include those not already closely aligned with government. The following suggested changes in the process are meant only for positions identified as "management" jobs in the White House and legislative branches. If the changed process proves effective, it could easily be expanded to cover other senior executive hires, such as those seeking to enter the civil service ranks of career employees.

Creating a perpetual candidate pool of men and women who are prequalified and prescreened would be a good first step. In doing this we would not only open access but also help reverse the trend of the ever-lengthening time it takes to staff key positions. If my experience is any indicator, there are many qualified people who are very willing to serve but have never been asked to do so. From the time it was announced that I was an appointee until today, dozens of people have approached me with an expressed willingness and enthusiasm to serve, in effect to "donate" their considerable talents—but even when I contacted the White House Office of Personnel Management on their behalf, there was either no follow-up at all or they were politely dismissed. I am, therefore, very confident that the numbers of people who would be qualified for such a pool are readily available.

But how do we identify them, and how do we get them into the mainstream of the process? There is already a well-established, broadly experienced structure in place that does this work daily for corporations and nonprofits. They are the professional executive search firms of the nation—the "head-hunters." Their involvement in the government staffing process would not be altogether new—in fact, an executive search firm senior partner actually ran the White House Personnel Office in the early days of President Ronald Reagan's first term. However, I would suggest a much broader and more permanent role.

Overall responsibility for the process would be assigned to the Office of Personnel Management (as distinguished from the White House Personnel Office). This would ensure that the process transcends administration changes. The executive search firms would be asked to assign one or two professionals to a nonprofit consortium that would become the implementation vehicle for this process. The consortium's expenses would be funded by the government. These people could be rotated or permanent, depending on the circumstances. The job of the consortium would be:

- Identifying qualified candidates. Potential candidates would be suggested by other sources, of course.
- Developing specific position descriptions for a wide range of "politically" appointed jobs. This would obviously be done in conjunction with appropriate government personnel people and other experts. If successful, the process could serve as a source for permanent career positions as well—but it would be best to limit it to political appointees to start.
- Screening and interviewing all candidates, regardless of their source. This is a very critical role because these professionals are not only capable of matching a candidate's experience with those set out in the job description, but they are also skilled at identifying personality

and style characteristics of individuals that are often just as important as the specific subject matter knowledge and experience.

- Conducting background checks and interviews. Again my own experience while at GSA was that this phase of the process, done within the government, took much too long and also often failed to uncover or highlight important issues that later proved embarrassing to the administration and/or the candidate. The disclosure of an "ethics" issue after the candidate has been nominated or even after the intent to nominate is announced is much too late. In my view almost all of these situations are the result of a flawed interviewing and screening process. Professional private sector search firms could do a much better job. National security clearances would still have to be done by the responsible government agencies, although much of the information gathered in the course of the regular background checks would be material and should not have to be duplicated. The FBI and others may argue this point, but I believe that after some experience with and an objective review of the search firm's process, even the FBI would accept the findings in most cases.

The foregoing process would have at least two major advantages: First, the candidate pool would be the result of an ongoing process providing a constantly updated list of prescreened, qualified candidates. The mad rush every four years would be avoided and any new administration would be able to fill its key appointments within a month or two. Second, although the typical candidates (i.e., big donors, campaign workers, "friends of the family," and recycled politicians) would not be excluded from the process, they would automatically be put into the same process with all others. Only those who met the predetermined qualifications and were evaluated according to those qualifications would survive.

Thus, when the process is in place, we would have a perpetual pool of approximately 2,000 to 3,000 men and women who have expressed a willingness to serve (not necessarily a commitment—but at least a strong interest). The candidates would be Democrats, Republicans, and Independents, and would have met a predetermined set of qualifications demonstrating professional management experience and expertise as defined by the position description mentioned earlier. They will have passed a background check (excluding national security issues).

The Opposition

The major opposition to this recommendation would probably come from within the Democratic and Republican political establishment—that is, those people who make a living from the political process. That means almost all of the political operatives, including members of Congress. The insiders will argue that to effectively operate inside the Beltway requires experience. They will point out that the system is so unique and complex that it would take an outsider too long to learn to be effective. Something along the lines of what Tip O'Neill, longtime Democratic Congressman from Massachusetts (and Speaker of the House, 1977–1987), used to say when advising new House members: "You must go along to get along."

The counterargument is that we would be *adding* experience to the process, not *replacing* it. Experience that is needed but not currently in place. Although there would certainly be some learning involved, unlike political or policy positions, most of the non-government newcomers' knowledge and experience would be directly transferable to their new jobs. Finally, of course, change will not occur if the only process known to new appointees is the one that is already in place. Creative new thinking can only come from those not vested in the status quo.

Other objections, I am sure, will come from those who question the injection of private sector executive search firms into the process. The counterargument is that these companies represent a profession that performs all of the tasks involved in the selection process all day, every day—not just once every four years.

What Will It Take to Get It Done?
How Can We Get Started?

Getting qualified management people into the key politically appointed executive branch positions could probably be done by a presidential executive order—and that may be a place to start. An incoming or sitting President could order that those jobs designated as management-critical be filled by people who had the prerequisite skills and experience. Just having these individuals in the deputy positions of the twenty-six cabinet and key agency posts would be an effective beginning. It would be preferable to have the whole process, including the pool creation as well as the legislative jobs, all put in place at the same time—but that is probably not politically feasible. In fact, I suggested this first step, the appointment of qualified management people to the deputy positions, to President Clinton in 1995. I remember that he didn't respond for a moment—his facial muscles flexing as they often did when he was thinking—and then he said something to the effect that he had no doubt it would be a great help in improving the management of the government, but at this time he couldn't afford to spend the amount of political capital it would take to get it done. He also said, "We've got too many other priorities—I just can't do it now." He obviously did not want to consider this idea, so I did not pursue the issue.

The point is that—although technically this first step could be taken unilaterally by the President—without more broadly based political support it would be very difficult to do. One can only hope that as the problems become more evident these proposals will get a higher political priority.

An adjunct to the above approach, and one that should be implemented in parallel, would be the creation of a separate list of individuals who would be willing to serve, but, for one reason or another, would not want to commit to four or more years. They represent another huge pool of talent that would make a big contribution—but are also usually shut out of the process simply because no one knows who they are, where they are, or that they would be interested. Every day specific management issues arise across the government that would benefit from the knowledge and experience of trained management people—if only for a few weeks or a few months. The unmitigated complete mess that we see in many of the federal computer systems (the FBI's antiquated system being one very troubling case) is an example of a problem awaiting effective management solutions. Other examples include the nonintegrated law enforcement systems that can't cross-check immigration applicants with terrorist lists, the IRS system that has "lost" thousands of taxpayers over the years, and the outmoded tracking systems of the Environmental Protection Agency. All would benefit greatly from outside management help.

The process for qualifying and background-checking this group of individuals should be less complex and time-consuming than for the longer-term appointment candidates. They could be organized by specific areas of expertise (such as information technology, health care, etc.), with the lists made available to agencies and Congress. With proper safeguards the lists might also be made available to the dozens of Washington-based consulting companies who currently get contracts to solve many of these issues. This would open these consulting jobs to thousands of experts around the country.

There probably should be a separate process using local congressional and senatorial offices as the accumulation point and for prescreening of interested people. In any event, I believe there are additional thousands of capable Americans who would be enthusiastic about serving their government—if only they had the chance.

What Else Can Be Done to Jump-Start the Infusion?

Every day, across the country, American companies present management courses of one sort another for their employees. Why couldn't these companies open these courses and allow some number of qualified federal workers to attend? Fortunately, not all federal workers reside in Washington, D.C. In fact almost one-third of them live and work in cities and towns across the country. As we have seen, all of the evidence shows that federal workers are just as smart and dedicated as the rest of the American workforce; they just lack management training and experience. This approach offers a way to infuse that training into the already existing work-force. Appropriate fees could be charged, but I suspect that the real incremental cost of adding a few people to each class would not be very much. As an incentive, a tax rebate might be offered. We already offer tax incentives for the training of a wide variety of people—why not add federal employees to the list?

Doing this would not only expose the federal worker to needed, up-to-date management techniques, but would also expose private sector management to high-caliber federal employees. Private sector management might also get a better understanding of the unique management problems facing the federal worker, and vice versa, and then each could offer the other some constructive suggestions rather than just the usual criticism. It might be interesting to see what could happen if each institution actually began to listen and talk to the other! If this could be done in companies across the country we could jump-start the educational process within the federal structure at the same time that we were making more of the country's management experts available to government.

Opposition would come from those who are afraid that federal workers would be "contaminated" by business "scoundrels." Again, the "try it, you may like it" approach might be the best path. If one or two companies—GE or Ford, for example, two companies known for their great internal training programs—would sign on for a trial, who knows? We might even find that the two institutions actually had something in common.

Training the Next Generation— The Colleges' and Universities' Role

So far, I have suggested approaches that deal with those already in the federal workforce. But what about the next generation of leaders? How can we give those planning to enter the political structure some training and experience in professional management?

My responsibilities in reinventing government meant that I would sometimes visit colleges and universities to talk about the need for management-trained people in government. This would normally end up with my speaking to gatherings of students and faculty in either the schools of management or the schools of public policy. What quickly became a pattern was that the schools of management—although acknowledging the need for management skills in government—had little or no formal coursework dedicated to the subject. In fact, too often the students and faculty would treat my subject with interest and respect, but would find no connection with what they were doing. I was more surprised to find that in the schools of public policy the subject of professional management was treated with suspicion at best and often outright hostility. There seemed to be an inherent mistrust of management, and managers were viewed as people who would somehow contaminate the policy process. (This was even before the corporate scandals of 2001–2003.)

Although a few of the nation's public policy schools—such as those at the University of Michigan, the University of California, and Harvard's Kennedy School—have courses in governmental management, the primary focus of the curriculum is on *creating* policies rather than providing the tools necessary for their effective *implementation*. Many of the management courses, in my judgment, deal more with the administration of existing systems than with teaching the fundamentals of professional management. Some business schools also offer courses with titles such as "Intergovernmental Relationships" and "Government and Business." The focus here is more on how businesspeople should deal with governments, with very little if anything covering the need for professional management in government.

The reasons for the lack of academic focus on the subject of professional management in government seem fairly obvious. The public policy schools see their primary role as developing students with an understanding of the criteria for developing good public policy. They may give lip service to the need for effective policy implementation, but these schools lack the qualified faculty whose primary knowledge base would have to be in management.

Even more fundamental is the fact that, in my experience, many faculty members do not recognize the need for management training and therefore—just as in government itself—there is a very small constituency for the initiative. Business schools, on the other hand, certainly have the trained faculty, but see their role as developing students whose careers will be in the private sector. Although trained in management, they have little or no academic credentials in government. Some business schools have attempted to add special programs in not-for-profit management, but they have met with little success because they are generally treated as academic stepchildren and consistently receive second class citizen stature in terms of funding and quality of faculty.

Within government itself, there are a wide variety of offerings, usually with titles that include "Public Administration." These courses, however, primarily cover the existing rules and regulations and do not even attempt to deal with the fundamentals of professional management. Therefore, after we left Washington, Janice and I decided to endow a chair at the University of California–Irvine, named the Roger W. and Janice M. Johnson Chair in Civic Governance and Public Management, to try to shed some light on the subject.[65] Professor Dr. Martha Feldman, a noted scholar with a specialty in governmental organizational issues, was appointed to the position.

In parallel with the activities associated with establishing the chair, I began teaching courses in UC–Irvine's School of Social Ecology and later in the Graduate School of Management that directly addressed the issue of managing in a governmental environment. The Social Ecology course material, which I developed specifically for this purpose, exposes the students to some basic management skills and philosophies, such as organizational structuring, planning and budgeting, setting standards and measurements, as well as related human resource and communication skills. The GSM course deals more with the issues covered in this book.

---

[65] See Appendix 28: Letter from President Bill Clinton to Roger Johnson (Re: Endowment).

Each of the courses involves visiting lecturers—including senior community leaders such as corporate CEOs, senior university officials, and executive directors of not-for-profits, as well as Congressmen and mayors. The Social Ecology course purpose is not only to expose the students to basic management principles, but also to demonstrate, by actual testimony and interaction, that these principles are essential to the success of any enterprise—not just a business. The primary message to the students is that the country suffers much more from bad implementation of good policies than it does from bad policies, and that professional management represents the skills they need to ensure that their policies and programs are effective.

In the Graduate School of Management I also present the flip side—that government/politics is not some remote world, that government has a major impact on both their personal and professional lives, and that they ignore it at their own peril. "Politics" is not a dirty word—the political process is fundamental to our democracy. To ensure the continued success of our "great experiment," they must be active participants.

I have had exceptional response from the students during the six years that I have been teaching the courses. More surprising, in those six years I have yet to find one graduate or undergraduate student in Social Ecology that had even one hour of management coursework prior to attending my class. In the Graduate School of Management, I also found that students have had little or no formal exposure to the management issues in government.

Each of the nation's public policy schools needs to develop a required core curriculum in professional management at both the undergraduate and graduate levels. Each business school should offer a required course whose content explores the relationship between government/politics and management. The courses of both the policy schools and the business schools should be open to each other's students.

The courses could be developed by the management faculty or could be created by drawing on advice and guidance from nearby management schools. Local successful managers should also be used in curriculum development as well as in teaching. Advice from government-related institutions such as the Council for Excellence in Government and others could also assist in the course definition. A more ambitious plan would be for one of the government-related organizations to undertake the development of a minimum standard curriculum that could be used as a starting point by each of the schools.

It would also be very useful if these courses were packaged so that they would fit a seminar-type structure that would be offered to local political/career incumbents. This would represent another outreach vehicle to help accelerate the process.

★ ★ ★

Although none of the foregoing suggestions will be easy to implement, I hope that they at least represent logical and realistic approaches to the problem. I hope that the case I have made for the necessity for change will encourage others to come up with many more creative solutions. In the final analysis, all of us—and our children—will benefit from these changes in government. It is up to us to lead the charge!

II

GETTING POLITICAL SUPPORT—THE TOUGHEST PROBLEM!

THE MOST DIFFICULT TASK WILL BE TO CONVERT the periodic political support for effective management into sustained, enthusiastic effort—that is, making good management a major national political issue. Currently such support only surfaces in times of acute financial need or in connection with scandals, and quickly disappears once the particular crisis abates.

This was never more evident than in the first term of the Clinton-Gore Administration. At the time, our national annual deficit was over $300 billion and the economy was in the midst of a recession. The President and Vice President had made "reinventing government" a significant part of their campaign and had turned that campaign rhetoric into a major initiative once they took office. Even with all of these big financial issues, including top-level political pressure, the overall political support all but disappeared once the financial crisis left the headlines.

I have come to the conclusion that the reason for this was quite simple. No one made a case that saving money and improving government operations could be turned into a political advantage. Why was this? It appears that we have been operating with two fundamentally false assumptions—that politicians want to save money, and that there are political incentives that make good management a major priority. I believe the converse is true: Political people want and need to spend money, and there are currently no strong political incentives to encourage good management. For instance, no one has ever "connected the dots" showing that management flaws were at the center of most of our government's biggest operational failures—from NASA's space disasters to 9/11 intelligence failures to the wide range of flawed computer systems.

Spending money is the primary source of political power—for good or bad. For "good" it is needed to fund the plans and programs that political people propose as they run for office. The "bad" money is needed to fund special interest programs, which all too often are the payback for political support. Therefore, to ask a political person to save money is like trying to make a stream flow uphill. To some extent we private sector businessmen have been trying to do just that. It is much like the mistake that many of us make when telling those involved in government that it should be "run like a business." They know that government is not a business and therefore dismiss the suggestions and the suggestor as irrelevant; we just "don't understand the problem."

If You Can't Fix It—Feature It!

The solution may well come from applying the familiar adage, "If you can't fix it—feature it." Politicians don't get too excited about saving money per se. But they do get passionate about programs. So let's turn the savings into a source of program funding, rather than savings that just removes money from the budget. The savings would go to fund the expansion of already successful programs, or the initiation of new ones that had been stalled because of the lack of funding. Since money is always in short supply, we should make the case that good management will not only result in more effective program implementation, but will also free up funds that could be redeployed.

I believe, for example, that by showing how $100 billion could be saved by better management of the federal procurement process, and how the $100 billion savings could then be applied to a medical program for senior citizens—without raising new taxes—politicians could be persuaded to support the infusion of more trained managers into government. If it can be demonstrated that professional management processes could lop off *another* $200 billion just by streamlining current government management processes, and that the savings would then go to fund Social Security—we should be able to get the needed political support for the necessary management changes. Savings in and of themselves might even be made politically exciting if it were proposed that a tax reduction program would share—let's say fifty-fifty—with any "savings." Tax reduction would become just another "program" to be paid for by more effectively managing the existing programs.

I can almost hear the screams of protest that my suggestions will generate:

1. "A save-and-spend Democrat isn't much better than a tax-and-spend Democrat!"
2. "Why not just cut the budget?"
3. "Let's just cut the revenue off—lower taxes—that will automatically shrink the government without all of the fuss."
4. "We'll never get this government beast under control until we cut off its food supply" (which can be translated as: "until we cut off revenues that come from taxes").
5. "If we can just cut off the source of money—we won't have to worry about good management—they'll have a lot less money to mismanage or waste!"
6. "Why wait until after they get the money? Just don't give it to them in the first place."

This all sounds very logical, and I must admit that for much of my adult life I shared this ideology. Over time, however, and through more direct experience with the process, I came to believe that there are valid arguments against this line of thinking.

First, for at least the past fifty years we have had no broad national consensus on the role of government. In simple terms (probably oversimplified)—each side of this issue tries to be "fiscally responsible" by cutting the other side's programs. One side sees national defense as a major issue and continues to press for more advanced (read *very expensive*) weapon systems—both defensive and offensive—while trying to control the spending on welfare programs that it believes are largely wasteful. The other side sees much of the military spending as excessive and wasteful, while spending on domestic human needs should be significantly increased. Which side you're on is not too important, because the fact is that there is enough support for both sides so that neither gets all of what it wants, but each gets enough to cause a continuous increase in spending. There is also considerable evidence that the public pressure for more and more government services will continue to drive this upward spiral regardless of the outcome of the traditional left-versus-right debates.

Furthermore, the federal government is the only institution that does not, at some point, have to balance its budget—that is, match income with spending. Income and spending in the federal government are not connected. We have seen time and again that reduced revenues only mean increased debt—debt that can grow and grow. We just keep increasing the debt limit! It's like having a no-limits, open-ended line of credit. We even have a significant body of politicians who say that the level of the national debt is irrelevant—since we "owe it to ourselves." Interestingly, that philosophy only seems to be applicable when the deficit is due to *defense* spending. Going into debt to provide expanded health care or prescription drugs does not seem to be as "good" as defense debt.

This line of thinking also ignores the basic laws of supply and demand, which operate just as much with money as they do with any other commodity. When the economy tries to expand at the same time the government is taking billions out of the available capital supply, the cost of the capital that is left rises rapidly, potentially and prematurely cutting off an economic recovery.

In any event, the record shows that cutting revenues does not automatically translate into smaller government—let alone better managed government. So, if that's the tool that is relied on, we get the worst of both worlds—bigger debt as well as a continuing non-managed government!

I don't believe that balanced budget legislation is the answer. There are too many uncertainties that could face the country. The legislation would just get pushed aside anyway.

The answer to the "connecting the dots" issue is to bring people into government with proven skills in identifying the root causes of problems and with the experience needed to implement basic changes in the management systems. America certainly has them by the thousands—men and women who operate the most successful economic engine in history, men and women who guide the biggest and most effective not-for-profit organizations in the world. We need to find a way to inject some of these people into the process that reassigns one-third of our nation's income!

Washington, D.C.—"The Nonworking City"

The definition of Washington as a "nonworking" city is not mine. It was the observation of a French minister of economics during a lunch at the State Department honoring the visit of French President Jacques Chirac in 1995. We were discussing the differences between the countries' political atmospheres and the minister said, "You realize that the United States is the only country, except for Brazil, that does not have its government in a working city."

I asked for clarification, and he continued: "In Paris, when our politicians go to work or go home, or when they go out socially, they are always in the midst of people who do not work in or around government. This helps keep our politicians in touch with the realities of normal life, and that is also true in London, Tokyo, Madrid, Rome, Berlin, Stockholm, Cairo, and every other country, except Brazil, that I can think of. In Washington all that your political people see or talk to are others in the political arena!"

I had not focused on this fact before, but the implications were quite obvious. In my view, the French minister's observation went a long way toward explaining the "beltway" mentality, with its seemingly increasing isolation from the country. Janice and I had seen this at work many times in Washington when we attended cocktail and dinner parties. Almost everyone present would have some connection with government. They were either in the current

administration or had served in a prior one. They were lawyers, lobbyists, and journalists—all tied to the politics of Washington. Even
the businesspeople were almost exclusively serving the federal
marketplace. Thus, it is not surprising that the discussions—even
the "social" ones—always turned to politics. The same topics would
come up time after time, with the same analyses and the same solutions. It makes for very comfortable conversations, but adds nothing to the debate on serious issues. This would not be so much of
a problem if it weren't for the fact that the attendees at these parties were the same people who, the next day, made federal policy.

At one party, frustrated by the same old topics and arguments,
I suddenly interjected what I thought would be a good idea—to
have everyone in government, except the President and his immediate staff, relocate their operations to Peoria, Oklahoma City, or
Kansas City—somewhere in the middle of the nation. That would
make the government much more accessible to its citizens. There
was a brief, bemused silence—and then people went on with their
conversations.

The suggestion to move to Peoria probably wasn't too practical, but other moves might be. Three-quarters of the GSA employees do not work in Washington. They are scattered throughout the
country, primarily because that is where most of the federal buildings are. I found these employees, in general, to be more creative,
more flexible, and certainly much more customer oriented than
their colleagues in D.C. To me this is not at all unusual. The head-
quarter staffs of corporations and nonprofits that operate nationally or internationally are always being criticized by those "in the
field." Some of the criticism is due to the fact that the headquarters represents the "boss," but much of it is justified. For a number of reasons, these companies and nonprofits have been shifting
away from large central headquarters and placing more responsibility in the locations that are closer to the customers. The accelerated pace of telecommunications has also facilitated this trend.
The result is usually a more creative, efficient, customer-oriented
organization.

Although the Clinton-Gore reinventing team made a run at
decentralization, it met with so much opposition—even open hostility—that the initiative quickly died. However, I am convinced that

this is a concept that would yield very big, positive savings as well as improved customer service. For example, I was convinced that although the GSA already was decentralized, we could have done even better. Moving all of our activities, except for a small group of high-level policy experts, into the regions could have reduced the headquarters (D.C.) GSA employment to fewer than 500 people, with an overall reduction of another 1,000 to 2,000 jobs.

I am convinced that similar reductions could be made in dozens of other federal agencies. Why do we have thousands and thousands of Department of Agriculture employees in Washington? I looked, but I didn't see many farms on Pennsylvania Avenue.

The same is true for the Veterans Administration, the IRS, and the EPA. The vast majority of our veterans, taxpayers, and environmental problems are distributed around America, but those advising and implementing their policies all live within a couple of square miles of each other—in that D.C. place. The situation was ludicrous—as the "keeper" of government office space, I was constantly getting long lists of reasons why each agency not only needed more office space in Washington, but also why it was imperative for each of them to be within walking distance of the White House.

The need for all of these people to be in Washington is based solely on a combination of political egotism and a lack of experience in structuring effective organizations. We can solve most of the ego problems by letting the Cabinet secretaries and their senior staffs stay in Washington where they could still talk to and comfort each other—but let's get the federal implementers out there with their customers. The decentralizing of most of Washington would have a significant long-term positive effect not only on efficiency and customer service, but also by making government jobs and assignments more accessible to experienced and talented ordinary citizens.

Making "Results" a Part of All Regulations

Although we have made some progress in reducing and simplifying federal regulations—examples of which are in Chapter 6—there is a lot more room for improvement. If changes are made, I am sure that the new management-experienced and trained people who begin entering federal service will continue that effort. In addition and, in parallel, it will be important to ensure that a new sense of "responsibility for results" be institutionalized. Therefore, I suggest that it be a requirement that each regulation contain a section that specifies the expected results for the regulation, a definition of the measurements to be used, and a specifically named government position that is responsible for ensuring the effective implementation of the regulation, periodically reporting on its status and the results.

An obvious objection will certainly be: "But many regulations are too general and can't be measured."

My response is that if it is that general, then it should be rewritten to be more specific. I suggest that if the expected results of a regulation cannot be measured in some fashion, the regulation is useless and should not be implemented!

Measurements do not have be numeric—they can even be opinions of others. For example, a regulation associated with tax-payers filing electronically might—in fact, should—include a measurement that asks taxpayers what they like about the system and what they don't like. This is just another reason why we need people with experience in establishing appropriate measurement systems in government.

If we can put some of the above suggestions into practice, I believe they will help bring a better balance between the purely political interests of those in government and the longer-term interests of the country. In the final analysis, however, it will have to be an enlightened and engaged citizenry that ensures that result.

The Disenchantment Factor

Although some skepticism is a healthy tradition in our democracy, there is a lot of evidence that healthy skepticism has turned into unhealthy cynicism. Many suggest that the basic cause of this disenchantment is a belief that the government can't get anything right anyway, so why bother to get involved.

The resulting abdication of a majority of our citizens from the processes of democracy could leave the system vulnerable to disproportionate control by special interest groups. And in fact there are many signs that this is already taking place. When this happens, the system of checks and balances put in place by our founders is impaired or rendered ineffective. In the final analysis it may be the most compelling reason to make major reforms in the management processes of our government.

★ ★ ★

I hope that the issues I have raised will result in some serious introspection by those in the political process who, down deep, know that "something is wrong" but do not see a way out. To them I would say—there are literally thousands of men and women in America who would love to help, but they can't find a way in. Please help clear a path for them. They will help you govern better!

To those with the needed skills and experience in the nongovernmental institutions of America who may also be cynical about the chances for change, I say this: People involved in the political process are just as smart, dedicated, and hardworking as you are—they just lack your capabilities in the areas of management. Take a step toward them—offer your help—but do it humbly with due respect for what they know and do. Who knows? Maybe someday the government will be a model of effective management that we can all admire.

APPENDICES

Appendix 1

 WESTERN DIGITAL

WESTERN DIGITAL CORPORATION 8105 IRVINE CENTER DRIVE
IRVINE CALIFORNIA 92718 TELEPHONE 714 932 7800 FACSIMILE 714 932 7820

ROGER W JOHNSON
CHAIRMAN OF THE BOARD
PRESIDENT AND
CHIEF EXECUTIVE OFFICER

November 26, 1991

Mr. Safi U. Qureshey
President & CEO
AST Research, Inc.
P. O. Box 19658
Irvine, CA 92713-96658

Subject: Looking for a Leader - Identifying Alternatives

Dear Safi:

- Restore solid economic growth to America!

- Directly attack the crucial social problems in America!

- Capitalize on an unparalleled opportunity for meaningful world peace!

We believe that these are not incompatible objectives. They are not "too expensive." They can be pursued in parallel. We also believe that to achieve them will require a different kind of political leadership - different from what we see in Washington today.

Maybe it will come from a re-awakening of the current leadership - maybe it will have to come from new leadership.

In any event, we believe it is critical to begin looking seriously at alternatives. Therefore, we invite you to meet Arkansas Governor Bill Clinton at 8:00 a.m. on December 6th in the Sycamore Willow Room of the Pacific Club.

We have talked extensively with the Governor and believe he would provide just such an alternative.

Please call Maralyn in Roger Johnson's office (714/932-7800) or Jane in Kathryn Thompson's office (714/380-1488) for reservations. We look forward to seeing you there.

Sincerely,

Kathryn G. Thompson

Roger W. Johnson

Appendix 1 (continued)

Looking for a leader?
We are!

Kathryn Thompson and Roger Johnson

invite you to meet

Governor Bill Clinton, Arkansas

Candidate for the Democratic Presidential

Nomination

8:00 a.m. Breakfast, December 6

Pacific Club

Call Maralyn Olsson (714/932-7807) or Jane

Rosenbloom (714/932-1488) for reservations

We need to evaluate alternatives

Appendix 2

PERSPECTIVE ON THE PRESIDENTIAL RACE

Jumping Parties Over the Economy

A longtime Republican compares economic programs and finds that Clinton's is the one with vision, and is workable.

By ROGER W. JOHNSON

The Bush Administration claims to be a friend to America's employers, but its policies over the past four years have been a disaster for business, nationally and here in California. When it comes to the critical issue of economic growth, which this presidential election will be decided upon, the Administration has taxed, spent and borrowed to a fair-thee-well, putting to shame the ghosts of Democratic administrations past.

As a result, there's a serious lack of credit in the capital markets; long-term interest rates remain too high because there's no confidence that the Bush Administration will address the deficit issue, and with this huge debt, the world's lending institutions have no incentive for taking the risk of lending to businesses. The Administration still does not have a clue about the seriousness and complexity of these economic ills or their relationship to key social and infrastructure problems. Sadly, it has no real plan to solve them, only negative attacks on any new ideas as immoral, unethical or un-American.

On the defensive, the Bush campaign has unleashed a faulty critique of Bill Clinton's plan for economic growth that in the words of the Wall Street Journal is "couched in harsh, misleading language that may not stand up to scrutiny." Indeed not. The Bush campaign has alleged that Clinton "proposes the largest tax increase in American history." But the evidence suggests that the Republicans themselves have raised taxes more often than Clinton has. In

fact, as recently reported in the Boston Globe, senior Bush officials have admitted that they are lying about their claim that Clinton raised taxes 128 times in Arkansas. When asked why they continue their attempts to mislead the public, they said "because it works."

As a businessman, I have studied the Clinton plan and concluded that it is realistic and well-thought-out, with tax reductions and increases and true investment targeted in the right places. The Bush campaign's "tax-and-spend" charges aimed at discrediting the Clinton plan are simply fallacious. They ignore the $104 billion in tax cuts over four years that the Clinton program contains. These tax reductions include $60 billion for middle-class relief, $12 billion for an earned-income tax credit for the poor and $25 billion for an investment tax credit for corporations.

My reading of the Clinton plan indicates that taxes would be raised only on the very highest 2% of income earners, those who earn over $200,000 per year. I believe that many taxpayers in that category would view such an increase as a worthy investment if their hard-earned dollars were part of a realistic, integrated plan to rebuild our infrastructure and revitalize our economy.

I am one who would be paying more taxes under the Clinton plan and, of course, I would rather not. But our problems are deep and long in the making; we must begin finally to take corrective action, which includes creating some new revenue. I am convinced that increased taxes on higher-income individuals is the least harmful way to accomplish that much-needed piece of the plan.

The Clinton plan would promote private investment through tax incentives to business and direct investments in better transportation, job training and education. Economic growth and jobs

would be stimulated through an investment fund that would help to replace lost military prime contracts with new businesses in products that are competitive in world markets.

Perhaps most important of all, the Clinton plan also specifies how these investments in the future can be made while gradually reducing the federal deficit to the $100-billion level by 1996—another fact that demonstrates the ill-fitting nature of the old "tax-and-spend" Democratic hair shirt this time around.

As a Republican who has voted for every GOP presidential candidate since Eisenhower in 1952, it has been an eye-opening experience to find that a Democratic governor from Arkansas has a far better understanding of what America needs than does an incumbent Republican Administration. It was Ronald Reagan's challenge in the 1980 campaign to assure the American public that his election would not result in an overly aggressive approach to nuclear arms strategy. Today, it is Bill Clinton's challenge to overcome the Democrats' reputation of fiscal irresponsibility and convince voters that he will not tax and spend our way to further deterioration.

After many conversations and a great deal of reading and analysis, I am convinced that neither Clinton nor the people around him bear any resemblance to previous Democratic administrations that advocated redistribution of wealth and welfare economics. In Bill Clinton, I believe we finally have someone who has melded the best of sound economic thinking with a prudent program of social responsibility.

With all of our problems, the United States still represents the best force for good in the world, all we're missing is a strong visionary leader with a strategy and plan to move forward. Bill Clinton is that person.

Roger W. Johnson is chairman of the board of Western Digital in Irvine.

Appendix 3

Republicans celebrate in Arkansas

By David J. Lynch
The Orange County Register

LITTLE ROCK, Ark. — Orange County Republican Roger Johnson shouted and clapped along with a delirious crush of Democratic VIPs on Tuesday night as Arkansas Gov. Bill Clinton swept to a resounding victory.

"I feel very good tonight, very encouraged and excited," an ebullient Johnson said above the din.

Johnson and his wife, Janice, watched the election returns at a posh reception at the Excelsior Hotel, just one block from the Arkansas statehouse.

Throughout the night, shouts and cries of glee rang out from the crowd of more than 1,000 Demo-cratic financial contributors and supporters jammed into the hotel's restaurant.

Out of the White House for 12 years, the Democrats became progressively more vocal as the evening wore on.

For Johnson, the moment was equally sweet.

Just one year ago, the Republican chief executive of Western Digital Corp. in Irvine publicly broke with the White House over President Bush's handling of the economy.

"I don't feel I broke with anyone," Johnson said. "My party broke with me, sometime in the last four to six years, and moved extremely to the right."

Johnson and seven other promi-nent Orange County Republicans helped convince voters that Clinton was not a traditional Democrat.

Costa Mesa public-relations executive Robert Nelson was also in Little Rock for the festivities.

Johnson moved easily through the crowd, greeting top Clinton campaign officials, including adviser Warren Christopher, on a first-name basis.

Johnson said he thinks Clinton faces stiff challenges.

The president-elect must avoid short-term quick fixes on the economy, he said. And Clinton must keep popular expectations reasonable while convincing people that his election does not mean a return to old-style Democratic policies, Johnson said.

Appendix 4

Administrator
General Services Administration
Washington, DC 20405

July 21, 1993

The Honorable Albert Gore, Jr.
Vice President
The White House

Subject: NPR - Early Observations

Dear Mr. Vice President:

Commenting on such a complex process after only a couple of weeks of detailed involvement might seem presumptuous - however, I have found that many times the view of an outsider/newcomer has been very useful to me - it is in that vain and with that hope that the following is offered.

First, I have been very impressed with the quality of the people involved; the breadth of issues being addressed and the depth of analysis and discussion. I have been particularly impressed with the obviously heavy personal level of involvement of the Vice President - and each of you, and this is <u>not</u> going unnoticed through the rank and file of the agencies. In fact this is the single most frequently mentioned positive as I talk with people here and in other agencies. These people have seen programs come and go but they've never seen the senior people themselves involved. Although it will be more difficult as time goes on - I believe it is essential that this continue thru all aspects of the reinventing process - (i.e. eight years plus).

Secondly, the spirit/will to change - among the team members is exceptional. In many cases there is an excitement that I would have loved to see in my own companies. They have been let out of jail - the inmates really are going to get a chance to run the asylum!

This leads however, to a concern and a suggestion - I have only two at the moment.

Suggestion (1) Change is obviously always difficult - no one really wants disruption, but it is made ever more difficult if it is presented or perceived as a criticism of the past, rather than a natural process needed for the future. I have been concerned reading some of the interim recommendations - particularly the executive summaries that begin with some fairly scathing condemnations of past practices. Those who we're asking to change will read this as a personal criticism and we'll needlessly set off more defensive reactions. Asking incumbents to make big changes is very very hard -- for this very reason -- they generally can't separate the acceptance of the "new" from it being a repudiation of the past -- i.e. themselves. That's why in private business most big changes come with fairly deep personnel changes as well. We don't have that opportunity and therefore selling change as a positive natural forward force is even more critical.

If this makes sense, I suggest we each being to emphasize this and quickly review the written material in that light.

Appendix 4 (continued)

Vice President Gore
Page 2

     Suggestion (2) This observation goes way beyond the NPR. It is almost impossible for me to get people to discuss end results vs. process. I have found almost no meaningful quantitative measurements and/or standards. There is very little mentality for committing or measuring anything but least of all cost improvements! I am concerned that even in the NPR discussions I get a sense that the objectives are "freedom" and delegation for their own sake - we seem to be missing commitments for savings.

     Suggestion: Could we ask the teams to also present the two or three key measurements that we will need to assure that their recommendations -- when implemented -- are doing what we want? (I have asked my senior staff at GSA to do this for FY94 and 95 as part of their budget process.)

Sincerely,

Roger W. Johnson

cc: Elaine Kamark
       Phil Lader
       Jim King

Appendix 5

Starting the Body Count

By Al Kamen
Washington Post Staff Writer

Just when it seemed that things would calm down on the personnel front (which, admittedly, would be bad news for this column), President Clinton comes through. Out goes Defense Secretary Les Aspin, putting a whole new departmentful of senior jobs up for grabs.

The embattled nomination of Morton Halperin for an assistant secretaryship may be the first of many casualties of the Bobby Ray Inman regime at the Pentagon, given word yesterday that Inman would have wide latitude to reshape the operation there.

By the way, is this the same Bobby Inman who just five weeks ago was telling us how he didn't miss Washington, not even a little bit, not for a moment, how he was enjoying his work putting together high-tech companies, making all that money and was glad to be gone and wouldn't think of coming back?

Nah. Must have been another Bobby Ray. Common name down in Austin, we're told.

Washington, Where the Hit List Hits Back

■ Like other federal agency heads, Roger W. Johnson, administrator of the General Services Administration, was working hard to find additional ways to cut his budget.

Johnson, a California business executive and former head of Western Digital Corp., drew up a list of federal construction projects that appeared either unnecessary or too large, including new federal courthouses in Phoenix and Charleston, W.Va.

Last week he had his staff notify the staffs of the senators with projects on his list, including Arizona's Dennis DeConcini (D) and West Virginia's Robert C. Byrd. DeConcini's courthouse would be delayed and Byrd's would be killed, the senators' staffs were told.

The phone calls went flying into the White House. DeConcini runs the Senate Appropriations subcommittee that controls the White House budget. The immensely powerful Byrd is chairman of the full committee. The staffers were told that mid-level White House folks had been alerted to, as one source delicately put it, "the problem," and that "a number of administration officials had talked to Johnson without success."

It was decided that Johnson, apparently trying to do things according to what made economic sense, needed to get what the source said was "some clear guidance" from the White House.

Enter Mr. Clear Guidance, in the form of White House senior adviser George Stephanopoulos, who sources said called Johnson this week to explain the difference between doing business according to what makes sense and doing business in Washington.

Latest word was the two courthouses will proceed as planned. Welcome to Washington, Mr. Johnson.

3 Reasons Why Clinton Didn't Light Up

■ Some reporters at the White House Christmas party for the news media on Wednesday thought the decorations and trees looked spectacular but that Clinton looked a bit pale and maybe puffy.

The ready explanation was that Clinton is in fact very allergic to all those decorations. Another explanation was that he may have looked a bit distracted because minutes earlier he had announced Aspin's resignation. A third possibility was that he was stunned by such a large concentration of egos in one place.

The Neverending Story

■ Clinton's decision to make Philip Lader the White House deputy chief of staff has prompted some changes of plan in the White House personnel shop.

Lader, formerly deputy chief at the Office of Management and Budget, was taking over the personnel shop before he got his new job, but he's still working on some personnel matters. Meanwhile, senior adviser and former personnel boss Bruce Lindsey is still involved in some personnel matters—although he's supposed to be moving to more political work and to the job he had during the campaign of being the "body man"—meaning joined to Clinton's hip and available to get things done quickly. And deputy personnel boss John Emerson, who was to be leaving with Lindsey, is still sort of in the personnel shop too.

This, senior officials say, is all going to get sorted out shortly.

Meanwhile, the new White House personnel procedure—called "last one standing gets the job"—appears to have settled on Patrick J. Griffin, Washington lobbyist and former aide to Byrd, to replace Howard Paster in the legislative liaison meat grinder.

Wife Of . . . Dept.

■ Oops. We forgot to mention that Susan J. Blumenthal, the physician who was named Tuesday to be deputy assistant secretary for women's health at the Department of Health and Human Services, is the wife of Massachusetts Rep. Edward J. Markey (D).

He's Leaving Too, but Not With Aspin

■ Lost in the shadow of the Aspin departure was the resignation of Assistant Agriculture Secretary Eugene Branstool as head of marketing and inspection services.

Branstool, who was chairman of the Ohio Democratic Party last year, told the Associated Press that his resignation was unrelated to recent complaints by the Ohio Department of Agriculture and state cattle groups that appropriate procedures were not followed in putting a friend of Branstool's on an industry board. Branstool is leaving on Dec. 31 to go back to his farm in Ohio.

Appendix 6

Administrator
General Services Administration
Washington, DC 20405

5 January, 1994

The Honorable Janet Reno
Attorney General of the United States
Department of Justice
Washington, DC   20530

Dear General Reno:

As you know, several weeks ago I became aware that, for many years, previous GSA Administrators had been granting waivers allowing federal agencies to sell old and/or surplus fire arms to dealers in the private sector.

This is to confirm our several conversations that on December 13, 1993, I issued a directive rejecting requests for new waivers, rescinding old ones and restricting any future weapons re-sales to transfers between federal agencies only.

I appreciate your and Director Freeh's support and cooperation in this matter and thought you would be interested to see that we have stopped over 60,000 weapons from dispersal to the public (see attached list).

Even though we "lost" approximately $5 - 10 million in potential sales revenue, I am confident that hard dollars saved from the cost of crimes avoided, as well as the human misery avoided, offsets by an order of magnitude these lost sales.

Thank you for your help and support.

Sincerely,

ROGER W. JOHNSON
Administrator

Enclosure

Appendix 6 (continued)

General Services Administration
Federal Supply Service
December 9, 1993

FACT SHEET

ISSUE: Exchange/Sale Waivers for Unneeded Federal Weapons

BACKGROUND: The Federal Property Management Regulation (FPMR)
                       Parts 101-42.1102-10(A-C) state, in part, that weapons no
                       longer needed by an agency may be transferred only to
                       those Federal agencies authorized to acquire weapons for
                       official use. Weapons may not be donated and may be sold
                       only for scrap after total destruction. Additionally, FPMR
                       Part 101.46.202 states, in part, weapons are ineligible for
                       exchange/sale.

DISCUSSION: Since 1982, GSA has granted 20 exchange/sale waivers for
                       weapons (handguns and rifles). Thirteen of these waivers
                       have been granted during the past 3 years.

WAIVERS GRANTED: A list of all waivers granted for exchange/sale of weapons
                       since 1982.

Agency	Quantity	Type	Date Granted	Date Expired
Secret Service	Unspecified	Handguns & Rifles	9/16/82	Open
Customs Service	Unspecified	Handguns & Rifles	1/13/83	12/31/87
U.S. Marshals Service	Unspecified	Handguns	9/17/84	Open
Immigration & Naturalization Service	1,450	Handguns	5/30/85	Expired
Customs Service	Unspecified	Handguns & Rifles	10/19/87	12/31/89
Energy Department	550	Handguns & Rifles	6/30/88	Open
Drug Enforcement Agency	541	Handguns	3/17/89	Expired

Appendix 6 (continued)

Agency	Quantity	Type	Date Granted	Date Expired
FBI	9,600	Handguns	4/16/90	Open
USDA	130	Handguns	11/9/90	9/30/93
State Department	600	Handguns	2/13/90	Open
Interior Department	20	Handguns & Rifles	12/7/90	Open
Immigration & Naturalization Service	16,000 3,000	Handguns Shotguns	1991	12/31/93
USDA	325	Handguns	7/24/91	9/30/93
Internal Revenue Service	4,000	Handguns	8/15/91	6/30/94
State Department	2,600	Handguns	6/08/92	10/31/92
Internal Revenue Service	4,000	Handguns	9/29/92	Open
Customs Service	15,000	Handguns & Rifles	4/30/92	3/01/94
U.S. Marshals Service	4,000	Handguns	2/02/93	9/30/96
U.S. Marshals Service	85	Uzi's	10/20/93	9/30/96
Total:	61,901+			

WAIVERS PENDING: A list of waiver requests for exchange/sale of weapons.

Agency	Quantity	Type	Date of Request
State Department	255	Rifles	10/06/93
Customs Service	15,000	Handguns & Rifles	11/23/93
Immigration & Naturalization Service	9,000 3,000	Handguns Rifles & Shotguns	11/1/93
FBI	9,600	Handguns	11/15/93
Total:	36,855		

SUBMITTED BY: Lester D. Gray, Jr.
Director, Property Management Division (FBP)
(703) 305-7240

Appendix 7

The Orange County Register **STATE and REGION** Friday, Jan. 21, 1994

GSA's Roger Johnson castigates Washington for plethora of red tape

GOVERNMENT: He offers business-inspired suggestions for streamlining the system.

By JEAN O. PASCO
The Orange County Register

NEWPORT BEACH — Washington is so mired in bureaucratic roadblocks and nonsensical rules that attempts to reform government are doomed without sweeping change, the administrator of the General Services Administration said Thursday. Roger Johnson, formerly chief executive officer of Western Digital in Irvine, said President Clinton's administration is attempting to tackle issues critical to business but is bumping up against a wall of resistance.

"The administration is changing the agenda on policy issues but the city is forcing it through the same process," Johnson said at a breakfast gathering at the Pacific Club.

"The business of government stinks. The process leaves you screaming within the first hour."

Johnson, one of the first Republican business leaders to support Clinton, said he's launched a program with business executives to persuade them to lobby for government reform. What is needed, he said, is a program in which CEOs can be lent temporarily to government to clean house.

Among the changes needed now, he said:

▶ Convincing Congress that agency heads need the authority to reduce jobs within government by offering employee buyouts. Employees who aren't productive or whose work isn't needed should be culled instead of the current system that gives longtime employees ironclad protections from layoffs. It won't help government to reduce employees when the ones left aren't doing the work needed, he said.

▶ Producing a capital budget for government buildings. Currently, each building is the product of a law and the entire cost of the building is included in a single year's budget. Johnson said his proposal to buy space to replace 48 properties coming off leases in the next two years was rejected, even though it would have saved $8 billion over 30 years. The reason: The entire cost of the purchase would be counted in the budget, exceeding an imposed cap on allowable increases.

Johson said a separate review of about 100 federal buildings pinpointed proposed savings of $650 million. But it won't be easy; he said he has to go back to Congress to get approval to rescind some authorizations for the buildings — involving changing about 70 laws.

"The process is so complicated, it's a wonder you can do anything at all," he said.

The bureaucrats running government — from agency middle management to congressional committee staff members — aren't bad people, he said.

What they lack is a basic understanding of what it takes to successfully operate a company, said Johnson, the administration's only former Fortune 500 CEO.

"They've worked in the government process so long, they have no concept of things you and I take for granted as common sense," he said. "There's no point in the process taking place that says, 'How did you do?' "

Appendix 8

Reinventing government
Procurement horror stories draw Feds' scrutiny

By Gary H. Anthes

WASHINGTON

Procurement expert Bob Dornan told the story of a U.S. Navy official who called him recently in a PC crisis.

Apparently the official's unit had for years purchased PCs from Gateway 2000, Inc., and the Navy had found the machines capable, cost-effective and easy to buy.

"But then a procurement official — in his infinite wisdom — decided to put it out for bids," explained Dornan, senior vice president at Federal Sources, Inc. in McLean, Va., a consultancy specializing in federal information systems procurement. "They ended up with rotgut PCs. There were 10 of them stacked up in the [official's] office; she couldn't even take them out of the

GSA administrator Roger W. Johnson: *'We haven't been delegating; we've been abdicating'*

boxes because they didn't have the Underwriters Laboratory certification. But they were cheaper."

Everyone has a favorite horror story about how the government messes up when

Procurement, *page 29*

Appendix 8 (continued)

News

Procurement

CONTINUED FROM PAGE 1

it buys things — from computers to toilet seats to space telescopes. IS technology — because of its complexity and its rapidly changing nature — has proved especially troublesome for Uncle Sam, whether buying a handful of PCs or multibillion dollar custom systems.

"What we buy costs too much, [the process] takes too long, and we don't even get access to some of the best technology because many companies refuse to do business with us," said Roger W. Johnson, administrator at the U.S. General Services Administration (GSA), which is chartered by law to oversee the government's IS purchases.

Faced with procurement lead times frequently measured in years, users are often saddled with technology a generation or two out of date, Johnson said. "A CEO of a large technology company said to me, 'Roger, I hope when you go [to the GSA] you don't change the rules, or I'll lose my only market for excess and obsolete inventory.'"

The system also takes its toll on managers at user organizations, according to Roger Cooper, deputy assistant attorney general for information resources management (IRM) at the U.S. Department of Justice. He said he spends 25% of his time on IS procurement, time he should spend on managing IS operations. "If you are trying to do big systems in the government and you are not a procurement expert, you will almost inevitably fail," Cooper said.

Cooper and other IS managers said that struggles with the procurement machinery — and worries about serving up on this or that regulation — consume time that would be better spent on accomplishing the agency's mission.

Army's David Borland: *'Let's not mess with the rules anymore. We're just beginning to understand them.'*

Procurement procedure OK

Despite these and other criticisms, not all observers agreed that federal IS procurement practices need a top-to-bottom overhaul. "I don't think the system is as broke as people make it out to be," Dornan said. "I don't see radical change as either possible or necessary."

For example, Dornan pointed to the controversial bid-protest process and to a popular perception that every major federal buy gets mired in wrangling among the parties. He said that out of 10,000 or so information technology procurements that were subject to protest in 1992, just 123 resulted in protests that had to be settled by judicial process, and 78% of those were decided in the government's favor.

The number may be small, but it is the largest and most visible deals that get mired in controversy, observers said.

While opinions differ as to where the system is faltered, numerous factions are hell-bent on fixing it. Thanks in large part to Vice President Al Gore's "reinventing government" crusade, which devotes considerable attention to the topic, procurement reform is all the rage here.

Examples of this include the following:
• Several procurement-reform bills are pending in Congress. One would raise the threshold for streamlined small purchases from $25,000 to $100,000, reform the bid-protest process and simplify in various ways the interaction between buyers and sellers.
• The Office of Management and Budget recently announced that it will start requiring contracting officials to explicitly consider a vendor's performance on earlier government work before granting new contracts. It also is developing guidelines to permit greater dialogue between buyers and sellers during the procurement cycle, and it plans to curtail the use of vendor audits by the government and require ments for vendors to provide internal cost data.
• The GSA is pursuing a number of initiatives, from a fundamental overhaul of procurement philosophy to electronic commerce. On April 1, a bulletin board system will begin listing prices of 150,000 PC products from 437 vendors. The aim is to increase competition and reduce administrative burdens on buyers and sellers.

According to Joe M. Thompson, the GSA commissioner for IRM, electronic shopping will lead to reduced prices by allowing more vendors to participate in the process and by helping to maintain a competitive edge by enabling vendors to lower their prices easily and more quickly.

Without such a system, in a recent 12-month period the government bought 17,000 copies of WordPerfect 5.1 at $262 per copy. Meanwhile, according to the U.S. General Accounting Office, it was available to the public at discount outlets for $244 and to the state of Texas for just $223.

Terry Miller, president of Government Sales Consultants, Inc. in Great Falls, Va., said many of the reform initiatives miss the mark. He said most procurement snafus are not due to inherent flaws in the system but to errors by officials who are poorly trained in IS procurement. "Most agencies don't understand you can't use the same guy to buy kerosene" and LANs, he said. "We don't need a new piano; we need a better trained pianist."

"Let's not mess with the rules anymore," agreed David Borland, director of the U.S. Army's Information Systems Selection and Acquisition Agency. "We're all just now beginning to understand them. If we keep on changing them, we'll be constantly trying to learn them while we do business."

Nevertheless, the consensus in Washington seems to be that reform should focus on the rules. "We have bad procurement systems and good people," Thompson said.

Asking questions

Performance-based procurement is a theme that knits together many of the current reform efforts. It is based on a philosophy that federal IS users and the public will generally be better served by a procurement framework that focuses on results, rather than adherence to regulation minutia. The GSA is moving to embed that concept in its delegation of IS procurement authority to other agencies.

When an agency comes to the GSA seeking that delegation it is usually handed the money — no questions asked, Johnson said. "We should — and will be — asking, 'Are you going to be able to process claims with fewer people? Will you improve customer service? What are the results?' We haven't been delegating; we've been abdicating."

Federal IS officials would like to apply that principle within their agencies, but they concede that measuring performance is not as easy as filling out a procurement checklist.

"We're trying to work the problem right now," said Jane L. Sullivan, director of IRM at the U.S. Department of the Treasury. "We want to delegate [procurement authority] and empower our bureaus more where their performance has proved itself. How can we set up measures to do that? How do you define performance? It's a hard problem, but we have to do it."

The Army marches to a different beat

The Army has a reputation for running a top-notch procurement shop in its 120-person Information Systems Agency, which now manages $6 billion in IS contracts. Much of the credit goes to its director, David Borland, said Terry Miller, president of Government Sales Consultants.

"It's the best buyer of [IS] today," Miller said.

Borland shrugged off the compliment and said he has no silver bullet, just management stability and old-fashioned leadership. He has been at the agency 18 years and his eight deputies combined have some 100 years of tenure there, he noted.

"We have knowledge of the market," Borland said. "We know the players and they know us. We never surprise anyone. It's like we're at a dance and everyone knows the steps." He visits key executives at vendor companies constantly, he said, and he rarely gets a formal protest over a contract.

Not all of the credit

Miller said there are other explanations for the agency's reputation for having satisfied users and nonlitigious vendors. He said it is one of just 15 procurement shops — out of some 2,500 in the government — that buys only information technology.

It is also one of the few that combines contracting, legal and technical people under the control of one person. Miller said he recently saw a request for proposals from another agency that was put together by user representatives in Alabama, buying specialists in Tennessee and lawyers in the Pentagon. "That's a recipe for disaster," he said.

— *Gary H. Anthes*

IS purchasing challenges government

In a recent Information Technology Association of America survey of 24 senior government IRM officials, 67% said they thought the climate for IS procurement reform had improved. Only 25% said no; 8% said maybe. To understand the challenge of federal procurement, it is helpful to look at some of the following numbers:
▶ The federal government buys $200 billion worth of goods and services annually, using 142,000 procurement officials armed with 4,500 pages of regulations in 2,500 procurement shops. It spends $25 billion on information technology — an amount that is growing steadily by $1 billion a year. *Sources: National Performance Review; Federal Sources, Inc.; Government Sales Consultants, Inc.*
▶ "A vice president at DEC told me a few years ago

that if we just took the boilerplate — 200 pages of requirements for things like small and disadvantaged business plans and 'Buy-American' plans — out of our terms and conditions, he would cut all of his bids by 10%," said Roger Cooper, deputy assistant attorney general for IRM at the U.S. Department of Justice.
▶ In the first nine months of fiscal 1993, vendors returned $1.4 billion in payments received from the Pentagon, saying they had not submitted bills and were not owed the money. *Source: Sen. John Glenn (D-Ohio), Jan. 27, 1994.*
▶ A Defense Department Acquisition Streamlining Panel recently completed a congressionally mandated perusal of Pentagon procurement practices. Its recommendations filled 1,800 pages.

— *Gary H. Anthes*

Appendix 9

said California Deputy Gen. William G. Prahl, who represent the state. If the ides with Tuilaepa, it could ew sentencing hearings for e 374 inmates now on Death

case comes before the high t a time when most Ameri- re demanding swifter pun- t for violent criminals, not rocedural rights for defend-

the court has been quietly g toward tightening the rds for using the death pen- Although all nine justices nd the U.S. Constitution, in ic, permits capital punish- they continue to seek a to ensure that it is imposed nd rationally.

justice thinks that is not e. Justice Harry A. Black- nnounced last month his
Please see APPEAL, A26

wn Proving diging at nd Raising

JL JACOBS N MORAIN AFF WRITERS

RAMENTO—Few politi- are as prodigious at fund as state Treasurer Kathleen now on a quest to become or.

mbly Speaker Willie —no slouch himself when it to raising campaign mon- eaks of her as a "fund-rais- hine."

evening cocktails or morn- ee, at $500-a-plate lunches, -country calls from her car at gala banquets, Brown ly uses her charm, family tions and disarming direct- perform a job that some ans view with disgust— money, lots of it.

's not afraid to ask the
Please see BROWN, A28

From O.C. to D.C., It's Downhill All the Way

■ **Politics:** Washington intrigue dismays, disgusts Janice Johnson, the wife of a top Clinton appointee.

By ANN CONWAY
TIMES STAFF WRITER

When President Clinton tapped Roger W. Johnson of Laguna Beach to head the Gen- eral Services Administration last year, it was with the idea that the Orange County busi- nessman would help reinvent government by eliminating waste and trimming expenses.

His wife, Janice—reluctant to leave her position here as a prominent social and arts fund- raiser, but anxious to join her husband—moved to Washing- ton eight months ago

Last week, an angry and disillusioned Janice Johnson

returned to Orange County to visit friends and lashed out at what she feels is a back-stab- bing political climate that is trying to reinvent them.

"The harassers on Capitol Hill can all go jump in the Potomac," she said in an interview with The Times while her husband was in Sacramento on govern- ment business. "When I flew into Orange County on Monday, I thought 'Oh boy, what a sight for sore eyes, why in the devil did we ever leave?' "

Janice Johnson was reacting to recent allegations that her husband, the Administration's highest ranking Republican— had misused tax-supported
Please see JOHNSON, A20

KAREN TAPIA / Los Angeles Times
Janice Johnson: "I guess Roger and I were very, very naive."

As U.S. Lea Somalia Br for Rough

By MARK FINEMAN
TIMES STAFF WRITER

MOGADISHU, Somali edge of Medina marke block from the perime main military compoun is leaving behind, Mah hamed sat at a batte table, selling the last of can garbage that has fed and tens of thousands of more than a year.

They are the leavin military MREs—Meals Eat. They have fueled street market in Medina 15 months in which Mo his fellow merchants bo from the back of Soma trucks that hauled the t American force that o bered more than 20,000 t

As the final few hund began heading home th including about 225 wh Saturday—Mohamed's p soaring.

Marble cake in an oliv went for $1.10. A tiny Louisiana Hot Sauce wa and a miniature packet sauce fetched 30 cents.

"The prices of ever going up now that the are leaving—no more su hamed said, noting sad stand is among the las that once supported th Somalis

"No one knows what now," he added. "But e afraid."

As Mohamed prepare up shop, it was clear th was leaving behind far garbage and soaring pric

Signs of deepening growing street violence
Please see SOM

Appendix 9 (continued)

JOHNSON: Potomac Power Play

Continued from A1

travel funds to visit his Laguna Beach home. Questions were raised about five of the nine official trips he scheduled during his first seven months in office. She was also upset that certain members of Congress and their staff, whom she declined to name, have told her husband they "would get him" because they are unhappy about his cost-cutting tactics.

Of the trips, she said, "One time the President asked him to come. Once, Al Gore asked him to come. He came home when I told him I was evacuating our house during the fires and he paid for that trip. During two other trips, he conducted a lot of GSA business. He has done absolutely nothing wrong."

Last week, Roger Johnson asked the GSA's inspector general to examine his travel records and vowed to reimburse the government for any expenses deemed questionable. In the meantime, the agency's chief financial officer issued a memo that Johnson's "actions were consistent with federal travel regulations."

Of threats about his cost-cutting measures, she said. "What has happened is he has taken a lot of the pork barrel away. That has prompted at least three congressmen to threaten him with, 'I'm going to get you,' which really means, 'send you back where you came from.'

"Like Roger says, 'You know who your friends are in Washington, because they stab you in the chest instead of the back.'

"Now, isn't it funny that they are looking at his travel expenses, instead of looking at all the money he has saved the taxpayers? They don't seem to care about that.

"We left Orange County because Roger really thought he could make a difference, help change things, and he is. But they—the far left wing and the far right wing—don't want change. It's too threatening."

Despite the ongoing politics and their frustration at the slow-moving process, the couple plans to remain in Washington.

"I guess Roger and I were very, very naive. Very naive. We're a little disillusioned. But, it's un-American to let the bad guys win, isn't it?

"So, we'll stick it out. As long as the President wants Roger, as long as he can make a contribution. If it comes to the point where he can't, where the congressional committees won't let him, then we'll come home."

Unhappy with President Bush's seeming disregard of the country's economic woes, the Johnsons in 1991 joined forces with other Orange County Republicans to support Clinton, long before the Arkansas governor made his official bid for the presidency.

Soon after he took office, Clinton appointed Johnson, formerly chief executive officer of Western Digital Corp. in Irvine, to his post.

Janice Johnson said the forces aimed at toppling her husband are also aimed at the Clintons. They are being attacked via the Whitewater controversy because, she believes, Clinton has brought popular issues to the fore, with promising results. Clinton has fought for a crime bill, Hillary a health care package. "They have taken all of the good ammunition away from the Republicans," she said.

"It's power harassment and very distracting for the President. Can you imagine what it's like? How can he go into a meeting, say with Hussein, and not be thinking about it?

"There's a whole attitude in

'There's such an old boy's club here—a generation that's about a half a generation older than we are—that control the Congress. They're men and they just can't wait to get' Hillary Clinton.

JANICE JOHNSON
Wife of Roger W. Johnson, head of
General Services Administration

Washington that you're guilty unul proven innocent. Maybe they [the Clintons] should have been more up front about it, said, 'Here's what it is, take it or leave it,' but I don't think they realised they were" not being forthcoming.

"The Clintons were sent to Washington as a mandate for change and that's the last thing anybody—the insiders—in Washington wants. They [insiders] are more interested in the power and the process because the process takes so long and involves so many jobs." She has watched in disbelief as members of the Administration have dropped by the wayside.

"There's such an old boy's club here—a generation that's about a half a generation older than we

are—that control the Congress. They're men and they just can't wait to get her [Hillary]."

Janice Johnson has had ample opportunity to become acquainted with the First Lady. She has dined with her in the First Family's private quarters. And it was Janice Johnson who helped organise a lunch for Hillary Clinton during a campaign swing through Orange County. From the moment they met, Johnson has been impressed by Hillary Clinton's sincerity and intelligence.

"Hillary is extremely bright and capable," Johnson said. "She wants to get her health care, or some health care package, through. Talk about powerful lobbies. Look at all of the people she's threatening with

...ys Dismay GSA Appointee's Wife

these changes."

In recent months, Johnson said she thought about trying to unseat Rep. Robert K. Dornan (R-Garden Grove), who is running for reelection this fall.

"I toyed with the idea," said Johnson, who is known here for her organizational ability. But she has put the dream to bed. "Not after being in Washington for eight months," she said with a sardonic smile.

"Pragmatically, the only way I could win would be to run as a Democrat. [Janice Johnson is now a registered Democrat; her husband remains a Republican.]

There's no way I could have beat him in a Republican primary. With the money he's got? No way I could have done it. Plus, I would have had to move to that district. It would have been tough."

Meanwhile, she has been appointed by the President to serve on the Committee for the Preservation of the White House. Jane Alexander, chairwoman of the National Endowment for the Arts, has invited her to join the National Symphony board.

"I was vetted [evaluated] by the White House, though it's not official yet. And the symphony position has not yet been ratified," she said.

In recent weeks, she has helped Alexander find artwork for the offices of Cabinet members. "We're calling it the Art on the Walls Project," she said. "Atty. Gen. Janet Reno wanted some art. [HUD secretary Henry G.] Cisneros wanted some. I've had a good time with that. All of a sudden I am more into the visual arts than the performing arts."

Generally speaking, Janice Johnson has been welcomed to Washington with open arms. "One of Hillary's assistants has made sure I have met people. She has paved the way, made it easier for me. There are some really good people in town."

Appendix 10

GSA   NEWS   FROM   A   DEMOCRATIC   PERSPECTIVE

News Bulletin -Denver April 6, 1994

Johnson, the GSA housecleaner: Back in the spring of 1993 when the AFGE union said they were looking forward to a new Administrator coming on board that would clean house at GSA, they were referring to one that would clean out the Republicans that had been dumped there and then had burrowed-in to management positions over several Republican administrations. Little did they realize that another Republican would be coming in and instead of cleaning out the Republicans this Administrator is cleaning out the recent White House appointed Clinton Democrats! In our April 4th and previous Bulletins, we told which ones he has fired, which ones he has targeted, which ones are leaving in disgust and the unnamed others who want the White House to help them find other positions. And the Republicans while all this is going on? They are sitting back looking like the cat that just swallowed the canary.

We are committed to putting a Democratic balance back into GSA which for too long has been a Republican dumping ground. Mr. Johnson's housecleaning operation goes contrary to that effort. By now it should be very clear to every Democrat that before any progress can be made toward a balance at GSA, Roger Johnson has got to be asked to leave or be forced out.

Johnson, the GSA recruiter: It appears Mr. Johnson's plan is to replace everyone with people that owe their jobs to him rather than the President. He doesn't want to have anyone in GSA that is able to call the White House. He knows he can't get away with promoting or bringing in more Republicans, so he is trying to recruit friends and acquaintances he has met in the past or around Washington who happen to be Democrats. Mr. Johnson wants Shirley Geer, from the World Resources Institute in Washington to be his new Public Affairs person and is pressing the White House to get her cleared. He is talking to Barbara Silby, Vice President of the American Business Conference about being his new Chief of Staff. We can't imagine why Ms. Silby would want the job but if she takes it, one of her first assignments as the "hatchet-person" for Mr. Johnson will be to help him push "Hap" Connors and Emily Hewitt out and then make another run at Mr. Ratchford. That's going to put her in a bad light as far as we're concerned and when the backlash comes, she would most likely be asked to leave along with Mr. Johnson.

Mr. Johnson is trying to woo others, telling them how well liked he is by everyone, etc. etc. Mr. Johnson is an excellent salesman, be it used cars, corporate bonds or Western Digital stock, but we would not recommend anyone buy anything he is pushing. We don't think Ms. Silby is going to accept his offer and there is no question she would be better off to stay with Barry Rogstead at the American Business Conference. As for Ms. Geer, if she isn't having second thoughts by now, she should be having them. We have more information on his recruitment activities but that's enough for now.

Appendix 10 (continued)

Johnson, the GSA "plumber":   Washington times Reporter John McCaslin, in his widely read column "Inside the Beltway" for April 5, confirmed from another source that Mr. Johnson had in fact tried to determine from which fax machine CROSSWIND was being circulated. Mr. McCaslin's other source said, "There was quite an effort to determine from where it was faxed..." The source would not or could not confirm if Mr. Johnson's witch-hunt went any further. And the leaks go on...

Johnson, the GSA destroyer: On Friday April 1, Mr. Johnson overruled his entire staff and was the only voice in favor of a decision which people believe will unnecessarily cripple the agency. Many, and this was no small meeting, went away from the meeting shaking their heads puzzled over his motive. We know what he is up to but before we lay out his latest plan, we are going to wait until our friends in Congress come back from recess.

We would like to remind people that it was just a few days ago at the Government Operations Committee hearing on March 24, that Chairman Conyers likened Mr. Johnson to a corporate raider viewing GSA "as a hostile corporate takeover that will be finished only when the agency is broken up and sold off." This is a very important observation which tends to get overlooked amongst all the other adverse comments that were said to Johnson in that hearing. People should also be made aware that Mr. Johnson did not show any signs that he had undergone any miraculous conversion when he came away from the hearing. People that saw him afterwards said he was not humbled by the confrontation. He was very very angry and determined to find another way to get what he wants. GSA beware!

Editor: We are going to give Mr. Johnson a chance to "pause and reflect" and reconsider if what lies ahead for him is worth it. Are Representatives Brooks and Conyers going to let up? Is the press going to back off their inquiries? Is AFGE's Bruce Williams going to go away? Is the CROSSWIND Network going to lose interest? Is it possible to win back the confidence of the GSA employees? Is the White House personnel office at some point going to be forced to take action? While Mr. Johnson is pondering these questions, we are going to take a break ourselves for a few days, unless of course something really good comes along which we just can't resist publicizing.   The network never sleeps and information is continually transmitted and shared.   We just don't publish everything.   Rest assured we'll be watching and we'll be back. In the meantime we truly hope Mr. Johnson makes the right decision.

CROSSWIND hereby places the above information into the public domain and grants unlimited license without compensation to anyone wishing to photocopy, paraphrase or quote all or any part of the above without any mention of CROSSWIND.

CROSSWIND
P.O. Box 260486
Denver, CO 80226

Appendix 11

Appendix 12

THE WHITE HOUSE

WASHINGTON

April 19, 1994

Janice Johnson
1406 30th Street, N.W.
Washington, D.C. 20007

Dear Janice:

Roger sent me the Los Angeles *Times* article
about you, and I just want to thank you.

I appreciate your candor and your honest
assessment of this town. At the end of the
day, though, I know you agree that the progress
we're making is worth it.

Hang in there!

Sincerely,

Bill

Appendix 13

Hillary Rodham Clinton

Dear Roger and Janice,

The President shared with me a copy of Janice's interview and, as the kids used to say, "Right on!" I don't think any of us realized the full extent of the changes Washington needed when we first started down this road together. Or that it wasn't just the Congress, but the press and permanent

establishment that would also be threatened. Well, all I can say is we are causing change and are paying the price for that, but I'm proud of your contributions and know that, in the end, the results will speak for themselves. Thanks for being our friends — Hillary

Appendix 14

EDITORIAL

Credit where it's due

You've got to hand it to General Services Administrator Roger Johnson. After his well-publicized knocks with Congress, he remains voluble and enthusiastic in his attempt to help change the way government information systems are planned, designed and purchased.

It would be overstating it to say the patrons of this lone Republican executive in the Clinton administration have been leaving him to twist slowly in the wind. But whatever emanates from the various administration-inspired National Performance Review reports seems calculated to shove Johnson into fights with Capitol Hill.

No one in the administration has dared question whether the Brooks Act itself is in need of updating, although it probably is. All that Johnson has contended is that the bureaucracy should cut itself a little slack in how to interpret the rules for buying computers and for GSA's oversight of that activity. But that brought on the wrath of Brooks Act author Jack Brooks as well as of John Conyers, current chairman of the House Government Operations Committee.

Now another NPR task force has recommended folding the GSA unit that oversees the FTS 2000 telecommunications contracts shop back into the IRM Service. The recommendation comes at a time when GSA is humming with planning activity for the post-FTS 2000 contract that presumably will be partly joined by DOD, *and* when GSA is losing some 25 percent of the IRMS staff nationwide through buyouts.

It was none other than Jack Brooks, former chairman of the Government Operations Committee, who insisted on a separate associate administrator for FTS 2000 in the first place.

So who does Johnson try to please? The administration with its NPR proposals, or the Hill, which will surely thwart what it will see as an attempt to weaken FTS oversight by GSA?

At a recent meeting of members of the Information Technology Association of America, Johnson said he's glad to take the "spears and arrows" on behalf of GSA as he tries to affect a cultural change in how the laws and regulations are applied.

Johnson may have underestimated the degree to which Congress likes to get involved in an agency's affairs. But he deserves credit for trying to make things better for those applying information technology in the government.

Thomas R. Temin
Editor
Internet: Editor@gcn.com

Appendix 15

GSA's Embattled Chief Enlists a Friend as Lawyer

THE REGULATORS, From D1

national caravan with maybe **Paul Newman** as spokesman.

The API, which has put its money on reformulated gasoline to help clean up the environment, said the report favors certain technologies, instead of simply laying out the pros and cons of different fuels and letting them compete.

"The government is trying to pick winners, and this is a strategy that is flawed," said **William F. O'Keefe**, executive vice president of API.

In written comments, API called the plan "brainwashing," with "unsubstantiated sales pitches" that try to convince Americans that the air is dirtier than it is and that newer cars, instead of just old clunkers, are polluting hogs.

Besides hiring Stone to write that report, DOE also hired the **Brand Consulting Group** to probe attitudes about alternative fuels. The price tag for both studies was $55,000.

Ann Negnauer, an official in DOE's **Office of Transportation Technologies**, said the Stone plan "is a preliminary balloon we have floated." She said API's concerns would be addressed.

Since January, DOE has held meetings with "stakeholders" such as API that are helping the department come up with an information program.

In the meantime, DOE may spend another $100,000 on public relations help with alternative fuels. Stone, which said full execution of the plan it presented may be costly, is a bidder.

ROGER JOHNSON, who has sunk deep into troubled waters as head of the **General Services Administration**, has hired a lawyer to help him out.

In the midst of an inquiry about allegations that Johnson used GSA employees to do his personal business, he has turned to **Albert J. Beveridge III**, a friend and prominent

BRUCE MORRISON
... Gramm puts his nomination in limbo

Washington lawyer who is founding partner of Beveridge & Diamond, former president of the National Symphony Orchestra, attorney to the Democratic National Committee and a notable participant in Washington social circles.

Johnson, a Republican who crossed over to the Clinton camp, came to town about a year ago from **Western Digital Corp.** in California. Beveridge said he was hired to show Johnson "how to conduct himself in Washington."

A more interesting explanation comes from the GSA public affairs office, which faxed this statement: "Mr. Johnson has never hired a lawyer in his life, but after being in Washington for a year, he began to feel left out. Since the Beveridges were already personal friends . . . he asked Mr. Beveridge to fill that void in his life."

PASSERSBY were doing double takes last week when they noticed that **Isaac Hayes** of

"Shaft" soundtrack and '70s soul music fame was signing autographs outside the **Resolution Trust Corp.** building.

Was this a Richard Roundtree comeback in "Shaft's Big S&L Score"? Shut your mouth! Rather, he was one of about a dozen demonstrators who say the RTC discriminates against minorities in awarding contracts.

For about four hours, representatives from a California company called **Title Recon Tracking Inc.** picketed the agency, handing out fliers that offered rewards for whistle-blowing and walking with signs that said, "Whitewater: The Tip of the Iceberg."

Title Recon, an RTC contractor, said it lost in a recent competition because the RTC didn't think its minority joint venture partner, the **Institute for Black Economic Independence**, had enough experience.

An RTC spokesman said the company didn't get the award because its bid was too high, but that the agency is reviewing the case.

ATTORNEY Bruce Morrison has fallen into Nominee Netherworld since Sen. **Phil Gramm** (R-Tex.) put a hold on Morrison's nomination to head the **Federal Housing Finance Board**, regulator of the **Federal Home Loan Bank** system.

Senate staffers said that when Morrison was a Democratic congressman from Connecticut he helped remove Gramm from the **House Budget Committee**. Allegedly, Gramm has not forgotten and has returned the favor: He was the only member of the Senate Banking Committee to dissent on the nomination.

A spokesman for Gramm said Morrison's qualifications were at issue. The rest is ancient history. Morrison had no comment.

This **Ricki Tigert**-esque situation leaves the FHFB with only two of five directors' positions filled.

Appendix 16

TO: Cindy Skrzycki

FROM: Roger Johnson

DATE: October 28, 1994

RE: October 28 Column

Dear Ms. Skrzycki:

How can hiring a lawyer - in Washington, D.C. of all places - be headline news? Not having a lawyer for a year and a half - now that was news. But I guess it is just an extension of the grossly distorted mind set in this town that chases fleas with great zeal while letting the elephants run wild. When are you going to move into some depth on the real story at GSA? I will warn you in advance, however, that you will probably discover one or two positive results. If you think you can handle that, please call me.

Appendix 17

Administrator
General Services Administration
Washington, DC 20405

November 18, 1994

Honorable Albert Gore
Vice President of the United States
1600 Pennsylvania Avenue, N.W.
Washington, D.C. 20500

Subject: Affirmative Action Program for Executives in Government

Dear Mr. Vice President:

Although business and government are quite different - and rightly so - the business of government, i.e., the management of the process and people, requires the very same skills and experiences as professionally managing any organization. Unfortunately, I have concluded after 16 months that there is a gross lack of professional management experience and skills in Washington resulting in a variety of poor management practices. The lack of these fundamental skills and resulting poor management practices produces needlessly complex and frustrating processes, as well as billions of wasted dollars. In my opinion, you have radically changed the policy agenda of our country. At the same time, The N.P.R. recommendations have provided the blue print for major changes in the process of governing.

I am concerned, however, that we do not have the managerial skills to effectively implement these changes.

Although no one action can cure this problem, I believe that I have identified some specific actions that could help a great deal.

Since coming to Washington, I have become more and more concerned with the dearth of people with real hands-on general management experience. I believe I am the only Fortune 500 CEO in government, for example, and I'd be surprised if there were more than a dozen or so people who have real general management backgrounds, i.e., full P & L and financial responsibility for multiple functional organizations (i.e., men and women who had personal responsibility for results!).

The basic principals of professional management, i.e., planning, organizing, measuring and controlling, are just as applicable, and probably need even better execution, in government that lacks the built in P & L and cash flow disciplines.

Appendix 17 (continued)

My concern stems not from the fact that I believe business executives are more intelligent, more patriotic or more anything except that they are better trained in the business of professional management. The task of organizing, i.e., the packaging of work elements in an effective manor - the planning process, whether annual budgeting or long range strategic planning - the concept of performance standards and measurement - each takes significant specific knowledge and years of experience to develop. They do not accrue to one simply because he or she has been given a job requiring management.

Therefore, just as we value diversity of race, gender, sexual preference, etc., I believe we should thoughtfully review the quantity and quality of diversity of general management experience and background in your administration. Having done my own survey, I've concluded that we lack this diversity and, therefore, need an Affirmative Action Program for industry and business executives in the federal government.

There are several inherent deterrents that uniquely discriminate against executives including the confirmation process. Other deterrents include:

Length of Assignment - Most of the general management people we would want are on a fast track in their organizations - a four year hiatus is almost always a preemptive negative to government service - two years may not be, particularly if we enlist the help of American companies.

Suggestion #1 - Select specific jobs, particularly in the "operating" agencies, i.e. GSA, OMB, OPM, SEC, certain White House staff positions and certain departments such as Treasury, Transportation, Commerce, etc. that will be two year appointments restricted to general management experienced people - a number like 50 feels comfortable.

Develop a pool of 200 - 300 candidates by working directly with American business, who, I believe, could be convinced to view the program as a combination of public service and experience broadening for their executives. There certainly would be issues of conflict of interest and "revolving door." However, I believe there are factors that could mitigate these issues. For example, lack of government experience, particularly government contracting, would be a plus in my view. In fact, it's just what we don't want.

Appendix 17 (continued)

Secondly, the positions selected would have primary responsibility for the management processes within agencies and departments vs. policy or contracting decisions.

Finally, with the positions pre-identified, measures could be taken to avoid specific conflict. To offset the shortness of tours, I would overlap by 6 months or even a year, i.e. a replacement would be named and in place 6 months prior to the incumbent leaving.

Suggestion #2 I suggest we select on a project basis vs. an ongoing position basis senior, retired executives who, perhaps teamed with young MBA's, be assigned specific projects. For example, there has been a continuous question in this agency as to whether the government should be in the automobile fleet management business. Why not have a private company who makes a living at it do it for us? All previous studies carry somewhat of the "fox watching the hen house" credibility concern. The analysis is relatively complex but quite definable -- an excellent 3 - 6 month task for a senior retired executive and a great learning experience for two or three MBA's. I am sure there are dozens of such issues that could benefit quite quickly from this approach.

In summary, Mr. Vice President, we are suffering greatly from the lack of diversity represented by the country's professional general management.

We extol the virtues of the free enterpriser, the entrepreneur, business like practices, opening international trade. We debate issues and pass laws that have a massive effect on these issues, and we are working hard to change the government's own way of doing business. Yet the halls and offices of government are almost completely void of the men and women who have created and who day-to-day make that system work.

I am convinced we need an infusion of these skills, experiences and thought processes as we move forward to make significant changes in the process of government via the NPR recommendations.

Sincerely,

Roger W. Johnson

Appendix 18

Administrator
General Services Administration
Washington, DC 20405

<u>Personal and Confidential</u>

To: Vice President Al Gore

Subject: 1996 Budget

Date: November 18, 1994

Dear Mr. Vice President:

The following recommendations concerning the 1996 Budget process are made from the perspective of an operations oriented CEO. I have made most of these suggestions to Alice Rivlin for the 1996 budget and many of them to Leon Panetta for the '95 budget. I have attached both letters and will therefore, not repeat the details here. I have also added some thoughts.

1) <u>Information Technology</u> - I am more convinced than I was a year ago that there is $5 - 10 billion available per year for at least the next three years. This reduction can be accomplished not only without hurting our initiatives but, in fact, helping them.

2) <u>Consumable Inventory Reductions</u> - I believe there is $20 - 40 billion cash savings available over the next 2-3 years. This is a "one time" real cash savings resulting from increasing the "turns" of the Federal Government consumable inventories from current turns of 2 - 3 to a conservative 4 - 6 turns a year and thereby cutting inventories by approximately 50%. Similar inventories in the private sector are turned 10 - 15 times. (The estimate of current consumable inventory levels is $40 - 80 billion.)

3) <u>Real Estate Conversions</u> - <u>expensive leases to government owned buildings</u> - This old issue could yield $5 - 7 billion over 20 years.

4) <u>New - Capital Planning/Budgeting</u> - This issue has been discussed and I am told - rejected by not only OMB but also the Economic Council. I believe that the arguments against the process are seriously flawed and result in part from some misunderstandings of how the proposal process would work. After a year and a half of watching the results of <u>not</u> having

Federal Recycling Program   Printed on Recycled Paper

Appendix 18 (continued)

such a process - I am convinced that there are several billions of dollars of saving that we could achieve simply by instituting the disciplines of a Capital planning process and not changing the "accounting" at all.

5) <u>New</u> - The relatively painless manpower reduction GSA achieved by enforcing a hard freeze on <u>all</u> new hires <u>and</u> replacements convinces me that similar actions could not only achieve 1999 manpower levels sooner, but in the process dramatically accelerate the re-engineering programs so desperately needed to achieve the real improvements in customer services the country needs.

6) <u>New (to most - but not to you)</u> -

a) Bring in a CEO to run OMB. <u>We don't need Government budget experts in that job - that is the problem!</u>

b) Add two or three CEO's of "non-financial" companies to Council of Economic Advisors. The issue is jobs and real competitiveness. Most of those on the Council have never created a private sector job in their entire career, nor have they directly competed nationally or internationally in the private sector.

c) Clearly designate the Vice President as Chief Operations Officer. (In my view the NPR assignment already gives you that role, but it needs to be "institutionalized."

I believe that these moves - controversial as they would be <u>inside</u> Washington would be hailed throughout the country. The administration would be saying "We've made a good, even great, start, but it is apparent that the country wants us to move faster and deeper. From our operating standpoint the N.P.R. already provides the specific plan. I believe the countries vote last week provides the mandate.

I look forward to further discussions with you on these issues.

Sincerely,

Roger W. Johnson

Appendix 19

Administrator
General Services Administration
Washington, DC 20405

June 22, 1995

The President
The White House
Washington, D.C.   20500

RE: Performance Agreement Status Report

Dear Mr. President:

I am pleased to provide you with the fourth quarterly status report on the activities that have been undertaken and/or completed related to the performance measures outlined in the Performance Agreement that we signed in March of 1994. Results are growing as progress on each of the measures continues.

GSA is currently revamping its strategic planning process to coordinate customer service, performance measures, GPRA requirements and the Performance Agreement with the budget cycle. We are in the process of drafting a new Performance Agreement for FY 1996, and it will be forwarded to NPR officials upon completion in accordance with the OMB prescribed timetable.

Sincerely,

Roger W. Johnson
Administrator

cc: The Vice President
       Elaine Kamarck
       GSA Leadership Council

Federal Recycling Program   Printed on Recycled Paper

Appendix 19 (continued)

GSA Performance Agreement
Annex: PERFORMANCE MEASURES, Fiscal Year 1994
Status Update for Quarter Ending 3/31/95
Note: Reporting on current activity is shown in bold italic.

During Fiscal Year 1994, GSA's performance will be measured by the successful accomplishment of the following specific measures:

1)   Put procurement performance measures for commercial information technology products and services in place for GSA and each agency that is delegated procurement authority.

First measure in place by: 3/1/94

First action completed before 3/1/94 in delegation of IT procurement authority to Social Security Administration to modernize its central facility.

There are currently 4 procurements in "Time Out", representing 4 agencies, and 6 others are potential "Time Out" candidates. GSA is working with 15 agencies to develop performance measures under 39 delegations of procurement authority. GSA also continues to work with agencies in the Time Out program, which was put in place in April, 1994. Time Out focuses on the largest and most important Federal information technology acquisitions, particularly those which have major problems. GSA has currently called a "Time Out" for five programs in four agencies. The results to date are that one program has been canceled, and significant redirection and downsizing has already occurred in three of the others. Another result of Time Out is that GSA expects $7 billion or more in savings from cost avoidances and deferred spending. Also, an additional $4 billion is still "on hold" pending GSA and the agencies reaching final agreements about the redirection of these programs.

Measures in place for all agencies: 9/1/94

2)   Reduce procurement cycle to less than eight weeks for all but major volume negotiated purchases. This includes commercially available commodities such as standard software packages, personal computers, copiers and furniture.

50% implementation: 12/30/94

Appendix 19 (continued)

ITS: For small purchases and MASC purchases, less than $50,000, adequately funded/justified SF49's received after October 1, 1994 have implemented the 8 week procurement cycle. The Federal Information Resources Management Regulation (FIRMR) was amended effective March 29, 1995. The rule change eliminated the need to synopsize Multiple Award Schedule orders over $50,000 and raised the maximum order limitation from $300,000 to $500,000. This reduced the procurement cycle to less than eight weeks for personal computers, and standard software packages.

FSS: An acquisition letter establishing this time frame was issued. Currently, FSS has a work measurement standard which profiles the work in process (WIP) for this category of procurements, and has consistently been less than the 45 day target (6 weeks). This new tracking system has been outlined, and a system design and implementation schedule projected for the fall of 1996.

100% implementation: 12/30/95

3)   Reduce procurement cycle times to less than six months for major negotiated volume purchases.

ITS: The Federal Information Resources Management Regulation (FIRMR) was amended effective March 29, 1995. The rule change eliminated the need to synopsized Multiple Award Schedule orders over $50,000 and raised the maximum order limitation from $300,000 to $500,000. This reduced the procurement cycle to less than six months for all items available under of Information Technology Multiple Award Schedules. This includes mainframes and associated products and services, personal computers, and standard software packages, as well as telecommunications products.

Prices under our Multiple Award Schedules are based on the Government's consolidated purchasing volume, and are equal to or less than the prices offered to commercial customers procuring under similar conditions.

Progress on this measure

100% implementation: 12/30/95

4)   Present real estate plans and programs to Congress that are in the best long term interests of government institutions and the American taxpayer and are consistent with the President's budget. GSA will demonstrate significant long term cost savings when compared with current practice.

First long term regional plans: 3/1/94

Appendix 19 (continued)

First action (s) taken by 3/1/94 with completion of internal analysis for National Capital Region long-range plan and commencement of discussions with House Sub-Committee on Public Works and congressional delegation from metro area. Plan includes implementation of new lease conversion program (contained in President's FY95 budget) to seek long-term savings through increased Federal ownership.

Outline of FY 1995 plan for National Capital Region was presented formally at hearing held by House Subcommittee on Public Works on June 16, 1994. Approach for community input/involvement for FY 1996 plan was also presented.

Regional offices presented Community Strategies (long-term plans) to the PBS Commissioner and the Planning and Project Review Board in April and May 1994. PBS selected 20 Community Plans to be presented to the Administrator for his approval. However, before these plans could be submitted to Congress, Administration initiatives regarding downsizing were accelerated. It was decided by the Commissioner that the submission of plans at this time would be inappropriate, because the space requirements of client agencies may be significantly changed during the planning window. Community Plans will be refined as updated space requirement information is obtained.

Complete by: 12/30/94

5)   Change binding procurements rules to guiding principles: increase procurement authority of customer agencies through delegations: expand electronic ordering systems: and ensure the most cost effective ordering and timely methods of supply distribution.

   a.   *The plan for the rewrite of the FAR has been developed, public comments were solicited by the end of June and a public meeting was held in mid-August. Comment period closed in early September and a review of the comments and responses to Federal Register notice is being conducted to determine re-write options. The basic outline of the plan includes only mandatory policies in regulation and proposes other vehicles for disseminating nonregulatory guidance.*

   b.   *GSA reviewed the entire FIRMR to assess its currency and relevancy. Regulatory changes that streamline the acquisition process are being implemented as a result of this review.*

   A one-year, single region pilot program within the Public Buildings Service is underway to evaluate the cost-effectiveness and other benefits of delegating small lease acquisition authority to customer agencies.

Appendix 19 (continued)

c.   *Model electronic ordering procedures and trading partner agreements
have been developed and are being tested in GSA laboratory.*

*Customers can currently order from the Federal Supply Service
electronically via FED/MILSTRIP disciplines and the Multi-Use File for
Interagency News. It is expected that in 1995 one hundred percent of
FSS orders placed with its vendors will be conducted electronically by
either Electronic Data Interchange (EDI) or FAX. The Information
Technology Service and FSS are working together to create and expand
the capability of Federal agencies to order electronically with GSA's
Federal Supply Schedule vendors.*

d.   *A report and milestone plans addressing improvements to the Federal
Supply Service distribution operations, with specific emphasis on
inventory reduction, faster customer service and greater reliance on
commercial distribution channels, has been finalized and is being
implemented.*

6)   Establish agency account executives to provide a "seamless" organization which
presents one face to the customer.

First account executives: 12/30/93

*First account managers assigned by 12/30/93. These national account
managers are charged primarily with liaison for long-range real property
planning. Customer research suggests that, at national level, a single account
manager representing all GSA's products/services is not desired. Major client
agencies are organized along lines similar to GSA structure (i.e., real estate,
information resources management, procurement and supply, etc.) GSA
customer contacts at local level will integrate service delivery.*

*Real estate has designated national account executives for 24 agencies.
These are staffed on a part-time basis by PBS executives. A number of
coordinating meetings have occurred with Commissioner Kimbrough and the
account executives. Monthly conference calls are in place and customer
agency visits are ongoing.*

Complete by: **COMPLETE**

7)   Establish reimbursable centers of expertise for several of GSA's operations. If
customer agencies desire, GSA will provide them with the information that they
need so that they can conduct business GSA has performed for them in the past.

Centers identified by: **COMPLETE for PBS
                                        In Progress for ITS**

Appendix 19 (continued)

a.   *Action complete by 3/1/94 with identification of 26 real property Centers of Expertise. All of these consulting services are available at present and new Centers of Expertise will continue to be identified as appropriate.*

GSA's Public Building Service began design work 1/94 in accordance with NPR timetable. The final list of the "Centers of Expertise" was concluded at the March Real Property Executives meeting. These centers will be integrated into the design of the New Real Property organization as indicated:

Portfolio Manager: Mega Project Pre Development (CO)
                    Project Financing (CO)
                    Environmental Executive (CO)

Fee Developer: Seismic Design & Engineering (Region (& CO)

Property Manager: Energy Usage Accounting System (Region 7)
                   Presidential Libraries R&A (Region 6)
                   Entomology (NCR)
                   Safety & Environmental Leadership (CO)
                   Energy Management Leadership (CO)
                   Cafeteria Design (NCR)

b.   *Established baseline performance of the ITS laboratory location including an analysis of the current costs, service capabilities, and customer satisfaction.*

Active client participation in the Lab has been accomplished. An Interagency Information Resources Management Council (IIRMC) was established to encourage and coordinate active client participating in the Lab.

Two telecommunications systems installations were established to compare provisioning methodologies. One system is being managed by GSA and the other system is being managed by another agency. Phase I of the GSA project was completed in December 1994, Phase II in March 1995, and Phase III is scheduled for completion in June 1995. The agency project will be completed at a later date.

8)   Establish a high level intra-agency forum to receive customer input, develop strategy for new initiatives and ensure client satisfaction. Conduct customer satisfaction surveys at all levels of GSA's operation.

In place by: **COMPLETE**

Appendix 19 (continued)

Action complete with creation in 12/93 of intra-agency working committee to report to agency Leadership Council. Committee prepared initial report on customer service surveys which was provided, pursuant to Executive Order, on 3/8/94.

GSA's Customer Service Plans for major business lines have been completed and distributed to regional delivery units for implementation. The plans contain customer service standards that must be communicated to customers, and reported on pursuant to the President's March 22, 1995, memorandum for Heads of Departments and Agencies. By September 1995, customer service standards for all business lines will be made available to our customers.

Fully functional by: 12/30/94

9)   Delegate significant authority to GSA regions to serve GSA's government customers better, provide first hand examples of effective government on a local level, and help restore the confidence of the American people that government can be customer-oriented and cost-effective.

Two regions (Regions 3 and 8) have been designated as Region-wide Reinvention Labs, to create a region-wide reinvention environmental in which all employees are empowered to identify and remove obstacles (that are not based in legislation) that inhibit optimal performance. These two labs serve as prototypes for change under which each region can re-examine the services it provides to determine how to best design an organization that will provide efficient and effective customer-driven service. The lab's results to date are impressive, and detail many ways in which service and efficiency have been improved. Plans are being prepared to "roll-out" the lab's successes nationwide.

As of October 1994, Regional Administrators have been delegated authority to manage their workforce within agreed upon FTE ceilings while measuring progress toward achievement of policy objectives in the areas of increased diversity, job mobility and training, improved supervisory ratio and collaboration.

Complete by: 6/1/94

10) Achieve a 95% approval rating by GSA's customers.

Complete by: 12/95

Appendix 19 (continued)

GSA has issued its customer service plan and the business line customer service plans. Regions will develop functional plans and establish baseline customer satisfaction measurements by September 30, 1995. Customer satisfaction will be assessed quarterly thereafter. In addition, each business line undergoing the FORM analysis is surveying its customers as part of that process. Preliminary results are positive: 88% of the Internal Computer Operations business line's customers reported that they are satisfied with service, as do 86% of Fleet Management's, 79% of Property Management's, and 70% of Commercial Broker's customers.

11)   Develop strategic and tactical plans that incorporate employee input and their vision of a quality workplace. Provide the resources for training to give employees the tools necessary to operate effectively in a reinvented GSA.

Ensure that the principles of quality management are intrinsic to reinvention efforts and the business process reengineering of GSA. Conduct routine internal surveys to determine employee satisfaction. Improve supervisor:employee ratio from current ratio of approximately 1:6. The ultimate objective is a ratio of 1:12   by 1999.

Complete by: 12/95

a.   *The GSA Strategic Plan is completed. It was developed with the participation of 200 GSA staff members. The plan was distributed to GSA employees in February 1995.*

b.   *Opportunity to serve on a training reinvention team was announced nationwide in July 1994, and hundreds of GSA employees responded. The team began its work in December 1994, with a report and recommendations anticipated by mid-1995.*

c.   *The GSA Quality Council has been expanded to include our union partners. The Council included a quality management message in GSA's Strategic Plan that was distributed to employees in February 1995.*

d.   *The Quality Culture Assessment and Climate Assessment Surveys are administered annually each January and the results used to assess employee satisfaction with the implementation of quality management, the work environment, goal setting, training, leadership, communication, and their jobs. The annual administration of the employee quality culture assessment is scheduled for May 1995. Results will be available to managers in late June and early July 1995.*

Appendix 19 (continued)

e. *The GSA streamlining plan documented results to date as well as yearly goals to meet the 1999 target. GSA has taken the lead in developing a guide to reduce the number of supervisory positions in the agency without adverse impact on existing grade levels. As of May 1995, the GSA supervisory ratio has improved from 1:5.8 to 1:6.2. Significant additional improvement is anticipated through buyouts and application of the above referenced guide.*

12) Develop performance measures that focus on outcomes and are consistent with the Government Performance and Results Act of 1993. Reengineer organization processes with employee and customer input and through reinvention laboratories. Provide benchmark data to determine best-in-class. Identify business areas where cost savings can be realized and attain these savings through negotiations with the private sector. Develop and introduce the use of a set of key result measurements for the agency.

Performance measures have been identified by all business lines and specific private sector firm's have agreed to be benchmarking partners for a number of critical activities.

The real estate organization in its entirety is a GPRA pilot and FY 1994 report, FY 1995 plan and interim report have been submitted to OMB.

Fourteen reinvention labs are underway, providing a test environment for innovative re-engineering processes. Quarterly progress reports are made, and a series of presentations for the Central Office have been completed.

As of November 1, 1994 Regional Administrators and Heads of Services and Staff Offices were delegated authority to manage within established FTE ceilings, within the framework of policy objectives relating to 1) reduction of the number of senior level positions, 2) improving supervisory ratios, 3) attaining a more diverse workforce, 4) ensuring a qualified, customer-oriented workforce, and 5) collaborating to effect change.

The real estate organization was realigned as of January 9, 1995 into business units (property management, commercial broker, fee developer and portfolio manager) analogues to those found in the private sector. This realignment will facilitate benchmarking and comparison and the adoption of industry best practices.

National Business process reengineering teams are analyzing all major work processes to identify the most streamlined, cost-effective method of performance. Targeted completion date is July, 1995.

Appendix 20

Administrator
General Services Administration
Washington, DC 20405

November 2, 1995

The President
The White House
Washington, DC 20500

Subject: Balanced Budget -- Suggested Additional Non-Program Reductions

Dear Mr. President:

Every time, as a CEO, I found it necessary to make significant cuts in our expenses my staff's initial response would too often be -- "well, what new products don't you want?" "Which sales offices should we close?" These responses were obviously trying to present me with unacceptable or very painful choices. My answer was always the same -- "if there are some products in design that don't look promising -- then cut out the engineering -- but don't cut any products that still look good -- additionally, we're not only <u>not</u> going to close sales offices, we're going to open some more in new market areas -- now tell me how you're going to do that and still take 20 percent out of the costs!"

Mr. President, you have given that same direction! You said that when you asked the Vice President to conduct the National Performance Review three years ago. You continue to set that direction each day. When you say in essence, yes, we must balance the budget, but we must also continue to invest in education, training and a variety of other areas that will assure our Nation's competitiveness in the 21st century. You have and continue to make the correct executive decision -- attempting to set us on the prudent correctional course. The problem is <u>we are not responding</u>. Now, obviously the Republican leadership is not going to respond, because in my view they are using balancing the budget as a disguise for dismantling programs, not fixing them. This is an ideological battle whose belief is rooted in the premise that the Federal Government should have little or no role in much of anything except national defense. The budget is not only a convenient weapon, but also provides a great cover that they hope will avoid debating their position on its merits.

Federal Recycling Program   Printed on Recycled Paper

Appendix 20 (continued)

-2-

Therefore it comes as no great surprise that they attack programs almost exclusively -- even ones whose demise will not really save much. But I'm afraid we/your Administration have taken the bait, and in the main, we are only defending programs. Certainly many of the programs deserve vigorous defense, however, if that's all we do -- we are missing an additional weapon -- a weapon that returns the debate to the budget -- by offering significant non-program related cuts.

We already have the primary non-program reducing blueprint in front of us -- it's the National Performance Review Report. I recognize that we already rightly claim $50 billion plus in resulting savings with $40 billion plus more to come. However, I believe we still have an additional $50 - $100 billion over seven years that we're not reaping that could be used in the final hard negotiations you have ahead on the 1996 Budget package. The savings come not only from non-program cuts, but also non-people cuts that accrue to us because you have set the Government on a reinventing path. I recognize that they will be difficult to get -- because you will have to take these savings out of the operating budgets of executive agencies and departments and we will each scream that we already have taken these into account. I'm sure most have reduced these areas to some degree, but not nearly what we should!

For example:

1. One-hundred sixty thousand fewer people heading for two-hundred sixty thousand fewer results in approximately 4 million fewer square feet of office space needed per year. At a conservative cost of $20 a foot that equals $800 million per year. Assume we can only capture 50 percent of this space, we still get $400 million per year or $2.8 billion over seven years. GSA is trying to put a program in place to capture these savings but without concerted senior support it will not happen.

2. These fewer people won't need desks, file cabinets, personal computers, travel, paper, phones (and phone calls) etc., the cost of outfitting a Federal worker is approximately a $5,000 one-time cost, and conservatively $1,000 ongoing. We should be able to capture the one-time savings for those agencies that are growing -- forcing the redeployment with obvious excess equipment and save the recurring costs of $260 million per year or $1.8 billion for seven years. Again, this cost will not be captured without a concerted intra-agency program.

Federal Recycling Program   Printed on Recycled Paper

Appendix 20 (continued)

-3-

Incidentally, in fiscal year 1994 we spent $2.1 billion on transportation, $2 billion on lodging, and $1 billion on meals or $5.1 billion for Federal workers' expenses while traveling on non-military missions. That's $2,200 per person! I'm sure that most of the reduced FTE were probably at lower levels, but even so a significant reduction in travel expenses should be flowing to us automatically.

3. Telecommuting - Some of us have been advocating expanded telecommuting for three years with only minimum success. Private sector data shows major savings in facilities and productivity improvements, as well as a variety of quality of life improvements. For example, these benefits have led AT&T (not a bastion of liberal social programs) to have 38 percent of its eligible workforce now telecommuting

By contrast we have, after three years, only approximately 300 Federal workers in 30 centers and even the goal of 60,000 workers by 1998 is far short of what we could and should do. Thirty-eight percent of the Federal eligible workforce would be approximately 250,000 people. The savings in space alone would be approximately $2 billion over seven years to say nothing of the demonstrated 20 percent productivity improvements as well as the enormous positive effect on families, children, and pollution.

4. Procurement Reforms and Targeted Cost Reductions - One of the most dramatic set of changes of your Administration has been in procurement reform, not only legislatively, but attitudinal. It probably can be argued that we are already claiming the savings in the cost of the procurement process itself within the Government, but I see no evidence of harvesting the savings in unit costs that should also come from these changes. These added savings come from two areas: (1) the same streamlined processes that saves the Federal Government money will also save industry money, and (2) the empowering effect that these changes should have on our procurement officials should make them more aggressive and effective negotiators. Obviously, industry will not volunteer these savings. In my experience it is a common management practice to challenge procurement teams with annual purchased material cost reductions that target at least to offset inflation and, in many cases, yield net savings of three to five percent. The Federal budget process, however, takes inflation rates as given increases and many then try to justify even more cost increases. A three percent reduction from current budget levels for all purchased goods and services would seem quite achievable. I'm not sure what 1996 and out years budgeted purchases are -- but the last data I saw they were approximately $200 billion per year.

Federal Recycling Program   Printed on Recycled Paper

Appendix 20 (continued)

-4-

Hopefully they are less due to the shrinking of Government -- maybe to
$150 billion. Just offsetting inflation by three percent of even $150 billion
equals $4.5 billion per year or $24 billion over seven years.

If we could get another 2 to 3 percent that could double. (Purchased goods
and services is the principal target of most CEO's for significant cost
reductions or cost control each year!) I'll bet if you and the Vice President
challenged the purchasing professionals directly, they would get you even
more!! These are top people and in my opinion have never been
invited/challenged in a mainstream initiative such as directly contributing to
the balancing of the budget.

5. Operating Inventory Reduction - There are $20 - $40 billion one-time
savings by increasing inventory turns of consumable inventory levels over
seven years. I have continued to point this out much to the distress of
many, but it is real and not hard to get at particularly if you turned loose a
team of private sector inventory control experts. "Just in time" inventory
programs have yielded large returns in the private sector.

They would need high-level support, particularly in the Department of
Defense (DOD) and specifically in the logistics management area of DOD.
Much of this inventory is turning 2 to 3 times, i.e. (4 to 6 months' supply) --
and should be turning 10 to 12 times (1.5 - 2 months' supply) without any
loss of readiness. The savings come from significant changes in the "time
to purchase" element of the process including charges in the "readiness to
supply" of our vendors -- not from selling off inventories!

Next steps: Using these areas as specific examples, I recommend you
direct the agencies and departments to take an additional $10 billion per
year ($70 billion for budget balancing purposes) out of non-people and non-
mission impacting expenses. I suggest that OMB allocate the reduction to
each organization heavily weighted on the basis of purchased goods and
services and consumable inventory levels. I suggest you charge the
President's Management Council with assuring that specific plans are put in
place and implemented. Additionally, you might consider asking a small
"Kitchen Cabinet" of CEO's - Paul Allaire, John Young, John Sculley, Jack
Welch, etc., to assist the President's Management Council with developing
the specific plans.

Federal Recycling Program Printed on Recycled Paper

Appendix 20 (continued)

-5-

I believe this approach has several advantages:

1.   I believe these savings (and a lot more) are there, but will not be achieved unless you specifically target them and have the active support of the department and agency heads. OMB cannot do this on their own.

2.   It puts the political focus back on balancing the budget and forces the Republican leadership to defend cuts in programs -- that are not needed to balance the budget.

3.   It will put new teeth in the reinventing initiatives and put it "front and center" politically where it belongs.

Respectfully,

Roger W. Johnson
Administrator

cc:
Vice President Gore
Alice Rivlin
John Koskinen
Laura Tyson

Appendix 21

Administrator
General Services Administration
Washington, DC 20405

January 17, 1996

The Honorable William J. Clinton
President of the United States
The White House
Washington, D.C.

Dear Mr. President:

Please accept my resignation as Administrator of the General Services Administration effective March 1, 1996.

In the last two and one half years the GSA has proven that government can work better and cost less without materially harming programs or people. Our employment levels are down approximately 4,000 people (20%) with no layoffs as of yet; operating expenses are down 17% and over $10 billion of the $64 billion of spending we have responsibility for either saved, avoided or deferred. In parallel and equally important, our customer service ratings have been continuously improving - including strong, bipartisan support from the Congress for our plans and programs.

These improvements were made by federal workers applying basic time tested professional management techniques!

Although there is much more that can be accomplished - most of the "next step" significant improvements will require a broad extension of these professional management approaches to many other areas of government that, given current conditions and political realities, will not, in my judgment, be accepted. Therefore, my own efforts within the GSA have reached a point of diminishing returns.

In addition, although I have tried to use it as such, the position unfortunately does not have enough visibility to provide an effective platform from which I hopefully could help change current attitudes. Changes that I believe deeply must be addressed if we are ever to create an effective governing management system commensurate with the needs of the twenty-first century. We must find a way to improve - by an order of magnitude - the management of political policy initiatives ranging from the complete revamping of the budget process to significant re-organization of the operating management segments of the executive branch and Congress. Failing to do so, I fear, will leave the

Federal Recycling Program   Printed on Recycled Paper

Appendix 21 (continued)

o alternative but to press for major and harmful reductions in the
s,   e of the programs themselves. This is unacceptable particularly since
th.   tens of billions to be saved simply by applying professional
ma   nent tools and techniques.

The Republi   's extreme right has already seized upon the country's
frustration with our   ibility to effectively manage the Federal structure and are
using the budget a   vehicle to impose their own ideologies, i.e., that the
Federal governme   should have little or no role other than national defense.

I also believe that the vast majority of the country does not want the
Federal government emasculated. However, if they perceive that they have no
alternative except to cut programs - more and more will support that approach.

We made a great start with the work of Vice President Gore and the
National Performance Review Team. Their results have been exceptional, given
the constraints   real management reform. I am afraid, however, that major
changes in ma   gement structures and techniques will also be pre-requisite to
achieving the   potential of those recommendations.

From a   ery different, yet equally important standpoint, Janice and I came
to Washington, D.C. with a simple and single objective - to do the best job we
could to help improve our country. However, we have watched, helplessly, as
you and the First Lady and scores of others, have been continuously and
ruthlessly personally attacked. As you know, I also experienced some of the
same and although our situation pales in comparison to yours it does underscore
the fact that if we are to attract qualified people to Federal service, we must
make the Washington political culture much more understanding, tolerant and
receptive of different backgrounds, not only in attitudes but also in specific rules
and regulations. I believe the country has no idea of just how intolerant and then
vitriolic and vengeful the status quo infrastructure of Washington has become
when faced with change or even a different opinion.

Therefore, I have concluded that I can be of more help to you and your reelection, as well as, to our government on the "outside," where I can use the
exposure and insight I have gained to provide a variety of audiences with, not
only a more accurate picture of the very real accomplishments of your
administration, but also identify the management problems that remain to be
solved along with several specific recommended actions.

Although my leaving will be little noted, I want to be clear for the record that my
comments are in no way critical of your leadership. In fact, quite the contrary, I
am more pleased today that I supported you than I was four years ago. I believe
it is essential that you serve another term and will be actively supporting your reelection.

Appendix 21 (continued)

On a more personal note, Janice and I thank you and Hillary for your personal support and friendship over the past four plus years and we look forward to the many years to come.

Sincerely,

Roger W. Johnson

cc: Vice President Gore

Federal Recycling Program   Printed on Recycled Paper

Appendix 22

THE WHITE HOUSE

WASHINGTON

February 22, 1996

The Honorable Roger W. Johnson
Administrator of General Services
Washington, D.C.   20405

Dear Roger:

I have received your letter advising me
of your resignation as Administrator of the
General Services Administration.   It is with
deep regret that I accept your resignation,
effective March 1, 1996.

I will always be grateful for your tremendous
energy and unfailing resolve throughout your
impressive tenure.   You have instilled a profound
commitment to improved and efficient management
within GSA, helping to fundamentally change the
way the government does business.   Thanks in large
measure to your efforts, the American people can
be proud of a federal government that functions
better and costs less.   I am confident that we
will build on your work in the years to come.

Hillary and I deeply appreciate your friendship
and tireless service, and we wish you and Janice
every future success and happiness.

Sincerely,

Bill Clinton

Appendix 23

THE VICE PRESIDENT
WASHINGTON

February 27, 1996

Honorable Roger Johnson
Administrator, General Services Administration
18th and F Streets, N.W.
Washington, DC 20405

Dear Roger:

President Clinton and I are sorry we were unable to attend your farewell dinner. We send you our best. We compared notes and agreed that you have been the most supportive Republican member of our administration. It wasn't even a close contest.

Since it has been my job to make government work better and cost less, I was especially grateful for your double-barreled initiative to (1) identify natural leaders of reinvention, and (2) to trim the size of the workforce. No one else had come up with the time-saving idea of combining both actions in one step. As a result, people like Gerry Turetsky, Julia Stash, Dan Neal, and Pat Keogh are not only acknowledged as government reinventors, they're permanently off the federal payroll.

Roger, both the President and I were wondering about your hair. While it raises many questions, we couldn't let you leave without clearing up one thing for us. If that's its real color, why *wouldn't* you dye it?

All that aside, I deeply appreciate having the chance to work with you. You were my key ally in the internal debates in the White House during the critical stages when reinventing government was either going to get off the ground or crash ignominiously. As a former CEO who understands the bottom line, you came in at the right moments with the decisive arguments.

Thank you for your help and friendship, Roger. Thank you for a job well done. Unfortunately, you can't bring your elephant collection home because I've just added them to the list of endangered species.

Sincerely,

Al Gore

Appendix 24

THE CHRISTIAN SCIENCE MONITOR

Roger Johnson recounts how he saved $11 billion in taxpayer funds by applying basic business principles

Mr. Fortune 500 Runs a Federal Agency

By Daniel B. Wood
Staff writer of The Christian Science Monitor

LAGUNA BEACH, CALIF.

ROGER JOHNSON has some good news and some bad news about how your federal government works.

"The good news is that your federal government is not being mismanaged," says the former head of the General Services Administration (GSA), back at his beachfront home here after a three-year stint running the $64 billion federal agency. "The bad news is that it's not being managed at all."

If that sounds like puff-chested hyperbole warmed over from a Ross Perot rally, read on. The Orange County Republican-cum-Democrat is not running for office and has a revealing story to tell.

After 35 years as an executive in several Fortune 500 companies, Mr. Johnson took his outside-the-beltway track record and put it to work *inside* the beltway at the GSA. That's the agency responsible for everything from paper clips to personal computers, federal buildings to phones – and a few of the $200 ashtrays you may have heard about. Now, after trimming $11 billion from the GSA budget and cutting 4,000 (out of 20,000) positions – without loss of services, programs, or laying anyone off – Johnson has resigned his position to write a book and hit the lecture circuit.

From the couch of his art-adorned home, Johnson delivers a punchline that might make a few ears twitch in both political parties: "From what I've just seen, bringing basic professional management principles to Washington could balance the budget in seven years, without cutting a program."

While some say that sounds ridiculous, others look at Johnson's track record in just three years in one agency and say he might not be far off. Either way, his experience sheds light on rampant waste in Washington. "Save a billion here and a billion there," Johnson is fond of saying, "and pretty soon you're talking big money."

"Roger Johnson brought a perspective to us that no one in Washington has had as long as I've been here," says Dennis Fischer, chief financial officer of the GSA, a 26-year, nonpolitical career official who has also served in several other departments. "He showed us a bunch of policy and political people how to organize and run themselves and saved literally billions in the process."

The ideas he used to do so are commonplace in managing businesses, schools, and hospitals, says Johnson, but practically nonexistent in the federal government. Among them:

• Using balance sheets to track inventory. (How many paper clips are on hand? What is the cost to store them?)

• Managing assets such as buildings and cars. (Are they cheaper to buy or rent? Are prices competitive with the private sector?)

• Capital planning and budgeting. (How much does a computer bought today save in workload costs over, say, the next five years?)

"People in Washington don't do any of these things, not because they are stupid or greedy or cor-

[PROFILE]

get more easily than a full purchase price. "In 20 years you've paid twice what the entire building would have cost to own," he says.

But such logic is commonplace in Washington because of "scoring" laws" used to legislate management behavior that elsewhere would be dictated by common sense.

Noting that the federal code regulating purchases now runs 130,000 pages, Johnson says: "You get piles and piles of rules and then have to employ whole new bodies of people to make sure they are fol-

'Bringing basic professional management principles to Washington could balance the budget in seven years, without cutting a program.'
– Roger Johnson, former head of the GSA

rupt," says Johnson. "They don't do it because they are primarily policy-oriented folks. They care more about issues of what to do in education, health, and welfare – not *how* to do it."

Johnson left the Clinton administration in March, he says, because he felt he could tell his story better and be taken more seriously if he were outside of government. He has said that his decision to step down was not related to a Justice Department review of his office accounts and that he has since been exonerated of wrongdoing.

Johnson insists his ideas are not rocket science, or even fancy ideas that only management gurus like Peter Drucker can understand.

An easy-to-grasp example is real estate. Half of all federal buildings are rented instead of owned because yearly leases (say $100,000) can fit into an annual federal bud-

lowed – congressional oversight committees, inspectors general, ethics committees."

"There is no doubt that what [Johnson] has achieved is very real savings and a model of what the government could well do if both Congress and federal managers put their minds to the business of results as opposed to simply thinking what their policies ought to look like," says Don Kettle, professor of public affairs at the University of Wisconsin, Madison, and a senior fellow at the Brookings Institution.

Johnson is not the first or only person to recognize the vacuum of professional management in Washington. With the mandate of "reinventing government," the Clinton administration has been attacking the problem head on with the National Performance Review (NPR) – a nonpartisan, 60-member task force of mid- to upper-level man-

agers. The task force is now in the process of untangling and reforming the massive sets of federal statutes that stymie the application of such common-sense principles.

Clinton tapped Johnson, a life-long Republican, for the NPR and the GSA in 1991, after long talks revealed a mutual desire for solutions that didn't neatly fit liberal or conservative ideologies.

Before coming to Washington, Johnson was chairman and chief executive officer of Western Digital Corp., a Fortune 500 high-tech firm in Irvine, Calif. He has held executive positions with Memorex Corporation, Singer Company, and General Electric.

Johnson says the story of his Washington experience is important not just for the billions of dollars involved but because "it goes to the heart of public cynicism about their government. People see things that make no sense and conclude that the place must be run by a bunch of idiots or crooks."

Quite the contrary, Johnson says. He says that federal employees were as hard working, competent, and honest as those he was familiar with in the private sector.

But not everything Johnson did was welcomed. A freeze of federal building projects already approved by Congress brought the wrath of several senators, and some Democrats tried to undermine his integrity with newsletters highlighting his Republican past. (A lifelong Republican, Johnson late last year aligned himself with a moderate wing of the Democratic Party.)

Johnson is proposing some of his own ideas about how to remedy Washington's ignorance of management principles.

• He is calling for American corporations who train their own personnel in management to voluntarily open their internal courses for free to government workers.

• He recommends a one-year swap of 500 to 1,000 of the top operating officials (chief financial officers, information officers, purchasing agents) between federal agencies and private corporations.

• He has suggested to President Clinton that top officials in Washington should not be hired unless they have experience running an organization of more than 2,000 employees and are fully conversant with basic management tools.

"We need to convince political people that it is in their best interest to have professionals running their operations because they can do much further on the dollars they have," says Johnson. Citizens have a vital role in this process, he says, and must question their representatives not only about policy or taxes but also about managerial oversight.

Appendix 25

MR. JOHNSON
returns from
WASHINGTON

In 1993, Roger Johnson went to Washington as President Clinton's highest-ranking Republican appointee. Now he's back, as Orange County's highest-profile Democrat

---

What caused you to switch party loyalties?

I first came to Orange County in 1982 as C.E.O. of Western Digital, a Fortune 500 high-technology firm based in Irvine. I was a Reagan Republican and still have great respect for the man. But in early-1990s conversations with George Bush, I sensed little connection with the basic problems facing our country. His decisions seemed to be driven by ideologies, not the merits of a particular program. So in late-1991, along with several other Orange Countians, I endorsed Bill Clinton for president. Then in April of 1993, President Clinton named me to head the 20,000 employees of the General Services Administration. That's the agency handling all government purchases, inventories, properties and services. It's a huge organization, operating on a $11.7 billion budget with responsibilities totaling $64 billion a year.

What were your impressions of government spending?

Our federal government operates with little regard for professional management techniques. Note I didn't say it should run like a business; government isn't a business. But that doesn't mean it can't operate off a credible balance sheet, initiate cost oversights and practice sound asset management. Because of the absence of such basic concepts, hundreds of billions of dollars are being wasted. I came away convinced that with proper management, the federal budget can be balanced within seven years. Instead, Congress appears intent on dismantling government by reducing, even eliminating, programs that have real merit. Medicaid, Medicare, plus basic

welfare and educational programs; they're all on the block. This isn't the way to solve our nation's problems. Programs should be eliminated because they lack merit, not in order to balance the budget. That's a basic tenet of sound management. But unfortunately, at present there is no political constituency for good management in government.

Yet in leaving Washington, didn't you only exacerbate this problem?

I was happy to go to Washington, and I'm happy to be back. While there, I reduced the agency's payroll from 20,000 to 16,000; trimmed the operating budget by 17% and cut computer, telephone and transportation expenditures by $11 billion. Our government needs a few hundred of me. But I became convinced I'd be more effective on the outside than on the inside. The President understood my reasons for leaving. He also welcomed my registering as a Democrat as I plan to unofficially campaign for him. I'll also speak on the need for professional management in government, probably do a book on the subject, and I'll be teaching a class at UCI on corporate and public leadership. Will I run for political office? I've no such current plans, but I learned long ago to never say 'never.' My point is, by leaving federal government I haven't abandoned the cause of professional management in government.

What are some insights of the workings of government you brought back?

I will say after 35 years of working with top executives in the private sector, Bill Clinton has the finest mind I have ever encountered. No comparison. He really chews on the issues; gets into their complexities. Sure he

Appendix 25 (continued)

changes his mind, what's wrong with that? Obviously he's a political person, yet there isn't a mean bone in his body. As for other individuals I dealt with, I found many who were extremely analytical; very capable. Al Gore is a tremendous asset to the president. And though I disagree with many of her positions, Barbara Boxer is an extremely effective Senator. As for Orange County's Congressmen, Rohrabacher and Dornan are both irrelevant, even to their own party. And although I don't agree with a lot of Chris Cox's policies, I do respect his efforts on the budget and litigation reform bills. The President was wrong to veto Cox's litigation measure. As for others who are doing good work and need our help: Senators Glenn of Ohio, Warner of Virginia and McCain of Arizona come to mind. Also, Congressmen Ron Packard and Nancy Pelosi of California, and Cabinet members Henry Cisneros and the recently appointed Mickey Kantor. I applaud the efforts of many people in Washington, what I found lacking was the work of the Washington press corps.

What do you mean by that?

Basically, the media deals only in the 'left' and 'right' of an issue, not its merits. It's either conservative or liberal. There is little substance in their reporting, only political expediency. For example, when I announced $1.8 billion had been trimmed from the government building program, the only questions were 'That's in Senator So and So's district, how will he react?' And, 'How will you respond?' Another example: There have been hundreds of hours in coverage of Whitewater; the hearings are packed with reporters. But welfare reform hearings are rarely covered, even though they involve thousands of lives and billions of dollars. As for who is doing a good job? I think Sunday's "Washington Week in Review" on PBS is excellent. Likewise for "The McNeil/Lehrer News Hour." And Jack Nelson of the *LA Times* and Charles McDowell of the *Richmond Times Union* are outstanding correspondents. And don't sell short the work of Judy Woodruff and Larry King of CNN, or our own Michael Jackson of KABC. My Washington interviews ran the gamut and these were some of the best.

Please summarize your concerns for the American system of government?

At worst, if present trends continue, we'll see a despot in the White House. This person wouldn't look like a tyrant, but would employ the divisive politics of blame. Immigrants, affirmative action, greedy CEOs or foreign nations would all be the scapegoats. At best, we'll see an increase in cynicism followed by drastic cuts in really good programs in health care, education and welfare. And who knows where this could lead? I'm convinced the American people are aware something is wrong, but they can't put their finger on it. They also know that dismantling government isn't the answer, which is why the Contract With America has stalled. My contention is a lack of professional management in government is at the core of America's problems.

- interviewed by Jim Wood

Appendix 26

Former GSA Chief Johnson Cleared in U.S. Ethics Inquiry

■ Politics: Ex-CEO at O.C. firm resigned from Clinton team in March 1996. He blames problems on those who resisted his reforms.

By H.G. REZA
TIMES STAFF WRITER

Roger W. Johnson, who went to Washington to help reinvent government but instead was hounded out of public service by Capitol Hill's cutthroat politics, was cleared Thursday of allegations that he used his powerful government position for personal gain.

John Russell, U.S. Department of Justice spokesman in Washington, said that Johnson, former head of the General Services Administration, was cleared in the latest probe. The investigation took more than three years to complete. Russell declined further comment.

The government's decision not to prosecute Johnson was bittersweet news for the former Republican who angered Orange County's GOP establishment by endorsing Bill Clinton in 1992. Johnson later joined the Democratic Party, but at one time he was the highest-ranking Republican appointed to the Clinton Administration.

Johnson, who resigned as GSA chief in March 1996, said he is still pained by the allegations of ethics violations that clouded his three-year tenure as head of the agency, almost from the day he arrived.

Please see JOHNSON, A32

JOHNSON: Ex-Chief of GSA Is Cleared in Ethics Inquiry

Continued from A3

He blamed his problems on career bureaucrats and politicians who resisted his reforms for the GSA, an agency viewed by many in Washington as wasteful and inefficient, and a political "system that lets a small minority of people destroy one by innuendo."

"This investigation is a good example of people chasing people merely to destroy them," Johnson said. "It was that from the beginning, and it went on for 3½ years, costing the taxpayers millions and me hundreds of thousands of dollars."

The latest investigation focused on allegations that Johnson used his executive secretary to draft memorandums to his personal business consultants. He was also accused of using her to oversee furniture delivery and plumbing work at his Georgetown home. In addition, Johnson was accused of using his government driver and limousine for nonofficial duties.

The GSA Inspector General's office had conducted an investigation of the allegations and forwarded its findings to the Justice Department for possible prosecution. A Justice Department official notified Johnson's lawyer Thursday morning that the agency had declined to prosecute.

In 1994, a GSA audit found that Johnson owed the government $72 for improperly using his government credit card and mixing personal and official business trips. Johnson had requested the audit in answer to newspaper reports that he had improperly billed the government for travel, phone and mail expenses.

He voluntarily repaid a total of $1,062, but the investigation also revealed that he was entitled to be reimbursed for expenses he did not bill the government for. The scrutiny Johnson faced as head of GSA motivated him to pay for all trips to California—including those that were business related—out of his pocket and to charge most phone calls from his office on a personal credit card.

At the time, GSA officials blamed Johnson's problems on "a lack of understanding about GSA regulations, as opposed to those in the private sector."

On Thursday, the 62-year-old former chief executive of Irvine's Western Digital Corp. said his Washington experience also included some gratifying moments. He went to Washington in 1993 as part of Clinton's team to "reinvent government."

"When I arrived at GSA, we had 20,000 employees and a $60-billion budget," said Johnson. "When I left, we had 16,000 employees, and I had lowered the agency's operating cost by 17%. None of the employees were laid off. Everything was done by attrition. I miss the days when we felt we were making a contribution to reforming government."

"I still talk to the president periodically and am able to play a small role in government," he added. "But I'm glad that I don't have to take the day-to-day problems home."

Still, Johnson left Washington with more than his share of bitter memories.

"The way the system works, it allows a very small minority to cause a great deal of trouble. They are immune from being held responsible for what they say or do," said Johnson. "It's a system that destroys people's lives by innuendo. It's a bipartisan disease."

Appendix 27

Trivial Pursuit

How the Scandal Mill Ran Chief of the GSA Out of Washington

Roger Johnson's Infractions Were Minor, but Probe Took 3 Years to Clear Him

Bathroom Door's Bad Karma

By EDWARD FELSENTHAL
Staff Reporter of THE WALL STREET JOURNAL

WASHINGTON — When Roger Johnson purchased a relic of one of the most corrupt conspiracies in American politics, he had no idea he would soon have his own chapter in the annals of Washington scandals.

As head of the U.S. General Services Administration, Mr. Johnson sat only a few yards from where the money changed hands in the infamous Teapot Dome bribery scam during the Warren Harding administration. Discovering a picture of the scandal's main figure at an antique store, Mr. Johnson bought it and hung it on the door of his office bathroom.

Roger Johnson

A short time later, Mr. Johnson found himself the object of a half-dozen separate probes of his travel practices, office expenses and financial dealings. Yet despite more than three years of intense scrutiny, Mr. Johnson has never been charged with a single violation. The main allegations — conducting personal business from the office and accepting free first-class airline upgrades — never involved much money. One early inquiry, in fact, found that the government actually owed Mr. Johnson for some expenses. And Mr. Johnson repeatedly tried to head off a protracted investigation, offering to cooperate and pay back anything he owed.

But Washington's investigative machinery went into full gear, fueled by leaks to news organizations and hundreds of faxes to the White House, Congress and Mr. Johnson's colleagues. By the time Mr. Johnson was cleared this spring, he had abandoned Washington and racked up $312,500 in legal bills and other professional fees connected to the investigations. The government says it doesn't know how much its work on the case cost, but with dozens of federal lawyers, investigators and other officials involved, the tally certainly was at least hundreds of thousands of dollars.

The implication was, "This guy is a monster. There isn't anything he's doing that isn't bad," grouses Mr. Johnson, who is 63 years old. "I went from despair to anger to complete, utter despair."

Scandal Fatigue

The Johnson affair shows how tangled such cases can become now that ethics controversies are such a pervasive feature of American politics. In contrast to past improprieties such as Teapot Dome, where the wrongdoing was blatant and well known, the scandals of the 1990s — from Whitewater to Newt Gingrich's troubles in the House of Representatives — have been murky and obscure. The result has been a kind of scandal fatigue, a combination of public confusion and apathy about what such incidents mean and how to handle them. Washington's ethics machinery, meanwhile, moves achingly slowly and has difficulty distinguishing the serious infraction from the trivial.

Even prosecutors and ethics officials concede there is a problem. With the constant investigative activity," says Stephen D. Potts, director of the U.S. Office of Government Ethics, "it's easy for these cases to take on a life of their own." Still, he adds he "can't really summon up a whole lot of sympathy" for officials who don't play by the rules.

Certainly, Mr. Johnson bears some blame for his troubles. A hard-charging former chairman and chief executive of computer-hardware maker Western Digital Corp., of Irvine, Calif., he came to Washington determined to enjoy the perks of office. From the start, he took some ill-advised liberties. For example, he had his secretary go to his new home to await a delivery — a clear violation of government rules barring subordinates from doing such tasks. And he says that when people inside the agency complained, his initial response was, "Of course she did. Why the hell wouldn't she?" He also had his government driver take his Mercedes-Benz to the carwash.

Business Practices

But Mr. Johnson says he stopped such practices once he discovered they were taboo in Washington. "All I did was bring my private business practices with me," he says. "When I found out you can't do that, I said OK."

A lifelong Republican with a deep enthusiasm for business, Mr. Johnson ended up in the Clinton camp after he became disillusioned with President Bush's handling of the economy. In late 1991, he told a newspaper that he would consider endorsing a Democrat. A few days later, Mr. Clinton telephoned, asking for his support in the coming primary elections.

Mr. Johnson organized a breakfast for the candidate and became enchanted with his intellect and nonpartisan rhetoric. Rallying the support of other major executives, Mr. Johnson delivered the Clinton campaign much-needed momentum when it was reeling from allegations about the candidate's sexual conduct and efforts to stay out of the Vietnam War.

Mr. Johnson's role in the election won him big points with the new administration, a debt that would come in handy as the allegations against him mounted. Indeed, the attacks on Mr. Johnson started within weeks after President Clinton nominated him in March 1993 for the top post at the GSA, a vast agency that oversees federal office space and handles government purchasing of everything from telephones to paper clips.

Angry that the job wasn't going to a Democrat, members of the American Federation of Government Employees protested. Faxes and mailings were dispatched all over Washington saying Mr. Johnson was unfit for the position. "The White House wants to use GSA as a place to put or dump Republican Roger Johnson," wrote union official Bruce Williams, who organized much of the opposition, in a letter to fellow GSA workers.

Anonymous View

Dennis Fischer, the GSA's chief financial officer, urged Mr. Johnson to brush the critics off. "Things like this will happen. Ignore it and it will go away," Mr. Fischer advised.

But the carping got louder. After Mr. Johnson was confirmed that summer, he became the subject of a regular newsletter called "Crosswind," an anonymously written publication describing itself as an "outgrowth" of the original union opposition, whose purpose was "to monitor and quickly publicize the adverse activities of Republican Roger Johnson."

It soon became obvious that much of what was in Crosswind was coming from GSA employees in Washington. A pattern developed: Allegations would be floated in Crosswind, picked up by the mainstream news media and then pursued by government investigators.

Internal Reviews

The pattern began less than a year after Mr. Johnson took office. The Wall Street Journal picked up on rumors that, on work-related trips paid for by the government, Mr. Johnson had visited his California home, where his wife, Janice, was still living. After the Journal obtained copies of his travel vouchers, Mr. Johnson requested two separate internal reviews of his travel, including a formal audit by the GSA's inspector general.

The first review, in March 1994, concluded that Mr. Johnson should repay the government $1,062. Almost half of that total had resulted from a clerical error; the rest was to reimburse the government for meals and other expenses on four trips where he had stopped over at his home. The review also found that the government had undercompensated Mr. Johnson by $353 for his airfare on one trip.

The inspector general's report, released a few weeks later, concluded that he in fact owed only $72.91. Largely dismissing the problems because of Mr. Johnson's "unfamiliarity with official travel rules," the report urged him to keep better records and not to dawdle in filing his expense reports. Nonetheless, Mr. Johnson, hoping to

Appendix 27 (continued)

put the matter behind him, paid the higher amount cited in the first review and asked a senior aide to handle his expense reports in the future.

Meanwhile, allegations were circulating that Mr. Johnson had been using government staff and resources for personal tasks. Again, Mr. Johnson requested an investigation by his staff, which concluded that he should pay $256.73 to cover the cost of overnight pieces of mail and personal long-distance calls.

Presidential Support

Already under political attack because of his efforts to downsize the GSA, Mr. Johnson was by turns repentant and despondent. He had trouble sleeping, and his asthma worsened, he believes, because of stress. In an interview with the Los Angeles Times, Mrs. Johnson said her husband's critics "can all go jump in the Potomac." Mr. Johnson sent a copy of the article to President Clinton, who responded with a note urging Mrs. Johnson to "hang in there."

Mrs. Clinton followed with a handwritten letter of her own: "The President shared with me a copy of Janice's interview," she wrote, "and, as the kids used to say, 'Right on!'" Friends say the Clintons' support helped mollify the Johnsons, since the president and first lady were facing so much ethical scrutiny of their own. "If Hillary can take this," Mrs. Johnson told her husband, "you can, too."

But Mr. Johnson was determined to dispel the cloud surrounding him. He tried, without success, to figure out who was publishing Crosswind. One GSA employee, suspected of leaks, was moved to a different department.

"Now [Mr. Johnson] is showing signs of paranoia as he goes around suspecting everyone of leaks, reminiscent of the days of the Nixon 'plumbers,'" reported a March 1994 edition of Crosswind. A week later, Mr. Johnson delivered what critics came to call his "Checkers" speech, a reference to Richard Nixon's famous effort to deflect an ethics scandal in 1952 by talking about his family dog. Putting aside his prepared remarks in a videotaped speech to GSA employees, Mr. Johnson gave a homey, spontaneous talk in which he suggested that people were out to get him because of his ties to the GOP.

First-Class Problems

Matters got worse that summer, when Mr. Johnson and Barbara Silby, his chief of staff, accepted free first-class upgrades from United Airlines on their way to a business meeting in Chicago. Mr. Johnson said the upgrades were offered to him because, as a former CEO, he had special status with the airlines. It was a major blunder. Since airlines are government contractors, taking such a gift risked raising eyebrows. The next day, faxed copies of Crosswind were already reporting the incident.

The immediate strategy was for Mr. Johnson and Ms. Silby to pay the airline for the difference between the cost of coach and first-class travel. Mr. Johnson says he still honestly believed that writing a check would end the controversy; Ms. Silby told a

colleague she felt cleansed, as if she been to confession.

But the news hit the mainstream p in August 1994, and soon a major invest tion was under way. Along the way, I neth Moreland and Samuel Besso, the (agents heading the investigation, cont ally found reasons to broaden their quiry. First, they discovered that Johnson had accepted free upgrades fi other airlines as well. Then in Septem Long Island Newsday reported that Johnson's secretary had logged dozen hours of official time drafting pers memorandums and that Mr. Johnson reaped a $1.5 million profit after West Digital "quietly extended" the deadline him to exercise some stock options. The vestigation was expanded further aft November article in the Washington 1 reported that Western Digital had g Mr. Johnson a $500,000 no-interest loan that he had remained a paid empl there for more than a month after he been sworn in at the GSA.

Chasing Fleas?

At this point, Mr. Johnson, who been relying on advice from aides White House officials, decided it was t to get a lawyer. When the Washington) disclosed that he had done so, Mr. Joh became enraged. He wrote to the repo "How can hiring a lawyer – in Washing D.C., of all places," be news? "I guess just an extension of the grossly disto mind-set in this town that chases fleas great zeal while letting the elephants wild."

The disclosures about Mr. Johns dealing at Western Digital got the at tion of Mr. Potts, whose office monitors financial affairs of agency heads. Potts wrote a letter in October 1994 seek extensive information about Mr. Johns severance package. Mr. Johnson's lawy fired off a response, denying that any l were broken. They never heard back.

Meanwhile, the investigation took new directions. The Securities and change Commission was explor whether Mr. Johnson violated securit fraud laws when he exercised his stock tions; the SEC concluded he didn't. And cause some of Mr. Johnson's corresp dence was missing from his files, questi arose about whether his chief of staff, Silby, was impeding the investigation – allegation she steadfastly denied.

All of this was now consuming a gr deal of energy. Agents Moreland and Be alone logged hundreds of hours and sp thousands of dollars on travel to cond interviews, according to governm records. Mr. Johnson spent 19 hours in f mal investigative interviews in early 1 and dozens of hours more going over the legations with lawyers, reporters aides. Twice, he threatened to quit.

During one meeting with reporters, N Johnson angrily stormed out of his offi into the nearby bathroom where his Tea; Dome memento hung. "Why the hell a body comes in here other than professio politicians is beyond me," he shouted his way out.

Out to Justice

David Krakoff, Mr. Johnson's m lawyer, begged the inspector general's fice not to refer the case to any oth agency once it reached its findings. But May 1995, the entire file was sent for f ther review to the criminal division of t Justice Department. GSA officials insist they had no other choice.

Soon after, agents Moreland and Bes began exploring yet another issu whether Mr. Johnson violated a law invo ing federal procurements when he (cepted the free airline upgrades. Mont went by and Mr. Johnson and his lawy heard nothing, except that the two agen were continuing to investigate.

By early 1996, Mr. Johnson had h enough and announced that he would lea the GSA. Although he spoke proudly of 1 accomplishments at the agency, where 1 sliced spending by about $10 billion a eliminated 4,000 jobs through attrition a buyouts, he was bitter. "The country h no idea of just how intolerant and then v riolic and vengeful the status quo infr structure of Washington has become," 1 wrote the president.

He and his wife sold their Georgetov house, which they had originally plann to keep even after Mr. Johnson left offic and moved back to California. Mr. Johns set up shop as an independent business a viser. "We'd get up in the morning ai say, 'Thank God, Roger's not in the pap today,'" Mrs. Johnson says.

End of the Case

Finally, in November 1996, Mr. Johns found out that he wouldn't be prosecute But there was a catch: The case would l referred to the part of the Justice Depa ment that handles civil litigation. That c vision would decide whether to sue M Johnson for his alleged violation of the pi curement law.

Six more months passed; then the d partment told Mr. Johnson's lawyer that wouldn't file a civil suit. The investigatio were over.

Despite everything, the Johnsons ha ker for Washington. Their oceanfro house in Laguna Beach is brimming wit memorabilia of their time here, and phot of political bigwigs are plastered like wal paper around Mr. Johnson's office. He sti talks with boyish enthusiasm about moto cades and Air Force One.

Would he ever go back into goveri ment? "Never, ever, ever," he says, "u less the president calls."

Appendix 28

THE WHITE HOUSE

WASHINGTON

March 20, 1998

The Honorable Roger W. Johnson
Roger W. Johnson and Associates
Suite 1260
600 Anton Boulevard
Costa Mesa, California 92626

Dear Roger:

    I am delighted to take this opportunity to commend you on
your endowment of the Roger W. and Janice M. Johnson Chair in
Civic Governance and the Social Ecology of Public Management,
at the University of California, Irvine.

    I have long admired your commitment to building a government
that works better and costs less. As your efforts at the General
Services Administration demonstrated, it is possible to improve
service and lower costs for American taxpayers. Making our government operate better remains an important goal for me and the Vice
President, and I am confident that the new and innovative academic
discipline you are developing will make important contributions
not only to enhancing the effectiveness of our government but
also to restoring the faith of our citizens in it.

    I look forward to your leadership as we work to serve the
American people.

Sincerely,

Bill Clinton

BIOGRAPHY

Roger W. Johnson is one of a very small group whose career includes executive positions in four institutional segments: CEO of a Fortune 500 company, head of a major federal agency, as well as significant leadership roles in nonprofit art organizations and a major public university.

The first Republican appointed to a top post in the Clinton Administration, Mr. Johnson was sworn in as the Administrator of the General Services Administration (GSA) in 1993. As the number one official at GSA, he directed all functions assigned to this independent agency of the executive branch—which at the time employed some 20,000 people and had an annual budget of $11.7 billion and financial responsibilities of $60 billion. He was also a member of the President's Management Council, tasked with ensuring implementation of the reinvention initiatives, and was appointed by the President to the National Economic Council. Because of Mr. Johnson's extensive background in reinventing large, complex, global organizations, President Clinton depended on him to create positive change at GSA and deliver to the American taxpayers an agency that is viewed as the world's standard of excellence.

In 1998 Mr. Johnson and his wife Janice created the Roger W. and Janice M. Johnson Endowed Chair in Civic Governance and the Social Ecology of Public Management at the University of

California–Irvine. Also, since leaving the Clinton Administration in March 1996, Mr. Johnson has become a member of the Board of Directors for The Needham Funds Inc., New York, New York; Sypris Solutions Inc., Louisville, Kentucky; Insulectro, Lake Forest, California; Maxtor Corporation, Milpitas, California; and Computer Access Technology Corporation, Santa Clara, California. In addition, he is a member of the Executive Committee for the American Entrepreneurs for Economic Growth. He has recently been appointed a Regent Lecturer of the University of California–Irvine, teaches a graduate course "New Leadership Roles," and is a trustee of the UCI Foundation Board and most recently at Claremont Graduate University. Mr. Johnson has also appeared as a speaker and lecturer at various forums in California and elsewhere. He served from 1998 until 2000 as the Chief Executive Officer of the Young Presidents' Organization (YPO International), a private, not-for-profit education association of approximately 8,500 presidents and chief executive officers worldwide.

Prior to coming to Washington, Mr. Johnson was Chairman and Chief Executive Officer of Western Digital Corporation, a Fortune 500 high-technology firm based in Irvine, California. During his tenure from 1982 to 1993, Western Digital grew its revenues from $30 million to more than $1 billion and became an international leader in the disk drive industry. The World Trade Center of Orange County named him International Businessman of the Year in 1984, and the *Los Angeles Times* named him Technology Executive of the Year in l986. During this period he was appointed to the University of California–Irvine Board of Trustees, and was a founder of the University's CEO Roundtable. He also served as a member of the Executive Committee of the Orange County Performing Arts Center and as its Vice Chairman of Development, and was a member of the Pacific Symphony Orchestra Board of Directors.

Before joining Western Digital, Mr. Johnson was President of the Office Systems Group of Burroughs Corporation and Executive Vice President and Chief Operating Officer of Measurex Corporation. Additionally, he has held executive positions with Memorex Corporation, the Business Machines Division of the Singer Company. Following college he spent three years in the

General Electric Company's Management Training Program. He remained with GE for fourteen years in a variety of management positions.

Mr. Johnson was Vice Chair of Economic Issues for the American Business Conference, an organization based in Washington, D.C., consisting of 100 chief executives of the fastest growing midsize companies in the nation. He also served on the Board of Directors of AmeriCorps Communities, the American Stock Exchange, Pacific Scientific Company, American Woman's Economic Development Corporation, Quintec Industries Inc., and is a member of the Black Chamber of Commerce of Orange County.

He has been acclaimed for his personal and professional accomplishments as well as his involvement in arts and philanthropic organizations. In recognition of their significant contributions, Mr. Johnson and his wife Janice have been recipients of many awards including the prestigious Living is Giving Award from the Volunteers of America Association.

Mr. Johnson has been interviewed on all the major television networks including ABC's *Good Morning America,* CNN's *Larry King Live,* and CNBC, and he has conducted many interviews on talk radio shows such as the *Michael Jackson Show* in Los Angeles and the nationally syndicated *Judy Jarvis Show,* as well as dozens of interviews with the print media.

Born in Hartford, Connecticut, the son of a labor union president, Mr. Johnson received a Bachelor of Business Administration degree from Clarkson University in Potsdam, New York, in 1956, and holds a Master of Business Administration degree in Industrial Management from the University of Massachusetts. In addition, he was the recipient of the Irvine Medal from the University of California–Irvine in 1990, and an honorary Doctor of Science degree from Clarkson University in 1994. On the occasion of Mr. Johnson's receiving the honorary doctorate Clarkson University, President Clinton said, "Roger has brought the skills he developed so well in the private sector to his outstanding work at GSA, helping us to improve the way our government works. He has truly used his success to benefit others and I thank him for a job well done."

INDEX